Hiking
ROCKY MOUNTAIN
NATIONAL PARK

"The Dannens' trail expertise and gift for vivid wildlife descriptions make this book a must for the hiker's backpack."
—*American West*

"A very comprehensive guide to the trails."
—*Colorado Daily*

"Remains the most comprehensive trail guide available to the Rocky Mountain National Park. Written for both day-hikers and backpackers, it describes over 400 miles of trails in the park and in the adjacent Indian Peaks area."
—*Bookpaper*

"The definitive trail guide."
—*Kansas Motorist*

Help Us Keep This Guide Up to Date

Every effort has been made by the authors and editors to make this guide as accurate and useful as possible. However, many things can change after a guide is published—establishments close, phone numbers change, hiking trails are rerouted, facilities come under new management, etc.

We would love to hear from you concerning your experiences with this guide and how you feel it could be made better and be kept up to date. While we may not be able to respond to all comments and suggestions, we'll take them to heart and we'll also make certain to share them with the authors. Please send your comments and suggestions to the following address:

The Globe Pequot Press
Reader Response/Editorial Department
P.O. Box 480
Guilford, CT 06437

Or you may e-mail us at:

editorial@GlobePequot.com

Thanks for your input, and happy travels!

Hiking
ROCKY MOUNTAIN NATIONAL PARK

Including Indian Peaks Wilderness

Ninth Edition

Kent and Donna Dannen

FALCON GUIDES ®

GUILFORD, CONNECTICUT
HELENA, MONTANA

AN IMPRINT OF THE GLOBE PEQUOT PRESS

*To our parents,
who showed us ancient paths:*

Martha and Don Harward
Mary Ellen and Dwight Dannen

FALCONGUIDES®

Copyright © 1978, 1980, 1982, 1983, 1985, 1989, 1994, 2002
Morris Book Publishing, LLC

Drawings by Donna Dannen

All maps reproduced courtesy U.S. Geological Survey and USDA
Forest Service.
Maps on pages 24 and 114–15 created by Tony Moore © Morris Book
Publishing, LLC.

ISBN 978-0-7627-2245-7

Manufactured in the United States of America
Ninth Edition/Fifth Printing

Contents

List of Maps viii
Note on the Maps ix
Trailhead Locator x
Acknowledgments xii
Introduction 3
   What to Wear and Carry 4
   High Altitude Sickness 9
   Lightning: One Strike and You're Out! 10
   Hikers as Caretakers 15
   Rocky Mountain National Park Wilderness Facts 18
   Bear Lake Shuttle Bus Service 24

Rocky Mountain National Park

Mummy Range 27
Gem Lake Trail 27
   Nature Walk to Gem Lake (Montane Zone) 29
North Fork of the Big Thompson Trail System 37
Mummy Pass Trail 46
Trails North of Horseshoe Park 51
Cow Creek Trailhead 58
Chapin Pass Routes 58

Moraine Park 63
Fern Lake Trail System 63
Cub Lake Trail 67

Bear Lake Road 71
Hollowell Park Trails 74
Boulder Brook and Storm Pass Trails 74
Bierstadt Lake Trail 76
Glacier Gorge Trail System 78

Bear Lake Trailhead 91
Dream Lake Trail System 91

Flattop Mountain Trail System 94
Odessa Lake Trail 100

Longs Peak and Nearby Goals 103

East Edge 113
Twin Sisters Peaks 113
Storm Pass Trail to Estes Cone 117
Lily Lake Trail 119
Homer Rouse Trail 121
Lily Mountain Trail (Roosevelt National Forest) 122
Homestead Meadows (Roosevelt National Forest) 123

Wild Basin 125
Ouzel Falls Trail System 125
Sandbeach Lake Trail System 137
Finch Lake Trail System 140
Allens Park Trail 142
Horsetooth Peak and Lookout Mountain 143

Trail Ridge Road 145
Old Ute Trail 146
Tundra Nature Walk (Alpine Zone) 152
Deer Mountain Trail 162
Abandoned Road 164
Trails from Milner Pass 166
Timber Lake Trail 170
Trails from Never Summer Ranch 171
Baker Gulch Trail System (Arapaho National Forest) ... 173
Onahu Creek–Green Mountain Circle 178

Colorado River Trails 183
Red Mountain Trail System 183
Lulu City Trail System 190

Grand Lake 199
North Inlet Trail 199
Tonahutu Creek Trail 202

East Inlet Trail 203
Shadow Mountain and East Shore or Outlet Trails 207

Indian Peaks Wilderness

National Park and National Forest—
Two Administrative Styles 211

East of the Divide (Roosevelt National Forest) 217
Pawnee Pass Trail 217
  Nature Walk to Lake Isabelle (Subalpine Zone) 220
Mitchell Creek Trail 233
Mount Audubon Trail System 235
Routes from Beaver Reservoir 237
Middle St. Vrain Trail System 239
St. Vrain Mountain Trail 243
Arapaho Glacier Trail (Glacier Rim Trail) 244
Buckingham Campground Trails 248
Trails from Hessie 249

West of the Divide (Arapaho National Forest) 253
Roaring Fork Trail System 254
Buchanan Pass Trail 257
Cascade Trail to Pawnee Pass 261
Arapaho Pass Trail 265
Caribou Pass Trail 267
Corona Trail 271

Destination Tables 275
Destinations Index 298
Suggested Readings 305
About the Authors 308

List of Maps

Trailhead Locator xi
Bear Lake Shuttle Bus System 24
Gem Lake and Cow Creek Trails 26
North Fork of the Big Thompson 40
Mummy Pass Trail System 48
Trails North of Horseshoe Park 52
Chapin Pass Routes 60
Moraine Park and Old Ute Trail 64
Bear Lake Road and Bear Lake Area 72
Longs Peak and Nearby Goals and Glacier Gorge 107
East Edge 114
Wild Basin 126
Baker Gulch Trail System 174
North Inlet and Tonahutu Creek Trail Systems
    and Onahu Creek–Green Mountain Circle 180
Trail Ridge Road and Red Mountain Trail 184
Lulu City Trail System 192
Grand Lake Area—East Inlet 205
Pawnee Pass, Mitchell Creek,
    and Beaver Creek to Mount Audubon Trails 218
Middle St. Vrain, Beaver Reservoir Trails, and
    East End Buchanan Pass Trail 240
Arapaho Glacier Trail and Buckingham
    Campground Trails 246
Trails from Hessie 251
Roaring Fork Trail System 256
Cascade Trail to Pawnee Pass and North Section of
    Arapaho Pass Trail 262
Caribou Pass Trail System and South Section of
    Arapaho Pass Trail 270
Corona Trail 272

Note on the Maps

The maps for *Hiking Rocky Mountain National Park* were adapted from Resource Base Maps prepared by the USDA Forest Service, Region 2, Denver, and from the U.S. Geological Survey's topographic map of the park. We have made corrections to the original maps based on our hiking experience.

If you desire maps with a larger scale than those in this book, we recommend ordering 7.5-minute 1:24,000-scale quadrangle maps from the U.S. Geological Survey, P.O. Box 25286, Denver, Colorado 80255. Some quads are also available in area outdoor stores and in Rocky Mountain National Park book outlets.

The names of quads for Rocky Mountain National Park and Indian Peaks Wilderness Area are (in descending order of usefulness) McHenrys Peak, Longs Peak, Trail Ridge, Fall River Pass, Allens Park (spelling differs here from our text because USGS and U.S. Postal Service spellings differ), Isolation Peak, Estes Park, Grand Lake, Mount Richthofen, Ward, Monarch Lake, East Portal, Nederland, Bowen Mountain, Glen Haven, Pingree Park, Comanche Peak, Chambers Lake, Clark Peak, Trail Mountain, Granby, Strawberry Lake, Gold Hill, Raymond, Panorama Peak, and Crystal Mountain. Circumambulating these maps when they are laid out together is a pretty long hike in itself.

Trailhead Locator

MUMMY RANGE
1. Pingree Park (9,030')
2. Corral Creek Trailhead (10,000')
3. North Fork Trailhead (7,960')
4. Cow Creek Trailhead (7,840')
5. Gem Lake Trailhead on Devils Gulch Road (7,740')
6. Twin Owls Trailhead (7,920')
7. Lawn Lake Trailhead (8,540')
8. Chapin Creek Trailhead (10,640')

MORAINE PARK
9. Cub Lake Trailhead (8,080')
10. Fern Lake Trailhead (8,155')

BEAR LAKE ROAD
11. Hollowell Park (8,400')
12. Bierstadt Lake, Boulder Brook–Storm Pass Trailheads (8,850')
13. Glacier Gorge Junction (9,230')

BEAR LAKE TRAILHEAD
14. Bear Lake (9,475')

LONGS PEAK AND NEARBY GOALS
15. Longs Peak Ranger Station (9,400')

EAST EDGE
16. Lily Lake (8,927')
17. Lily Mountain Trailhead (8,780')
18. Homestead Meadows (7,360')

WILD BASIN
19. Copeland Lake (8,312')
20. Finch Lake Trailhead (8,470') and Wild Basin Ranger Station (8,500')
21. Allens Park Trailhead (8,526')

TRAIL RIDGE ROAD
22. Fall River Pass (11,796')
23. Ute Trail Crossing of Trail Ridge Road (11,440')

24. Beaver Meadows (8,440')
25. Deer Ridge Junction (8,930')
26. Milner Pass (10,750')
27. Timber Lake Trailhead (9,000')
28. Never Summer Ranch (8,884')
29. Baker Gulch Trailhead (8,864')
30. Onahu Creek Trailhead (8,765')
31. Green Mountain Trailhead (8,794')

COLORADO RIVER TRAILS
32. Colorado River Trailhead (9,010')
33. Lake Agnes Trailhead (10,300')

GRAND LAKE AREA
34. Tonahutu Creek and North Inlet Trailheads (8,545')
35. East Inlet Trailhead (8,391')
36. East Shore Trailhead (8,391')
37. Green Ridge Campground (8,400')

INDIAN PEAKS, EAST OF THE DIVIDE
38. St. Vrain Mountain Trailhead (8,800')
39. Camp Dick [Middle St. Vrain] (8,638')
40. Beaver Reservoir (9,161')
41. Mitchell Creek Trailhead (10,480')
42. Long Lake Trailhead (10,480')
43. Rainbow Lakes Campground (9,960')
44. Buckingham Campground (10,121')
45. Hessie (9,009')

INDIAN PEAKS, WEST OF THE DIVIDE
46. Roaring Fork Trailhead (8,281')
47. Monarch Lake (8,346')
48. Junco Lake (10,040')
49. Rollins Pass (11,671')
50. Devils Thumb Park (9,660')

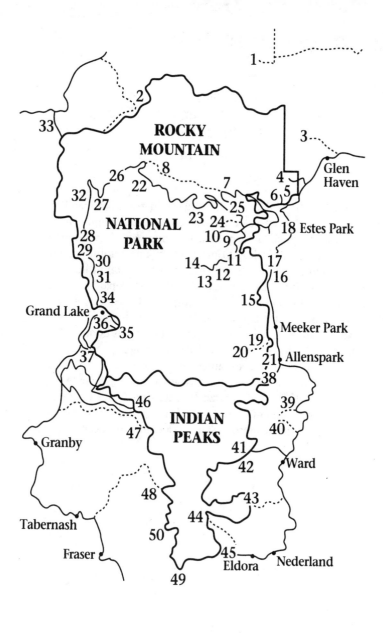

ROCKY
MOUNTAIN

NATIONAL
PARK

INDIAN
PEAKS

Glen
Haven

Estes Park

Meeker Park

Allenspark

Grand Lake

Granby

Ward

Tabernash

Nederland

Fraser

Eldora

Acknowledgments

Ask for the ancient paths
where the good way is; and walk in it
and find rest for your souls.

Jeremiah 6:16

The authors wish to thank fellow hikers in the National Park Service and USDA Forest Service who checked the manuscript of this guidebook, refreshed our memories, supplied information on recent and future trail alterations, made many helpful suggestions, and caught mistakes. The value of this aid cannot be overstated. The staff of Rocky Mountain National Park paid us a special compliment by vehemently debating among themselves their criticisms of our text (the war of the marginal notes). These proofreaders will see much of their own effort in this book as they read it from cover to cover—with sharp red pencils ready.

We have set some place-names in boldface type to make descriptions of various destinations easier to find. We made our decision about what to emphasize by intuition based on many years of answering hikers' questions. What to highlight was, in the words of George Armstrong Custer, a command decision.

Hiking
ROCKY MOUNTAIN
NATIONAL PARK

Sagebrush and Indian paintbrush

Introduction

On Rocky Mountain National Park trails, it sometimes seems as if the whole world has heeded Jesus's command to "rise, take up your bed, and walk." A conservative estimate indicates that 1.5 million people hike the park trails each year. In Roosevelt-Arapaho National Forest along the park's southern boundary, approximately 120,000 visitors hike the trails of the Indian Peaks Wilderness each year.

Obviously, there is a quality to these mountains that multitudes of people want to experience. Just as obviously, that quality eventually will be stomped out by lug soles if we are careless in our use of this spectacular stretch of the Rockies.

In writing this guidebook we have two goals, neither of which is to encourage more people to hit the trail (an activity needing no encouragement). First, we want the book to help both novice and experienced hikers to enjoy the backcountry more fully. Second, and even more important, the guide is intended to help everyone use the Rocky Mountain wilderness in a disciplined way so it will not be loved to death.

Understanding the ecosystems of Rocky Mountain National Park greatly increases the enjoyment of its trails. Accordingly, this guide contains three very detailed descriptions of parts of three different trails, called nature walks, located in the Mummy Range, in Indian Peaks, and off Trail Ridge Road. These walks, none more than 3 miles long, represent the workings of various life zones. By reading the three descriptions, hikers will begin to understand the ecosystems of other trails situated in the same zones.

All the trail descriptions are relatively detailed. In fact, knowledgeable fellow hikers in the National Park Service and USDA Forest Service who kindly reviewed the manuscript suggested that it might be too complete. They feel that knowing exactly what to expect takes some of the adventure out of backcountry experiences. Their criticism certainly is valid. Nevertheless, we believe that knowledge is usually preferable to ignorance. Although the information furnished here will eliminate some (but only some) of the physical adventure that accompanies error and uncertainty, it will also, through increased understanding, open additional paths of spiritual and mental adventure.

Frankly, though, this book can't cover everything because back-country management is complicated. The National Park Service tries to protect the landscape and the visitor from each other and, at the same time, to make re-creation (as well as recreation) possible for visitors. To meet the constantly changing demands of such a difficult task, the Park Service may change the details of its backcountry management.

We mention almost no trail signs in the guide. Signs are often present along the trails to help hikers find their way, but predicting exactly where signs will be and what they will say next week makes long-range forecasting of mountain weather seem sure and simple by comparison.

Another criticism of the original manuscript was that it contained information about trails that are harmful to the land—old trails running to destinations now served by newer paths built with land protection in mind. After considering each of the old trails carefully, we decided we agreed with the criticism, so we eliminated their descriptions from the book.

This trail guide is meant to be used during the five months of the year that are appropriate for hiking in the Colorado Rockies: June through October. We prefer post–Labor Day hiking because of the comfortable temperatures, yellow aspen leaves, and smaller crowds, but each month offers its own unique and worthwhile joys.

What to Wear and Carry

Among notices about gadgets, clothing, food, and miscellaneous exotic stuff for hikers to carry into the wilderness, we once saw an ad for a unique Colorado product: a down-filled necktie. No longer is there any excuse for sloppy hikers!

A certain amount of silliness is unavoidable as advancing

technology in materials and equipment design makes hiking and backpacking ever easier. As the number of potential customers for hiking products increases, the incentive for manufacturers to supply both quality and crud to satisfy hikers' needs and desires increases proportionately. Any detailed list today of what is needed in the Rocky Mountain National Park backcountry would be obsolete tomorrow.

Nevertheless, although the latest in equipment and clothing constantly changes, there are some basic requirements, since the human body and the mountain environment do not change much.

The park's mountain environment is made up of two important categories: terrain above tree line and terrain below tree line. The latter is more moderate. Venturing very far above the trees into the alpine zone necessitates more preparation for varying conditions.

As for the human body, it experiences two important states: comfortable and uncomfortable. The state of discomfort can be subdivided almost infinitely, with "sissy" at one end of the scale and "casualty" at the other. Most of us prefer to risk some discomfort during our backcountry experience than to shoulder the weight of extra gear. The trick lies in determining the degree of risk.

For instance, starting out for Dream Lake on a warm, sunny August morning without carrying sweater or rain gear is perfectly reasonable. The chances of a dangerous ambush by the elements are negligible. But starting out for Longs Peak on the same morning without the burden of extra protection for your body is foolhardy and could cause you significant harm. Between these two extremes range a number of less simple situations requiring decisions about what to wear and carry.

Below tree line it is possible, although unlikely, for the temperature to vary as much as 50 degrees Fahrenheit during a single day. The chance of being caught in an afternoon shower is fairly high, but the wind is usually not dangerous.

Wind, wetness, and temperature all figure in discussions about hypothermia, which used to be called exposure. The new terminology developed along with a better understanding of the weather conditions and physical stresses that cause this dangerous phenomenon. Essentially, the victim's internal heating mechanisms break down because of repeated draining away of body heat by combinations of low air temperatures, wetness, and wind. Hypothermia can occur in temperatures as high as 50 degrees and in locations below tree line. But it probably won't occur below tree line unless a nearly naked, fasting hiker, traveling alone off trail and unknown to anyone, suffers an incapacitating injury.

Below tree line, the risk of serious injury from exposure to inclement elements is not very significant. On the other hand, who wants to be even miserably uncomfortable? If you plan to be more than a mile from the trailhead, a cotton shirt, long pants, and rain gear are the minimum items necessary to avoid significant risk of discomfort. Additionally, sunscreen, food, water, a sweater, and a pack to carry it all in are advisable. And some hikers do manage to survive with less than fifteen pounds of camera equipment.

The alpine zone has greater extremes: The temperature varies much more than below tree line. Unfortunately, the sun will probably pour down in the morning when you are climbing and generating plenty of your own heat. In the afternoon, when you are descending and generating much less heat, clouds often will shade you while the wind picks up to a stiff gale.

While hiking above the tree line, therefore, you need to be able to add or shed layers of clothing. You should have some way of covering the full length of your arms and legs. Raingear helps to cut the wind. Gore-Tex hats and jackets are worth their expense for their ability to keep you dry and warm or cool, as circumstances require. A sweater is the minimum extra clothing you should carry just for warmth, and a hat, gloves, and jacket may be very welcome. You will need more water than when below tree line because deeper breathing and high winds suck moisture from the body.

Protection from the sun is vital in the shadeless environment of the alpine zone. People differ, of course, in their sensitivity to the burning of ultraviolet light, but tolerance experienced elsewhere is irrelevant at high elevations where thin air screens out far less UV radiation than at lower elevations. On snow, the exposure to UV is much greater than on earth or rock because the snow reflects back much of the burning radiation, greatly increasing the dosage you receive. In the Rockies many attempted suntans end up as sunburns. Colorado has the country's highest rate of skin cancer because thin air gives so little protection from radiation.

Do everything practical to keep the sun off your skin. Long sleeves and pants are obvious. When they are too warm, apply sunscreen lotion with abandon. Turn your collar up to cover the back of your neck. Wear a hat with a brim. Sunglasses are essential.

As frequently as people underprotect their skin while hiking in the mountains, they overprotect their feet. Plain old over-the-ankle work shoes with cork composition or rubber soles or even mere tennis shoes are adequate for most trail hiking. For off-trail hiking (for example, to mountain summits) or for backpacking—times when it is more important to keep feet dry—heavier (but not very heavy) hiking boots made of full-grain leather are helpful. The all-too-familiar neoprene lug sole is the best sole for traveling over rock, but it also causes wear and tear on meadows. Step as gently as possible in these areas.

Many hikers carry more food than they need. If you are enthusiastic about food, eating in the unequaled beauty of the wilderness certainly will enhance your gustatory delights. On the other hand, that same beauty can compensate for a good deal of deficiency in the food department.

High-calorie food that is bad for your health at home, such as hard candy or chocolate, could be just what you need for dragging your body up a steep slope. Most dried fruits and the multiple variations on the familiar mixtures of fruit, nuts, and candy are good.

Yet, if the truth be known, food is the least necessary item in the pack for all day hikes and for most backpacking trips. You should have some food, but you do not need much. Anybody can manage to skip a meal or two. From the standpoint of total joy derived from

Pika (cony)

a wilderness experience, an extra roll of film or a pair of gloves can be a good deal more important than an extra sandwich.

Furthermore, there is an undeniable relationship between amount of food consumed and amount of defecation, and human defecation has become a serious pollution—not to mention aesthetic—problem in Rocky Mountain National Park. Small garden trowels for the burying of human wastes are not carried and used with nearly enough frequency.

For this reason, it is much more important to carry water than to carry food. Do not drink from streams in Rocky Mountain National Park. Although you might get away with it for a while, making a habit of drinking unboiled or untreated water eventually will cause illness—usually diarrhea, and always at the worst possible time.

Just as preventing illness is preferable to curing it, preventing accidents is preferable to first aid. Still, one member of your hiking party should carry a first-aid kit. Adhesive bandages, in particular, are useful and have magic healing powers far beyond any rational explanation. First-aid knowledge is usually more important than first-aid supplies, and it is infinitely more lightweight. Our book list contains a good reference for wilderness first aid; it should be learned from rather than carried along. The extra weight would be no fun, and if you have to take time to look up a first-aid technique, you probably will be too late in executing it.

On the other hand, the book you are reading is well worth its weight in the energy you save by not getting lost. A map is the absolute minimum reference needed by hikers not intimately familiar with the terrain they hope to cover. You probably can get along without a compass if you can orient yourself in relation to prominent mountains, especially Longs Peak. But if rare low clouds obscure the peaks, a compass may help you to get out of the wilds at a time when you do not care to waste hours in being lost.

Finally, there is no need for such equipment as an ax, saw, sheath knife, or cavalry saber. The only necessary cutting tool is a pocketknife. Some multibladed pocketknives have a lot of useless extra stuff attached (a corkscrew?!), but screwdrivers, scissors, file, awl, magnifying glass, or tweezers can be very handy for makeshift repair of equipment or body.

Backpacking, of course, requires much more equipment than hiking: frame pack, sleeping bag, tent, stove, mattress, ropes, telescope, wet-suit, inflatable raft, hot air balloon, helicopter, whistle, four Sherpas, this trail guide, and a partridge in a pear tree. Further information on what backpackers need can be found in the excellent books on this subject listed at the back of our book. If they fail to mention a down-filled necktie, please remember that it is very hard for even the best of us to stay current.

High Altitude Sickness

Visitors unaccustomed to high elevations may experience symptoms of Acute Mountain Sickness (AMS). The Estes Park Medical Center describes the symptoms as being similar to the flu. Victims may experience headache, fatigue, dizziness, nausea, vomiting, breathlessness, diarrhea, loss of appetite, and lethargy. Symptoms should subside after 72 hours. Suggestions for alleviating symptoms include drinking plenty of water, eating a diet high in carbohydrates, decreasing alcohol and caffeine consumption, and avoiding smoking. The Estes Park Medical Center also warns that visitors with a history of heart or breathing problems should be careful not to overexert themselves at high altitudes where heart and lungs must work harder. It is possible that undiagnosed pre-existing heart problems may surface at high altitudes. If you experience chest pain, seek medical attention at once.

Lightning: One Strike and You're Out!

The weather was deceptively clear, even balmy, as we began to walk up Old Fall River Road after a successful climb of Ypsilon Mountain. This unpaved road, which climbs to 11,800 feet at Fall River Pass, had not been reopened to summer auto traffic. It had been necessary for us and our hiking companions to hike down the old road to Chapin Pass from the Alpine Visitor Center on Trail Ridge Road before ascending Ypsilon.

Climbing back to our cars, we were less than a half mile from safety when the sky quickly blackened and thunder echoed ominously. It was a difficult situation. We were much closer to the Alpine Visitor Center than to the tree line, yet the higher we climbed, the greater our danger of attracting lightning. Because all alternatives were bad, we decided to try to reach the visitor center from the east, before the storm reached it from the west. Of course, we lost the race.

Rain and hail pelted us in sheets. We tried counting five-second intervals between lightning and thunder to estimate the number of miles to where the bolts were striking; our count yielded only four seconds for the thunder to travel to us from the strikes. We hoped we could get inside an old cabin nearby that had sheltered road workers many years before, but it was locked (and has since been removed).

Under its eaves, we at least found protection from rain and hail. Because we no longer generated heat by frantically hurrying uphill, we began to chill. There were dry, warm jackets in our packs. Leaving hiking companions strung out along the cabin wall, we ran around a corner of the building; the recess of a door on the other side would give us a bit more shelter for putting on the jackets.

We had barely turned the corner when the universe erupted in one all-encompassing boom. Its volume knocked us to the ground. Back on our feet, we returned to our friends and found them thoroughly shaken. Lightning, they babbled, had struck right where we had been standing seconds before! Sparks had flown off and hit the individuals standing on either side.

No one was seriously hurt, but all of us were seriously terrified. Lightning does strike twice in the same place—frequently, in fact—and it was thundering all around. We scattered quickly for the lowest depressions we could find, trying to stay away from each other and from watercourses and rivulets that could conduct currents along the ground to us from lightning strikes.

Actually, our friends were wrong. Had lightning struck exactly where we had been standing, the hikers on either side would have been badly injured or killed. Lightning did hit nearby, though, and the strike's voltage had diffused through the ground along lines of least resistance, dissipating in strength as it traveled.

One line of this "step voltage" had radiated to a piece of an old shovel lying on the ground under the eaves. Had we not moved, it would have radiated to us instead and caused injury or death. Most people who are hit by lightning are victims of step voltage rather than of direct strikes. But the time between strike and conduction of step voltage is a very small fraction of a second, far less than human senses can perceive. It certainly seemed as though lightning had smashed directly into the midst of the group.

Rain pelted our hollows of scant safety, and we wished we had sleeping pads or climbing ropes to squat on for insulation from the ground and from more exposure to step voltage. Such equipment, unfortunately, is unnecessary for reaching the summit of Ypsilon Mountain. We could only stay as low as we were able, with as little of our bodies as possible touching the ground.

At last the storm passed over. Its fury had lasted a scant few minutes, but it seemed much longer. Looking west, we could see another storm following close on the heels of the first. Lightning was striking the Never Summer Range and heading our way fast.

We ran for the shelter of the visitor center at Fall River Pass. Running a half mile at full speed, laden with heavy boots and packs, up a 45 degree slope in oxygen-short air at 11,500 feet poses definite problems. On the other hand, flashes of lightning and extreme fear are marvelous incentives to effort. As we ran, we heard sirens wailing across the tundra and hoped that rescuers were coming for us.

We were on our own, and were nearly dead from exhaustion when we stumbled, gasping, into the safety of the visitor center. The second storm hit as the door swung closed behind us.

Nearly dead does not count. We learned then where the sirens were going: to a parking lot on Trail Ridge Road where a woman had been struck directly by lightning and killed. Standing on the equivalent of a mountaintop, she probably had died from an "upward stroke" of lightning. This type begins in the ground and sparks up to clouds. The huge amount of electricity exposes the conducting object (in this case, a human body) to a temperature as high as 50,000 degrees Fahrenheit. Death is almost inevitable.

The victim might have been struck by a "downstroke," with about the same result. Yet strikes that originate in clouds usually dissipate in the surrounding air so that the actual strike consists of only a few thousand volts. Seventy percent of the victims of downstrokes survive.

The amount of shock a person receives from voltage running along the ground depends on the nearness of the strike and on the conductivity of the ground surface. The chances of survival depend largely on the reaction of people nearby. The victim may look very dead because heartbeat and breathing are usually stopped at once by the electrical shock. Nevertheless, closed heart massage and artificial respiration should be commenced immediately. The heart frequently will start up by itself; the lungs will not. Although lack of oxygen for long periods can cause brain damage, victims have recovered completely after having had no oxygen for as long as twenty-two minutes. There are additional

12

injuries from lightning that may require first aid: burns, cuts, shock, internal bleeding, broken bones from falling. Some of them may be fatal if not tended.

It is easy to understand why many mountaineers are fatalistic about lightning. Their attitude is unfortunate, for it fosters carelessness, and there are some ways to avoid being hit. Obviously, you should not be the highest object around when a storm threatens. If at all possible, get below tree line. You will be very safe in a forest. This is quite different from huddling under a lone tree, which would make you an excellent candidate for receiving strong step voltage. If you can see an old lightning scar twisting around the trunk of a nearby tree, you are too close to the tree.

If caught unavoidably above the tree line by a storm, you should stay away from edges of cliffs and from high boulders; also stay away from rock debris and vegetation at the bottom of cliffs, for both conduct step voltage. Cracks and shallow niches in the mountainside also should be avoided.

The best procedure is to crouch among flat-topped boulders. Because such ideal places are scarce on the tundra, a depression may have to do. But depressions containing water are annoyingly uncomfortable and are dangerous because of step voltage.

Included here are a few extra hints for avoiding lightning in Rocky Mountain National Park. First, because storms tend to gather in the afternoon, you should begin hikes to peaks early enough to reach the summit and leave it by about 1:00 P.M. Having to end a hike by climbing to a trailhead above tree line, such as on the Old Ute Trail or Fall River Pass, is less than ideal.

Second, certain places apparently are preferred lightning targets and might be avoided during storms. On the list are Deer Mountain, Specimen Mountain, and Mills Moraine. Trail Ridge seems like a favorite target, but that could be because it swarms with so many potential victims. Longs Peak, of course, is the highest point anywhere around—except for the climbers who are standing on top of it.

All in all, lightning is nasty stuff. It is the only summer danger

Douglas-fir branch and cone

in Rocky Mountain National Park that a fit, properly equipped, and experienced mountaineer cannot overcome. Nevertheless, fear of lightning can inspire evasive action, which reduces the chance of being hit to acceptable odds. Only the foolish lack such fear.

Hikers as Caretakers

Rocky Mountain National Park is a better place now than it was when we first hiked its trails in the 1950s. The improvement has occurred despite a huge increase in visitation of all kinds and an explosion of backcountry use. Some evidence suggests that mushrooming crowds might have reversed the trend toward improvement and that the park is headed toward wilderness degradation. But the reversal is not inevitable. Better educated, more enlightened, more loving use of the land will preserve the park for future generations.

Although most of the park's improvement should be credited to the National Park Service, the time has passed when we should count on rangers to look after our wilderness interests. Every day we hear more calls in more areas for government to do this and that and to relieve individuals of personal responsibility. Because we hikers and backpackers value the freedom we feel in the wilds, we must accept the responsibility for taking care of the land over which we walk in Rocky Mountain National Park and Indian Peaks Wilderness.

As caretakers, each of us must act as though the salvation of the park's wilderness depends on us alone rather than on regulations for preserving the backcountry. Our wilderness will be preserved, in fact, only if we exceed the minimum requirements of regulations. For instance, to spread out the wear and tear of camping, the National Park Service requires that all backpackers obtain a permit, which allows backcountry camping at certain sites on particular dates. Favored sites fill early; call ahead for reservations (970–586–1242). Campfires are permitted only at sites equipped with steel fire rings. The regulations specify that only dead and down wood should be burned.

In reality, there is no room left in this park's backcountry for campfires of any kind, anywhere. Even the dead and down wood has a place in the ecosystem; each link in the chain of life is important to the whole. Research in other mountain wilderness areas has revealed that some insects that pollinate wildflowers nest in dead and down wood. When thousands of campfires consume all the dead and down wood—and insect nesting sites—within a wide radius of many campsites, they eliminate the insects and the plants as well, without a single blossom being stepped on.

The backpacking stove with liquid fuel is the hiker's only acceptable source of fire in the wilderness of Rocky Mountain National Park and Indian Peaks. Stoves are much more convenient and clean than campfires, so virtue has its reward.

We must pack out not only all we pack in but all the litter left behind by other hikers as well. Park regulations prohibit hacking trees, ditching tents, removing rocks from their natural sites, and blackening rocks in fire rings because these practices permanently inflict human presence on heavily used areas. But we should take greater care; at campsites we should wear moccasins or some other soft footwear to minimize the effect of concentrated walking.

When there is no outhouse, Park Service regulations call for human waste to be buried in the zone of decay 6 inches underground and at least 200 feet from all watercourses. We should do more. We should remove the ground cover intact with our trowel before digging a hole and replace it later, as cannily as a fur trapper used to hide his cache of pelts. Really good caretakers even cultivate backcountry constipation.

The hiker's role as caretaker of Rocky Mountain National Park extends further: We must abandon our normal reluctance to intrude on other people's activities. When we observe other hikers acting contrary to good wilderness ethics, we must take it upon ourselves to educate the offenders in the friendliest way possible about proper backcountry behavior. For instance, we can explain how hikers must travel on trails and not make shortcuts across switchbacks, because making shortcuts destroys vegetation and causes erosion, which will wash away the trails. And we can insist that wash water for dishes, bodies, and everything else be carried away from watercourses and campsites for dumping.

We need to educate ourselves extensively about the ecosystems of Rocky Mountain National Park wilderness so that we will not damage it out of ignorance. We must stress to fellow hikers the delicacy of all life on this austere land. We can point out how slowly plants grow in the mountains, especially in the alpine zone. By word and example we must urge the utmost care in subjecting mountain plants to the absolute minimum of stress, for their already stressful lives can stand little more. Where trails already exist, we will stay on them. Where there are no trails, we will avoid fellow hikers' footsteps to disperse and minimize the impact of our passing.

Hiking with dogs adds much to one's appreciation of the mountains by providing a nonhuman viewpoint. This benefit has been praised by many wilderness advocates, such as John Muir and Enos Mills, Father of Rocky Mountain National Park. For day hikes, dogs are the best pack animals, inflicting no impact on the wilds. Alas, those dog owners who allowed their pets to run at will, chasing wildlife and intimidating other humans, caused the banning of pets from Rocky Mountain National Park trails. To prevent this loss from occurring on other trails, canine hikers must be kept under control, which almost always means leashed, and prevented from pestering other hikers. Boarding kennels are available in Estes Park (call 970–586–6606 or 970–586–6898).

The role of caretaker demands that each hiker and backpacker make these sacrifices and more so the wilderness may live long after we are gone, just as it lived long before any people saw it. We must sacrifice out of love for the wilderness; it benefits us in many ways, and it is beautiful and needs our protection. As we urge others to practice good wilderness ethics, we must feel kindly toward them, for they are potential allies and fellow caretakers of Rocky Mountain National Park and Indian Peaks Wilderness.

Rocky Mountain National Park Wilderness Facts

In 2001, Rocky Mountain National Park approved a new Backcountry/Wilderness Management Plan, which is considerably weightier than this trail guide. The plan contains many facts and statements that we believe will interest hikers. We have listed these below, not always as exact quotes.

• On January 26, 1915, the Rocky Mountain National Park Act established Rocky Mountain National Park and its mission: "said area is dedicated and set apart as a public park for the benefit and enjoyment of the people of the United States, under the name Rocky Mountain National Park . . . regulations being primarily aimed at the freest use of the said park for recreational purposes by the public and for the preservation of the natural conditions and scenic beauties thereof."

• The Wilderness Act of 1964 secures "for the American people of present and future generations the benefits of an enduring resource of wilderness." By definition, wilderness is "a tract of undeveloped federal land of primeval character without permanent improvements or human habitation; an area where the earth and its community of life are untrammeled by man, where man himself is a visitor who does not remain; where the forces of nature predominate and the imprint of human activities is substantially unnoticeable; which provides outstanding opportunities for solitude and an unconfined and primitive type of recreation."

• Rocky Mountain National Park contains 266,714 acres, 60 percent of which is forest, 13 percent alpine tundra, 18 percent bare rock, and 9 percent mixture of habitats. A total of 93.5 percent of the park (248,464 acres) is recommended for immediate designation as wilderness; 0.4 percent (1,147 acres) has potential to be designated as wilderness; 1.1 percent (2,917 acres) was already designated as part of Indian Peaks Wilderness when it was brought into the national park as part of a boundary adjustment.

- Six wilderness areas administered by the USDA Forest Service are adjacent to Rocky Mountain National Park: Indian Peaks, 73,291 acres; Rawah, 73,068 acres; Comanche Peak, 66,791 acres; Never Summers 20,747 acres; Neota, 9,924 acres; and Cache La Poudre, 9,238 acres.

- Since the 1970s, there have been three Research Natural Areas within Rocky Mountain National Park: Paradise Park, Specimen Mountain, and West Creek. These areas were set aside as prime examples of natural ecosystems in the southern Rocky Mountains and are considered to have significant genetic resources that have value for long-term baseline studies. They are managed to provide the greatest possible protection of ecosystem integrity. Only foot traffic is allowed in these areas. Overnight camping is not allowed. Day use is not encouraged, and trails will not be constructed or maintained. An exception is the hiking trail to The Crater on Specimen Mountain.

- Although only 10 square miles of Rocky Mountain National Park have been surveyed for prehistoric or historic archaeological sites, more than 500 such sites have been discovered. Several thousand sites are estimated to exist. Historic cultural groups that visited the park on a seasonal basis from a time ranging from 6,000 years ago to the end of the nineteenth century include Ute, Arapaho, Pawnee, Sioux, and Apache.

- Several historic trails in the park were used by Native Americans until the 1800s. The Ute Trail (also called the Child's Trail) began in Upper Beaver Meadows and extended over Forest Canyon Pass to Beaver Creek north of Timber Creek Campground. Trail Ridge Road parallels much of the Ute Trail. The Deer Trail split from the Ute Trail at Poudre Lake and ran from Milner Pass to Deer Creek and the North Fork of the Colorado River. The Tonahutu Trail traversed Flattop Mountain to Big Meadows. The Dog Trail followed Fall River.

- Nearly one-third of Rocky Mountain National Park lies at

an elevation of more than 11,000 feet above sea level, the alpine tundra zone of vegetation. The Continental Divide bisects the park from north to south, dividing precipitation that flows to the Atlantic drainage from water that flows toward the Pacific. The eastern slope receives about 15 inches of precipitation annually. The western slope receives approximately 20 inches and deeper snows.

• The average summer viewing distance from Rocky Mountain National Park is 83 miles 50 percent of the time. Viewing distances can vary from a high of 120 miles on a clear day to a low of 30 miles on a high pollution day.

• Rocky Mountain National Park contains 147 lakes with a total surface area of 1,103 acres, and 473 miles of streams. Fifty-one of the lakes in the park contain trout. Early settlers—and even the National Park Service, as recently as 1968—stocked many streams with nonnative species of trout (e.g., brown, rainbow, brook) and moved trout to lakes and streams that lacked them. This is no longer acceptable or allowed. In order to restore the fisheries resource to original conditions, artificial stocking is only done to supplement or restore native cutthroat (greenback and Colorado River) to waters previously altered.

• Approximately 1,025 vascular plants have been identified within Rocky Mountain National Park. Moraine Park at one time had a nine-hole golf course, which closed in the late 1960s, but 20 percent of the plants in the meadow still are nonnative, including several noxious weed species. The park has 260 species of birds, 66 species of mammals, 11 species of fish, 5 species of amphibians, and 1 species of reptile (garter snake).

• Certain risks are inherent when visiting the habitat of wild animals. Visitors must be aware of potential safety and property damage hazards when traveling and camping in wilderness. Regarding public use, NPS Management Policy (6:8) states, "Park visitors must accept wilderness largely on its own terms, without modern facilities provided for their comfort or convenience. Users must also accept certain risks, including possible dangers arising from wildlife, weather conditions, physical features, and other natural phenomena that are inherent in the various elements and conditions that comprise a wilderness experience and primitive methods of travel. The National Park Service will not eliminate or unreasonably control risks that are normally associated with wilderness, but it will strive to provide users with general information concerning possible risks, recommended precautions, minimum-impact use ethics, and applicable restrictions and regulations."

• Annual visitation to Rocky Mountain National Park, which topped three million in 1994 and has remained at this level, is about the same as Yellowstone National Park, although Rocky Mountain National Park is about one-eighth the size of Yellowstone. Two park goals are to provide visitor access to the park resources to a degree that enables the visitor to understand and appreciate the processes they reflect and to provide the opportunity to sample fully the various geographic regions, geological features, and ecological attributes.

• The most important attractions at Rocky Mountain National Park are natural scenery, clean air, clean water, wildlife, tranquillity, undeveloped vistas, alpine tundra, and night sky. Forty-eight percent of park visitors regard hiking as their main activity while visiting the park. Scenery is the main attraction for 72.6 percent of park visitors. Photography is another main attraction for 48.8 percent.

• The average age of park visitors is 46 years. Thirty-six percent of the visitors are from the Front Range of Colorado. The average length of stay is 2 hours and 45 minutes for day users, 3.33 days for overnight users.

• The park's current trail system evolved from game trails used by the Native Americans, then explorers and herders, and finally adopted by the National Park Service, which now maintains 350.2 miles of trail in Rocky Mountain National Park. There are approximately 107 bridges and 190 footlogs in the Rocky Mountain National Park backcountry/wilderness.

• The administrative fee for issuing backcountry camping permits, which includes all nights of the permit and all people in the party, rose to $15 on May 1, 1997. The total number of backcountry campers that are permitted in Rocky Mountain National Park each night during the summer is 1,973. The total number of rock climbers permitted to hang on 11 bivouac sites during a given summer night is 88. The total number of winter campers permitted in the backcountry per night is 2,484.

• There are approximately 1,200 signs in the backcountry/wilderness. Designated campsites are marked with an 8-inch-tall silver metal arrowhead and post. Campers must camp within 15 feet of the arrowhead or on established tent pads. Access trails to the camp area and sites will be identified along the main trail with a standard wooden camp area sign indicating the camp area name. Access trails from the main trail to campsites will be marked with 4-inch plastic red arrowhead markers.

• Social trails are defined as those trails that are nondesignated and undesirable. They are trails made by people shortcutting to other campsites, water sources, and so on. They generally cause resource impacts such as soil erosion and vegetation damage. All attempts should be made to obliterate and rehabilitate any social trails in and around camp areas to prevent resource impacts and management problems.

• Users with horses, llamas, burros, mules, and ponies can use all stock campsites, with the exception of Aspen Knoll, Ute Meadow, and Haynack, which are designated for llama use only.

• Stock users are expected to clean up after their stock. This includes packing out any uneaten feed, spreading manure, and filling in any holes caused by pawing. Rocky Mountain National Park contains 62 hitch rails for livestock.

• Garbage containers will not be placed in the backcountry/wilderness. Burying of garbage is not allowed. All garbage must be packed out and disposed of properly in wildlife-proof containers. Nondegradable litter is common in all areas of visitation. Litter as it relates to climbing is deposited by climbers, climbing spectators, and at bivouac (bivy) sites. Ledges and the bases of cliffs have been found to have fecal matter scattered around. Some bivy sites pose a problem, since waste cannot be buried. Decomposition of waste is a problem at high elevations due to cold temperatures. Exposed waste poses health problems to other climbers or wildlife and aesthetically degrades the user experience.

• Human waste and the activities related to its disposal can result in significant impacts to wilderness resources and the visitors' wilderness experiences. Improper disposal of human waste can result in nutrients and pathogens contaminating surface waters, ground water, and soils. The presence and strong smells of toilet paper and fecal material on the soil, rock, or snow surface impact the aesthetics of wilderness. The level of visitor use is the primary factor affecting the degree of human waste–related impacts. Visitors are encouraged to pack out human waste when visiting areas where cat holes or other appropriate means of human waste disposal (e.g., privies, smear technique in sun-exposed areas away from drainages and travel routes) are not available or appropriate.

• Five methods of human waste disposal are lumped under the term Human Waste Management Systems in the Backcountry/Wilderness Management Plan. For instance, solar toilets above tree line in the Longs Peak area are human waste management systems. Appendix C, Table 11 of the plan identifies a total of eighty-three human waste management system locations.

Bear Lake Shuttle Bus Service

Rocky Mountain National Park offers free shuttle bus service to transport visitors through the popular Bear Lake and Moraine Park areas. Visitors can avoid the congested Bear Lake parking lot by parking at the Glacier Basin parking area and catching the bus to Bear Lake. Hikers can use the bus as transportation between

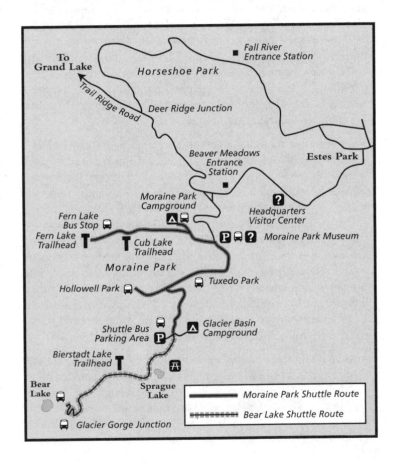

trailheads, facilitating one-way hikes, such as those beginning at Bear Lake and ending at Fern Lake Trailhead, Hollowell Park, Bierstadt Lake Trailhead, or Glacier Gorge Junction.

Bus service is daily in summer (beginning in June). The shuttle program goes to weekend-only service after Labor Day, serving visitors who want to view the aspens in their autumn colors during September. Schedules vary somewhat from year to year, but buses usually run every fifteen minutes from Glacier Basin in summer. The Moraine Park bus runs about once an hour.

The Bear Lake shuttle makes intermediate stops at Bierstadt Lake Trailhead and Glacier Gorge Junction. The Moraine Park loop starts at Fern Lake bus stop and runs to Glacier Basin parking lot with intermediate stops at Cub Lake Trailhead, Moraine Park Campground, Tuxedo Park, and Hollowell Park.

The shuttle bus program began at Rocky Mountain National Park in 1978 to reduce congestion along Bear Lake Road.

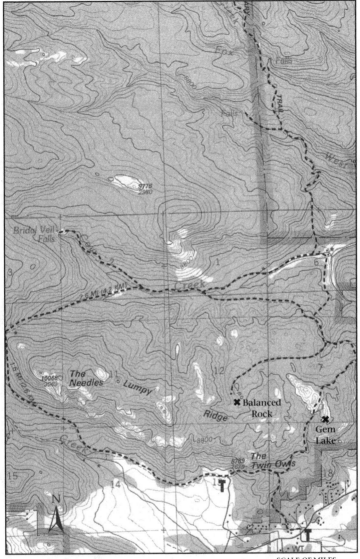

Gem Lake and Cow Creek Trails

SCALE OF MILES

0   1

ROCKY MOUNTAIN NATIONAL PARK

Mummy Range

The Mummy Range is the most diverse and complex hiking area in Rocky Mountain National Park. From trailheads scattered all around its base, a network of trails crisscrosses the mountains, giving hikers and backpackers wonderful choices of routes and destinations.

Gem Lake Trail

"How could 2 miles be so long? When do we reach the darned lake, anyway?"

Such reactions are frequent among the many hikers who are lured onto the Gem Lake Trail because it seems fast and easy—the lake is only a 2-mile walk from the two trailheads closest to Estes Park Village. The trail, however, winds through open southfacing ponderosa pine woods at a lower altitude than most park paths; thus, midday heat in summer can sap hikers' energy significantly.

Many folk are disappointed by the Gem Lake hike, but their disappointment arises from their inability to see and understand the fascinating natural events occurring at trailside. With a quart of water per person, three hours to spend, and a knowledge of what to look for, they would find the Gem Lake Trail unique and enjoyable. It is best hiked early or late in the day, not only for physical comfort but for grand vistas of dramatic light falling on the Front Range.

To reach the two Gem Lake trailheads, drive north on MacGregor Avenue (which becomes Devils Gulch Road) from the intersection of MacGregor Avenue and the US 34 Bypass of Estes Park. After about a mile, the road bends east at the entrance to MacGregor Ranch. One trailhead for Gem Lake is reached by driving through the ranch. You may have to open a gate; if so, be sure to close it behind you. Stay on the paved road (0.8 mile long), which dead-ends at a parking lot below Twin Owls, a large rock formation perched on Lumpy Ridge.

To reach the second trailhead, continue on Devils Gulch Road past the MacGregor Ranch entrance. After the road bends north again, you arrive at a parking lot on the left side of the road 1.8 miles from the middle of town.

Note: The National Park Service has proposed building a new Gem Lake Trailhead and eliminating the Twin Owls and smaller Gem Lake trailheads. If this is done, the new trailhead will be well marked along Devils Gulch Road and a new trail about 0.7 mile long will connect the new parking area with the current Gem Lake Trail near Twin Owls.

The first 0.8 mile of trail from the parking lot at the second trailhead passes through private land. Much of the access corridor is fenced on both sides as it crosses level open meadows. At the trail's second right-angle turn, look up at Lumpy Ridge. The highest "lump" to the left is Twin Owls, a favorite formation for technical rock climbers. From other viewpoints it really does look like two owls.

The next formation to watch for comes into sight as you approach a small creek bed bordered by moisture-loving white-barked quaking aspens. Before you reach the trees, look to your left to note on a ridgeline a trio of rock figures called Hen and Chickens. If you have the gift for seeing images in rock formations, you will find no better place to exercise it than on the trail ahead.

Soon the way grows steeper, and a pull on your water bottle may seem appropriate. There is no point in being Spartan about it; you should be carrying enough water to take a drink whenever you want one. After a couple of switchbacks, you arrive at last at the point where the trail from Twin Owls joins this one.

The trail from Twin Owls is a bit shorter than the one from Devils Gulch Road. Furthermore, its trailhead is 180 feet higher, and its path climbs more gradually. It is the somewhat easier way to Gem Lake, and it all lies within national park boundaries. If the Twin Owls parking lot is full, however, you might want to begin at the other trailhead.

Nature Walk to Gem Lake (Montane Zone)

The Twin Owls parking lot is a good place to visualize the broad outlines of the geology of Lumpy Ridge. Forty million years ago (give or take a day or two), the ridge top was part of an ancient plain. It was raised to its present position a mere five to seven million years ago, by which time the plain had been deeply penetrated by weathering, the process that breaks up rocks and decays them into soil. This decay had occurred along a network of fractures in the granite underlying the plain. As the sides of granite blocks outlined by fractures disintegrated, their unweathered cores remained as solid rock surrounded by weathered debris. The debris later eroded away, especially as the ridge was raised.

The cores are the "lumps" of today and also the huge boulders that eventually tumbled down the slopes of Lumpy Ridge. The boulders could easily be mistaken for rocks deposited by melting glaciers, but glaciers never extended to this spot.

The rounded appearance of the rocks comes from the way in which they weather. Masses of granite in areas of slight rainfall split off plates or shells in successive layers like those of an onion. The process, called exfoliation, begins when water invades tiny cracks in the granite and dries more slowly than on the surface. Some minerals in the granite are slowly dissolved by the water, forming a claylike material. The clay expands, pushing off granite plates parallel to the surface.

The action, of course, takes a very long time. We casually overlook millions of years here and there throughout Lumpy

Ridge geology. Human life is too short and human experience too limited to enable most imaginations to encompass so long a period of time.

The trail begins amid quaking aspens and large chokecherry bushes. The latter is the most common wild cherry (*Prunus virginiana*); varieties of it grow throughout most of the United States. It is a marvelous shrub. The long white flower clusters have an almost overpoweringly sweet odor in spring. The blossoms evolve to masses of dark purple or black cherries, much favored by birds and jelly makers. In fall the leaves of the bush turn orange-red.

In the drier areas along the trail, two kinds of juniper grow. Common (or creeping, or dwarf) juniper is a low shrub with short, sharp needles. Rocky Mountain juniper (often called cedar) is a small, many branched tree with flat scalelike foliage. The female plant of both kinds bears blue cones with a waxy covering that makes them resemble berries. Juniper "berries" are used to flavor gin. They are not tasty, and after an experimental nibble, few hikers venture to try more.

Wild rose is another common and edible-if-you-are-desperate shrub on the first part of the Gem Lake Trail. Rose hips, the seeds of its fragrant pink flowers, are well known as a source of vitamin C. These red fruits taste no better than bland, mealy apples; they also have annoying hairy seeds. So unless an advanced case of scurvy is causing your teeth to fall out, it would be best to leave the rose hips to grow prettily and to be eaten by the wildlife that favors them.

Growing among the rocks and in draws on the hillside is Rocky Mountain maple. Although the leaf's shape is familiar to most hikers, this many stemmed shrubby representative of a noble and valuable family seems like a stunted poor cousin. Well, it is the only maple we have, and we like it! It puts up with excessive dryness and poor soil that the big, showy maples never could tolerate. In size and shape it reflects the general harsh austerity of the West, yet in fall its leaves turn a showy red and yellow like the magnificent sugar maple of the East.

Ponderosa pine is the dominant tree in the montane zone of vegetation through which the trail passes. It has moderately long needles growing in bundles of two or three. The bark of young ponderosas is dark gray, and that of mature trees is thick, deeply grooved, and rusty red. These picturesque mature pines, which may be as old as 500 years, stand apart from each other, giving a ponderosa woods an open, parklike appearance.

Perhaps the most interesting inhabitants of ponderosa forests are the tassel-eared Abert squirrels. They are the most magnificent squirrels in North America and need no description beyond that of the children who call them "squabbits"—squirrels with rabbitlike ears. Aberts come in two distinct color phases, black and gray-and-white, and there are some dark brown individuals.

Tassel-eared Abert squirrel on ponderosa pine

Less spectacular but more pugnacious are the red squirrels, which are more gray than red. Chipmunks (striped back and face) and golden-mantled ground squirrels (larger, with striped back and plain face) also abound. In grassy areas near the base of the trail, unstriped Richardson ground squirrels are common. Locally they are called gophers. Yellow-bellied marmots, western cousins of the woodchuck, are often seen sunning themselves on rocks about a quarter mile up the trail from Twin Owls.

Common birds to watch for as you hike toward Gem Lake include tiny pygmy nuthatches, mountain chickadees, yellow-rumped warblers, gray-headed juncos, and raucous Clark's nutcrackers. Two thrushes seen more frequently along the lower part of the trail than in other areas of the park include Townsend's solitaire and the rust-and-blue western bluebird, which is not to be confused with the very common blue-and-gray mountain bluebird.

You may spot winged hunters soaring above the meadows of MacGregor Ranch, looking with hawk eyes for any of these small birds or mammals. Most common of the hunting raptors is the red-tailed hawk, which seeks squirrels for lunch. The much larger golden eagle also dines on marmot or even coyote. Birds are the preferred prey of the endangered peregrine falcon. Some parts of Lumpy Ridge may be closed to the public during spring and early summer to protect raptor nesting habitats. The exact sites change and are indicated by notices nearby; usually rock climbers more than hikers are affected by these closures.

In the moister areas among the ponderosas, Douglas-firs grow in groups or singly. Their cones, with three-pointed bracts protruding from under the scales, are quite distinctive. In the Pacific Northwest, the Douglas-fir grows to a huge size and is extremely important for lumber. In our semiarid climate, however, a specimen a yard in diameter qualifies as an old giant.

After a double switchback below Twin Owls and a stretch of trail running just inside the clearly marked park boundary, watch for an interesting antelope bitterbrush growing closely over a trailside rock on the left. Bitterbrush does not look unusual; it has many branches, small leaves, and small yellow blossoms in May and June. Yes, it tastes very bitter, but it is an important browse plant for mule deer. (In the second half of the nineteenth century, market hunters wiped out the antelope of the plant's name in the Estes Park area.) The warm period of each spring day is longer near the rock's surface, which reflects and absorbs heat. In response to the advanced season of this inch-thick microclimate, the branches of the plant growing nearest the rock are the first to leaf out and bloom.

By now, a pause to take a swig from your water bottle is probably welcome. The view over the pastures of MacGregor Ranch, established in 1874, is dominated by Longs Peak, the tallest peak in sight. At 14,255 feet, it is the highest point in Rocky Mountain National Park. Mount Meeker, to the left of Longs, is the park's second tallest peak—13,911 feet. To the right of Longs stretch other 12,000- and 13,000-foot summits of the Front Range.

Nearer at hand, the hillside is dotted with many dead ponderosa pines killed by mountain pine beetles. Now and then you will see lightning-killed trees too. Beetle trees are good hunting grounds for hungry woodpeckers such as common flickers, whose red wings and white rumps flash in flight. All the dead trees provide holes essential for nests of swallows, bluebirds, wrens, chickadees, nuthatches, and many more cavity-dwelling birds.

Farther up the trail, in especially dry and sunny areas, prickly pear cactus begins to appear. The blooms in June are a showy yellow and red. The big, nasty-looking spines at all times of year are a dramatic warning to keep away. But they are not dangerous, for you can see them. The real threat comes from the minute spines growing close to the surface of the fleshy stem.

In a national park, the prickly pear, like everything else, is of course left unmolested. Elsewhere, where it is more abundant, it is gathered and eaten, and then the small spines come into play. The big spines are easy to break or burn off, but the little ones seem immune to any type of removal. Most folks cannot even see them without a hand lens; under magnification the rows of barbs on each spine stand out like fishhooks. The barbs can work their way into the flesh of careless hands and cause pain for days.

The small spines were found by an archaeologist in 90 percent of the feces collected from ancient ruins at Mesa Verde National Park. Not content with the romance of examining centuries-old feces, the archaeologist tried eating fresh prickly pear with its tiny spines intact. Oddly, martyrdom for science was not the result. The only negative sensation was a prickling of the tongue. Please refrain from this kind of experiment though—especially in national parks!

A safer if not better-tasting addition to the Native American diet was squaw currant, which grows abundantly along the trail as it climbs the ridge. This bush has the typical rounded, lobed leaf of a currant and trumpet-shaped pink flowers that ripen to red berries. The berries are used by some jelly makers, but they need much spicing up to make the product more than insipid. They are, however, an important food for birds and small mammals.

As the trail bends to the left, it climbs across a gulch between Lumpy Ridge and a minor ridge extending south from the main slope. Although you might not be able to feel a change, you are entering a cooler, wetter climate. Plants are more sensitive to climate than are people, and here Douglas-fir is the dominant tree rather than ponderosa pine, which is adapted to drier slopes.

More water trickles into this gulch than is available to plants on the surrounding hillsides. The sides of the gulch are shaded during much of the day, and in winter the north-facing side receives hardly any sun. Each snowflake that is protected from the sun's direct melting rays serves as a tiny reservoir of water to nourish thirsty plants. Additionally, the shade slows evaporation at all times of the year.

The trees change again as the trail climbs over the minor ridge. The ridge top is exposed to high winds, especially in winter. Here grows limber pine (*Pinus flexilis*), whose tough, flexible branches bend easily in the wind but rarely break. This tree normally is associated with the tree line, several thousand feet higher on the mountains. Its needles are shorter than the ponderosa's and grow five to a bundle.

After crossing the ridge top, the trail from Twin Owls descends slightly to join the approach from Devils Gulch Road. Past the junction, the combined trail climbs eventually to the edge of an aspen grove in an often dry creek bed, where there is a heavy growth of bracken ferns. Soon excellent views beckon to the south and west, necessitating short detours from the trail. Looking south, you will see the bumpy summit of Twin Sisters across the valley east of Longs Peak. Lake Estes and associated civilization are obvious in the valley immediately below you.

Essentially similar views continue until the trail turns into a shady canyon with a small stream. The canyon is refreshingly cool, and out-of-place Engelmann spruce has found a foothold similar to its usual home higher in the subalpine zone. An occasional subalpine fir also grows here. Aspen, water birch, chiming bells, shooting star, and other moisture loving plants, along with mosquitoes, inhabit this oasis.

After crossing the stream, the trail is closed in by canyon walls. Exit is via two series of short switchbacks, at the top of which appears Paul Bunyans Boot, a rock formation that is a "must" photo. Chemical weathering even has put a hole in the boot's sole.

Natural sculpture and balanced rocks are common on Lumpy Ridge, as are potholes in the granite. On cliffs above Gem Lake, itself a big pothole, these formations of chemical and mechanical weathering seem too fantastic to be natural, more like a Disneyland invention.

The hollowing out of rock basins begins when falling rain picks up a little carbon dioxide from the air to form extremely mild carbonic acid. The acid tends to break down certain granitic minerals into various clays. Some of the rock surfaces are structurally weaker and more susceptible to this chemical weathering than are the surrounding surfaces. Further weak acids formed by accumulations of decaying vegetation can accelerate pothole formation, as can wind and frost wedging, expansion of ice that enlarges cracks in rocks. Weathering sometimes creates holes all the way through rock.

Below Gem Lake there are three series of short, steep switchbacks built to make the trail easier for horses, not for humans. The trail emerges from trees to run along steep-walled rock slabs, which collect the sun's warmth and radiate it back on hikers. You get steadily hotter, and then face one more long, dusty switchback to reach the lake—at last.

"Ugh, that's it?" is the standard reaction. Folks expecting a typical alpine lake are always disappointed. Gem covers only two-tenths of an acre, with a maximum depth of 5 feet and an average depth of 1 foot. It is stagnant, fed by rain and snowmelt, with no visible outlet. Various interesting but unglamorous creepy-crawlies call it home.

Yet Gem is a joy, for there is no other body of water like it in the park. White-throated swifts, uncommon elsewhere, dip and soar over the lake. Picturesque limber pines and Douglas-firs decorate the sandy shore. Stroll 200 feet to the opposite end of the lake, where pine branches will frame a photo of Gem with spectacular peaks in the background. Details of the patterns made by orange lichens on the rock cliffs provide additional good picture subjects. The examples of exfoliation and chemical weathering are unexcelled, and the acoustics of this natural amphitheater are such that your heartbeat seems to echo.

Around the corner of the cliff at the north end of the lake lies the easiest route of ascent to the top of the cliffs, about 200 feet above. It is worth the climb for the different photographic perspective of the lake (for which a wide angle-lens is helpful), fantastic potholes, and views of the surrounding peaks.

The trail continues north and descends a quarter mile from Gem Lake to a fork. The right branch is an unmaintained trail that cuts across private land at its bottom. Public access is disputed, and we recommend that you not bother hiking this trail.

The left branch descends a short way to level walking until

another fork is reached a half mile from the first. A left turn winds down among more Lumpy Ridge lumps into a gully containing the most interesting lump of all, **Balanced Rock,** about 2 miles from Gem Lake. Take the right fork, which descends to yet another split. The trail cutting right drops down to the old McGraw Ranch. Bear left to open meadows and the Cow Creek Trail. A right turn here takes you to Cow Creek Trailhead at McGraw Ranch. (At this trailhead is an emergency telephone.) A left turn leads to Bridal Veil Falls or Black Canyon. It is possible to trace your way down Black Canyon back to MacGregor Ranch, along the southern base of Lumpy Ridge to the Twin Owls parking area. This circle around Lumpy Ridge is roughly 9 miles.

North Fork of the Big Thompson Trail System

Everyone is destination oriented. This trail guide of necessity reflects the hiker's obsession with getting to a particular place. But on the North Fork trail system there is much to be said for no-particular-destination hiking. Most destinations are far from the trailhead. The national park itself is 4.4 miles from the starting point in Roosevelt National Forest.

The land around the North Fork of the Big Thompson River has been less used for day hiking than other sections of the park —Bear Lake or Glacier Gorge, for instance—because of the long distances to specific destinations. But backpacking has greatly extended the range of wilderness walkers, and travel along the North Fork is increasing.

It was the North Fork's remoteness that attracted one of the most colorful characters in Estes Park history in the 1870s. The Earl of Dunraven, an Englishman, had attempted to gain control of the Estes Park region to preserve its beauty and wildlife from despoliation by the three or four summer tourists who drifted in weekly. By fraudulent means, Dunraven gained title to enough land to turn Estes Park and the entire Big Thompson drainage to the north, west, and south (including the North Fork) into his own private hunting reserve.

When Americans paid no attention to his titles, land or otherwise, Dunraven saw that his plan would fail. He reversed his goals and opened a posh hotel to capitalize on the growing fame of Estes Park as a summer paradise. Meanwhile, he escaped the frustrations of civilization by building a hunting lodge for himself along the North Fork.

Dunraven's name lives on in a glade, trail, mountain, and lake in the North Fork drainage. His memory adds romance to an area that would be very pleasant and interesting even without a colorful history. The day hiker on the way to nowhere in particular will have an enjoyable trip along the North Fork.

To reach the trailhead, drive north from Estes Park on the Devils Gulch Road to the little town of Glen Haven. At a Forest Access sign about 2 miles past Glen Haven, turn left on unpaved Dunraven Glade Road. Somewhere along this road is the lost site of Dunraven's hunting lodge. Perhaps someday excavation for the construction of a new summer home will turn up the whiskey cache that the earl buried one fall and was unable to find the following spring.

A few miles down the unpaved road on the left-hand side is the Dunraven Glade Trailhead parking lot provided by the USDA Forest Service. On the other side of the parking lot, the **Dunraven Trail** begins by heading up a small ridge to enter Comanche Peak Wilderness. The path soon drops steeply down a forested slope to parallel the North Fork. To the left, the trail extends down through a deep, narrow canyon to Glen Haven—an easy, pleasant walk of less than 2 miles. To the right, the trail extends much farther than 2 miles, not all easy, but mostly pleasant.

Passage to the right does start out easily through the shade of thick blue spruce and Douglas-fir. In late August and early September, you may have trouble walking quickly past raspberry bushes laden with delicious fruit. As this beautiful canyon widens, the trail passes from national forest property to private land. While you are on private property, be especially conscientious about staying on the trail.

Before long, you find yourself walking on a four-wheel-drive road, which narrows again to trail dimensions until breaking out of the trees at **Deserted Village,** 3 miles from the trailhead. Wagons carried hunters to this turn-of-the-twentieth-century resort, which still has one cabin in more or less upright condition. A dysentery epidemic in 1909 had a poor effect on business, and the place was abandoned once and for all by 1914. The earl's hunting parties called this site Dunraven Meadows; a 1907 map labeled it Dunraven Park.

Lest you duplicate the unpleasant intestinal symptoms of wilderness visitors in 1909, do not drink the water straight from the North Fork. Treat it chemically and/or boil it first.

Ponderosa pines close in on the trail as the meadow narrows toward its upper end. Some of them have grown around strands of barbed wire that used to fence off someone's land interest. Dunraven probably did not bother to erect fences along the North Fork; people ignored his other fences anyway, running cattle over much of the land he claimed. His dream of preserving the wilderness and its wildlife for himself was a $200,000 flop. After one last hunt up the North Fork in 1880, he left the region for good. Preservation along a more typical American pattern was accomplished in 1915 with the establishment of Rocky Mountain National Park.

Almost a mile inside the park border, the North Boundary Trail begins on the left. Despite its name, it follows the eastern boundary south to Cow Creek Trailhead. This trail is described on page 43, but for now you may wish to note that it passes the North Fork patrol cabin less than 200 yards from its junction with the Dunraven Trail.

Past the junction, the trail along the North Fork is called the **Lost Lake Trail.** It proceeds along the bottom of the valley on a fairly mild grade for about 1.5 miles, then climbs steeply away from the river. At a spot 2.3 miles from the North Fork patrol cabin, the trail forks. The Stormy Peaks Trail (see page 44) is the right-hand fork. The Lost Lake Trail continues

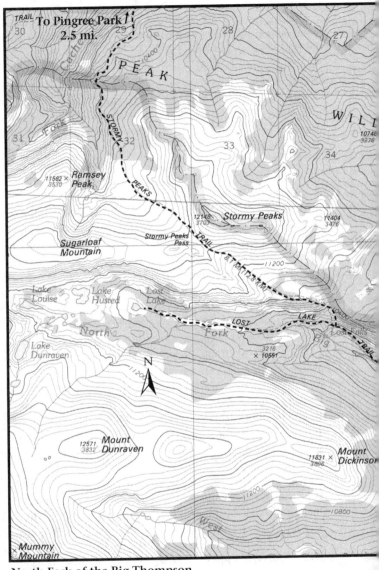

North Fork of the Big Thompson

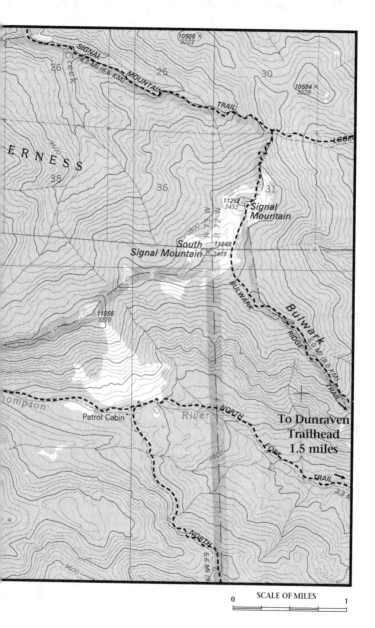

SCALE OF MILES

0   1

left over a relatively young terminal moraine, missing Lost Falls but passing through Lost Meadows. It parallels the creek to reach **Lost Lake.**

Lost Lake itself was once lost to the national park. After Dunraven gave up his dream, the need for preservation became evident. In 1911, a dam was built on the North Fork, enlarging Lost Lake into a reservoir. In the early 1970s, the National Park Service acquired the reservoir, and demolished the dam in 1985. Human alteration of the lake now is limited to the "bathtub ring" where high water killed the plants.

The trail fades away beyond Lost Lake, but easy routes exist to points farther on. Two lovely, unnamed alpine lakes sit on the other side of a ridge southwest of Lost Lake. There you are close to the base of Rowe Peak, and the rock cliffs of the mountains rise dramatically from the tundra.

The North Fork descends into the upper lake via a small noisy waterfall tumbling out of an interesting gorge that extends down from **Lake Dunraven.** Rather than climbing the gorge to Lake Dunraven, you may prefer to use it for your descent; a much easier route to the earl's lake begins at the outlet of the lower of the two unnamed lakes. After crossing the outlet, worm your way through the least dense section of krummholz, traverse the bottom of a talus slope, and then head straight up the ridge that hides Lake Dunraven.

To climb **Mount Dunraven,** continue up the ridge. After it becomes somewhat less steep, descend slightly and cross an unnamed drainage to reach and ascend the main bulk of Dunraven. Dunraven is the first summit on a spur extending east from the Mummy Range. The second is unnamed and in the way if you wish to continue along the spur to **Mount Dickinson,** at the end.

From the Mount Dunraven spur, you can climb to a saddle on the main section of the Mummy Range between **Hagues Peak** and **Mummy Mountain.** Although the approach from this side is less steep, these peaks are usually climbed from Lawn Lake because that approach is shorter (see Trails North of Horseshoe Park).

From Mummy Mountain you can descend to the Lawn Lake Trail via a south slope and the Black Canyon Trail. If **Lawn Lake** itself is your goal, carefully descend the steep tundra slopes from the Mummy-Hagues saddle (avoid cliffs by traversing a half mile west to descend less precipitous slopes below Hagues) to reach the route between Lawn and Crystal Lakes.

You can climb from Hagues to **Rowe Peak** and **Rowe Mountain** by dropping a few hundred feet to below the tarn at the base of Rowe Glacier. From there, climb steeply north to Rowe Peak. Losing and regaining altitude is easier than fighting the ragged spires on the knife ridge extending above the glacier between Hagues and Rowe Peaks.

There is a circle route back to Lost Lake via **Icefield Pass,** north of Rowe Mountain. Two more alpine lakes, **Lake Louise** and **Lake Husted,** add further joy to an easy meander across the tundra above Lost Lake.

Back at the North Fork patrol cabin, the **North Boundary Trail** heads south through fairly thick forest, crossing two streams as it winds steeply up a ridge. It descends to Fox Creek, then up and down again to West Creek, then up and down again to Cow Creek Trailhead, 6 miles from the North Fork.

As you can imagine, all this up and down becomes tiresome and dulls the mind to interesting details at trailside. Yet, because spectacular views are infrequent, sharp attention to detail is essential to make the North Boundary hike worth the effort. This trail is not the park's best for hiking; horse riders have it pretty much to themselves. But for hikers with both endurance and perception, there are some nice spots. It definitely should be hiked from north to south, so you will be climbing on the relatively cool, somewhat less steep northern slopes and descending the more open and warm southern slopes. Some details:

Fox Creek Falls is pleasant, though not spectacular. It is reached by a trail extending from private land at the Trail's End Cheley Camp, west of Glen Haven. It can also be reached from above by following Fox Creek down from where the North Boundary Trail crosses it, just outside the national park boundary.

Another trail junction comes up soon, this one with the **Fox Creek Trail,** on the left. Unless you have some personal reason for following Fox Creek to the east, there is little point in paying much attention to this trail, which soon descends a very steep slope through switchbacks. It is little used.

Past the Fox Creek Trail junction, the North Boundary Trail descends to West Creek. As you reach the valley floor but before you reach the creek, a spur trail cuts back sharply to the right, extending a half mile upstream to **West Creek Falls,** inside the national park. You have more than a mile of steep walking ahead to the south end of the trail, and the hiker's natural urge is to get on with it. Nevertheless, you may find it worthwhile to expend a little more effort on the pleasant side trip to these lovely falls.

The southern end of the **Stormy Peaks Trail** branches from the Lost Lake Trail immediately after a very steep section 7.6 miles from the Dunraven Glade Trailhead parking lot. Past the junction, the Stormy Peaks Trail is even steeper for almost a mile. The grade becomes less grinding near tree line, where you get a fine view of Rowe Peak and Rowe Mountain above Lost Meadows. (You may want a wide-angle lens for photos at this point.) **Stormy Peaks Pass** is another mile up a less steep section of trail. The effort required to make a short climb from the pass to the top of Stormy Peaks is amply rewarded by an excellent view.

From Stormy Peaks Pass you can skirt some rocky bumps for an easy walk west over the tundra to **Sugarloaf Mountain.** As you climb Sugarloaf, walk to the edge of the North Fork Valley for a spectacular view of the lakes below and the main peaks of the Mummy Range. From Sugarloaf you can descend via **Skull Point** and Icefield Pass to Lost Lake.

The Stormy Peaks Trail continues north below Stormy Peaks Pass. The path is faint in a few spots but easy and pleasant to follow downhill to the park boundary and out of the park through subalpine woods. The northern end of the trail is located at an entrance gate to the Pingree Park Campus of Colorado State University, about 7.5 miles from the Lost Lake Trail. The Stormy Peaks Trail affords good views of Pingree Park; its "campus" is more like a camp.

Stormy Peaks Pass is 9.7 miles from the Dunraven Glade Trailhead and just over half that distance from Pingree Park Trailhead. If your goal is the Stormy Peaks area, it is obviously easier to hike from the northern end of the trail.

To drive to Pingree Park from Fort Collins, take US 287 north to Colorado Highway 14. Drive 27.5 miles north and then west on CO 14. Two miles past Fort Collins Mountain Park, turn left onto Pingree Park Road (63E) and drive 14 miles south to Pingree.

From Estes Park or Loveland, take US 34 east to the Masonville Road, about 3 miles east of the Big Thompson Canyon. Drive on through Masonville to the spot where the road ends in a T. Turn left (west) and drive northwest along Buckhorn Creek. Keep on until you reach a fork in the road more than 10 miles from Masonville. The right-hand fork goes to Stove Prairie; take the left-hand (lower) fork west to Pennock Pass and down to another T, about 25 miles from Masonville. Turn left and drive approximately 5 miles on a two-lane gravel road to a fork at Pingree Park. Take the left branch and continue 500 feet to the entrance gate. A sign marks the trailhead on the left side of the road.

Some maps show **Signal Mountain Trail** heading from the Stormy Peaks Trail to the park's eastern boundary. This "trail" is hard to find and has disintegrated to the point where trying to follow it amounts to cross-country navigation. It can be traced in some sections (watch for old blazes on trees), but you will lose the path now and then and have to wander about, searching. When it disappears at last in an expanse of boulders accented with magnificent old limber pines, head for the ridge top and try to retrieve the trail there. It was never located where maps indicate, on the side of the ridge, and it disappears completely above tree line on South Signal Mountain. Head straight up to the summit or circle on its left (northern) flank to climb the slightly taller Signal Mountain just outside the park boundary.

The USDA Forest Service trail from Signal Mountain down to the North Fork is well maintained. It is steep in some stretches and very steep in the rest. As it descends Bulwark Ridge, most of the trail passes through open limber or lodgepole pine forests, which normally are sunny and hot. The trail is used mainly by horses; hikers ascending it face a difficult grind. Signal Mountain Trail ends at the unpaved Dunraven Road west of Glen Haven at a gate marking the boundary between Roosevelt National Forest and private property. The road at this point is closed to public vehicles, but the Dunraven Glade Trailhead parking lot is located a few hundred yards to the east.

Mummy Pass Trail

Mummy Pass Trail runs from the Long Draw Reservoir Road past the national park's northwestern boundary to a spot above Pingree Park, beyond the northern boundary. Both ends of the trail are in Roosevelt National Forest. The trail passes through what once was the remotest part of the park. The improvement of the road to Long Draw Reservoir to accommodate ordinary passenger cars has made the park's northwestern corner more accessible, but it still is relatively uncrowded and the best place to spot deer and elk. During hunting season it is heavily patrolled by rangers to frustrate the criminal intent of poachers.

To reach the Pingree Park end of the trail, from Colorado Highway 14 take Pingree Park Road (63E) 17 miles to the Tom Bennett Campground turnoff. A Forest Service sign marks the turnoff. Turn right past the campground, cross the South Fork of the Cache La Poudre River, and continue up around a curve to a fork in the road, where you can park. Walk up the left fork toward Cirque Meadows and Emmaline Lake. This trail is a road for another 2.5 miles to the beginning of Mummy Pass Trail. This county road, however, tends to deteriorate to a four-wheel-drive adventure.

The road fords Fall Creek, and about a quarter mile later the trail heads left (south) from the road. After zigzagging through subalpine forest for a couple of miles, it winds out of the trees and into the national park. Above tree line, the trail steepens somewhat until you reach the broad, nearly level top of a bench leading to Mummy Pass. On the way, you must descend into a lush little valley holding two ponds and a multitude of flowers.

After hiking out of the valley, you can turn right (northwest) off the trail and climb steeply over tundra to **Fall Mountain.** The opposite (northern) side of the peak is glaciated dramatically, as is the entire ridge leading northwest to **Comanche Peak.** On the way to Comanche, skirt the big rocks at the heads of the cirques that indent this ridge, but walk to the edge now and then for the view.

From the top of Comanche, it is a long way north to any higher mountain. It is also a long way down to Emmaline Lake, Cirque Lake, and other smaller tarns at the head of Fall Creek. These lakes can be seen from intermediate peninsulas that project from the Fall Comanche ridge, but the best view is from Comanche's summit.

A circle route back to Pingree leads east down the north ridge above the Comanche cirque. Below this ridge you will hit a trail from Emmaline Lake that leads to the four-wheel-drive road. Follow the road down to your parked vehicle.

Mummy Pass sits on a broad tundra plateau between the Hague Creek drainage and the South Fork of the Poudre drainage, 1.5 miles from the northern boundary. As the trail winds across tundra and through subalpine forest, you see the Mummy Range from a unique if not particularly spectacular angle. More scenic from the plateau is the Never Summer Range to the southwest, with dramatic Mount Richthofen and Nokhu Crags dominating the skyline. Just past the crossing of Mummy Pass Creek, 1.8 miles from Mummy Pass, you arrive at a junction where the Mirror Lake Trail runs to the right (north).

Because more hikers approach **Mirror Lake** from the western end of the Mummy Pass Trail, we will jump in seven-league boots to the **Corral Creek Trailhead.** To reach this trailhead, drive

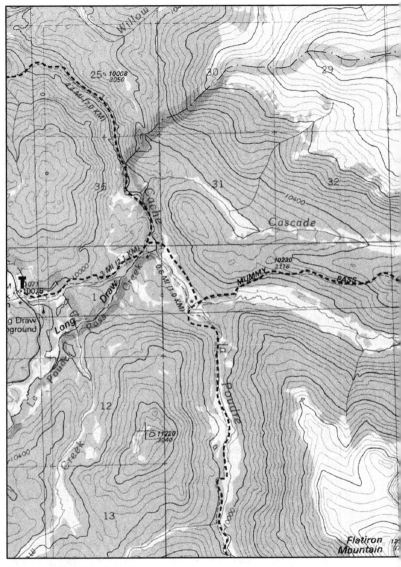

Mummy Pass Trail System

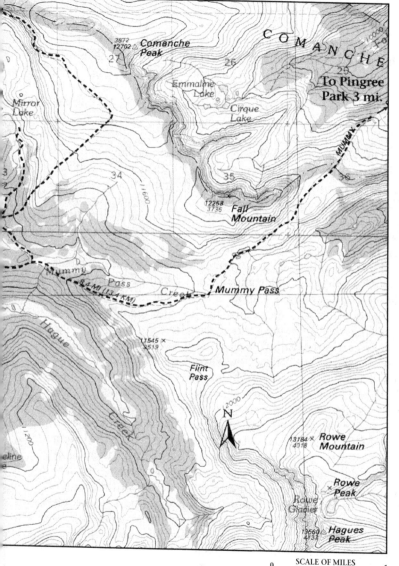

Comanche
Peak
3872
12702 △

C O M A N C H E

27
26
29

Emmaline
Lake

**To Pingree
Park 3 mi.**

Mirror
Lake

Cirque
Lake

Mummy

34
11,600
35

12258
3736
Fall
Mountain

Mummy
Pass
Creek

Mummy Pass

2.4 MI (3.4 KM)

Hague

11545 ×
3519

Flint
Pass

N
2000

Creek

13184 ×
4018
Rowe
Mountain

Rowe
× Peak

Rowe
Glacier

eline
e

13560 △
4133
Hagues
Peak

SCALE OF MILES

0   1

along CO 14, which runs between Fort Collins and Walden. About 4 miles north of Cameron Pass or 2 miles south of Chambers Lake, turn southeast onto the two-lane, gravel Long Draw Road (USDA Forest Service Route 156), which travels through Box Canyon and Corral Park, eventually ending at the western end of Long Draw Reservoir.

Drive about 8 miles on this road to the Corral Creek Trailhead and its parking lot. There is a campground, Long Draw, about a quarter mile south of the trailhead.

The Mummy Pass Trail begins as an old road following Corral Creek, but soon becomes a path. After less than a mile, you will reach the national park and a rather substantial bridge over the Cache La Poudre River. Another 0.6 mile of easy walking brings you to a junction with the Poudre River Trail. The Poudre River Trail (see Trails from Milner Pass in the Trail Ridge Road chapter) branches right (south); the Mummy Pass trail continues east.

The Mummy Pass Trail meanders north of Hague Creek along a gentle open valley until a left bend takes you steeply up through thick woods. The grade moderates at the ridge top, rising gradually to the junction on the left with the **Mirror Lake Trail**, 4.5 miles from the Corral Creek Trail.

The climb to Mirror Lake is an easy walk through subalpine forest until you reach a meadow where Cascade Creek flows still and wide, 0.7 mile from the Mummy Pass Trail.

There, branching sharply right from the main trail, a path heads straight up through the forest. Above tree line the route is steeper yet. Marked by cairns up the mountain, the trail levels west of Comanche Peak. There is nothing to be gained from striking out for the top of Comanche until the path flattens; premature departure probably will put you on an annoying false summit. Beyond Comanche Peak, the trail descends out of the national park to another junction; a sharp right turn there leads down, after about 4 miles, to Comanche Reservoir. This artificial lake is situated at the end of the road branching off the Pingree Park road to Tom Bennett Campground.

It may seem odd that some maps call the trail to Comanche Peak the Mirror Lake Trail when from the point of view of most hikers, it cuts away from Mirror Lake. The trail was named, though, when most visitors to the lake approached it from the north.

The final mile of the trail to Mirror Lake passes through forest and flowered marshy meadows before reaching its destination. The lake, a classic tarn, was scoured by a glacier in the rock of a long cirque. This is tree line, so the lake at its outlet end is bordered by both erect subalpine fir and the shrubby krummholz version of the same tree. The far shore is rocky and barren, bordered by steep cliffs and snowbanks. The peaks that tower over the lake are no less dramatic for being unnamed. The lake itself has been shortchanged with a very common name for an uncommonly beautiful place.

Trails North of Horseshoe Park

The Lawn Lake dam broke July 15, 1982. The resulting flash flood killed three campers, destroyed $30 million in property, and obliterated the streamside sanctuary of Roaring River that had taken 10,000 years to create. Heroic warnings by park rangers, sheriff deputies, and Estes Park police (all of whom knew that two law officers had died while out issuing similar warnings in the 1976 Big Thompson flood) prevented greater loss of life. A giant outwash fan west of Lawn Lake Trailhead testifies to the flood's power. The trailhead is a parking lot on the right (north) side of Fall River Road near the spot where the road branches off US 34.

The beginning of the Lawn Lake and Ypsilon Lake Trails is a series of switchbacks on a ponderosa-covered lateral moraine. Hikers cutting up or down across these switchbacks have caused severe erosion. The National Park Service is trying to restore vegetation and repair the damage to the land, so please do not take shortcuts.

As you climb, the flood damage in the valley of Fall River becomes increasingly obvious. Above the switchbacks, the deep,

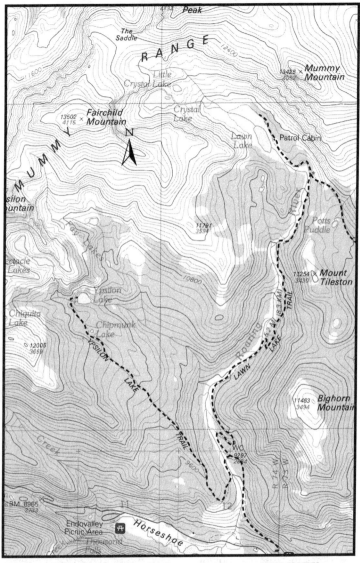

Trails North of Horseshoe Park

SCALE OF MILES

0   1

raw gorge gouged by the flood is visible below. Destruction of trees has opened a view of Ypsilon Mountain. Looking down the gorge reveals a new view of Longs Peak. Through a devastated sandy area, you approach the trail that branches left to Ypsilon Lake 1.3 miles from the trailhead.

A log bridge takes the Ypsilon Lake Trail across what once was an aspen cathedral along Roaring River and climbs a moraine through lodgepole pines. Once on top of the moraine, the trail levels a bit, still among lodgepoles. Some hikers find this section of trail boring despite occasional close views of the snow-filled gullies that form a huge Y on the face of Ypsilon Mountain.

When the trail descends to **Chipmunk Lake,** pause to take a photo of Fairchild Mountain reflected in this tiny pond (assuming it's a calm day). Then leave the trail and walk through the woods to the pond's swampy eastern shore. If the air is still, you will get numerous mosquito bites and a superb reflection shot of Ypsilon Mountain. A wide-angle lens is essential.

The trail ends on the west side of **Ypsilon Lake** amid large glacial erratics and subalpine forest. A waterfall tumbles down a steep slope nearby before the stream flows into the lake. It is a pleasant spot but, it lacks the majesty of **Spectacle Lakes**, a hard, steep half mile farther on. These lakes, which look like giant eyeglasses from the top of Ypsilon Mountain, sit on a ledge 800 feet higher than Ypsilon Lake. Above them rise dramatic Y-shaped couloirs on the classic glacial cirque that is the east face of Ypsilon Mountain. A photographer caught here without a wide-angle lens faces certain frustration.

There is no maintained trail leading to Spectacle Lakes, and all routes are very difficult early in the season. One of the least difficult is up the stream that flows into Ypsilon Lake. This route is steep above the waterfall and blocked by rock outcrops and glacial erratics. You will have to crisscross the creek to circumvent the obstacles.

In an often flowery meadow, the terrain levels, and the stream branches. The lay of the land will probably cause you to arrive between the two forks. You can follow the left fork to **Chiquita Lake,** about a mile from Ypsilon Lake. The right fork leads to Spectacle Lakes. Below the lakes, the stream tumbles through a waterfall from the shelf on which the lakes sit. Getting up onto this shelf involves a rock climb, which many trail-accustomed hikers find disturbing. It's probably easiest to reach the shelf by climbing to the left of the falls.

An alternative route that avoids the rock work begins by ascending a gully above the treeless northern edge of Ypsilon Lake. You can see the starting point from the trail at the western shoreline. The gully leads up to a ridgeline, where you turn left and climb above the trees. From this area, angle left again around to the west side of the ridge and descend to the lower Spectacle Lake.

This alternative route involves a greater total expenditure of energy than does the first. It also leads you to an inconveniently cliffy spot on the lower lake, from which it is difficult to reach the best vantage point, at the outlet. (Early in the season, an ice ax may be handy here.) On the other hand, this is the route for hikers who absolutely will not climb the slabs below Spectacle Lakes!

To reach **Fay Lakes,** three small bodies of water in the valley between Mount Ypsilon and Fairchild Mountain, follow the southern shore of Ypsilon Lake to its outlet. Cross over and make your way northeast through the forest, climbing steadily until you reach the stream from Fay Lakes, less than a half mile from Ypsilon Lake. Follow it upstream to the lakes, which are strung out at half-mile intervals.

From the turnoff for Ypsilon Lake, 1.3 miles from the Lawn Lake Trailhead, **Lawn Lake Trail** skirts an area where flood damage continues. The tons of rushing water cut a very steep-walled gorge through unconsolidated glacial debris. Of course, there are no plants to stabilize the steep walls above Roaring River. Rain and melting snow will continue to erode the walls, cutting them back into forest originally untouched by the flood until a less steep, more stable slope forms. Thus, earth slides will

Bull elk

be common along the gorge of Roaring River. If you are standing on the gorge lip when it gives way, you could become another flood victim. The Park Service has built new sections of trail to replace those wiped out or made unsafe by the flood.

After the trail veers east from the river, a set of two long switchbacks marks the beginning of gradually increasing steepness. Above these switchbacks, head uphill from the trail if you wish to climb **Bighorn Mountain** or **Mount Tileston.** The ascent is steep, without benefit of trail, and runs through fallen timber. Picturesque limber pines compose the tree line on Bighorn and Tileston. Mountain sheep concentrate on Bighorn, but you are just as likely, and perhaps moreso to see them from US 34 in Horseshoe Park.

Continuing up Lawn Lake Trail through more switchbacks brings you to a small basin and good views of the cliffs on Mummy Mountain to the north. A trail junction on the right, 5.6 miles from the trailhead, marks the beginning of the Black Canyon Trail (see page 57). Although Lawn Lake is 0.6 mile farther on, some maps refer to the trail between this spot and the lake as the Black Canyon Trail. This appellation arose in the early part of the twentieth century, when the trails were mainly horseback routes and the usual destinations were somewhat different from today's. In this book, Black Canyon Trail refers only to the path between Lawn Lake Trail and Twin Owls.

In 1902, a dam was built, enlarging Lawn Lake to store irrigation water until it was needed down on the plains. Improperly maintained by the irrigation company that owned it, the dam eventually washed out, leaving barren, rocky shores surrounding a much smaller lake. Above the former water line are lovely meadows where subalpine flowers mix with those of the tundra.

Fairchild Mountain and **Hagues Peak** tower above. They can be climbed by following unmaintained routes beyond the northern end of the lake and then up a much steeper grade. Four hundred feet above and a half mile beyond Lawn Lake, the route divides. The left branch heads uphill past an unnamed pond and **Little Crystal Lake** to **Crystal Lake.** Crystal Lake, which sits in a magnificent cirque on the side of Fairchild Moutain, is probably the deepest lake in the park.

If a mountain summit is your goal, you probably should not take the time to visit these lakes, wonderful as they are. You will get good views of them from the right-hand branch of the route as it ascends to **The Saddle** between Hagues and Fairchild. Well below The Saddle, Fairchild climbers should leave the beaten path as it angles to the right (north) in a relatively level alpine meadow. Bearing left, ascend the steep ridge that extends southwest to Fairchild's summit, a simple but strenuous boulder-hopping climb at this elevation.

If you wish to climb Hagues Peak or **Mummy Mountain,** head east from the main trail about 0.2 mile beyond the Crystal Lake junction. A natural ramp leads steeply to the saddle between Hagues and Mummy. Step gently on the tundra. From the saddle, it is a relatively easy hike to either summit. (See description of these peaks in the North Fork of the Big Thompson section.)

It is likely that the easiest route up Mummy and Hagues is not from Lawn Lake but from the **Black Canyon Trail.** East of its junction with the Lawn Lake Trail, where the Black Canyon Trail levels, strike off to the left (northeast) through struggling pines over large rocks to tree line. Pick out the least steep route to the top of Mummy; the summit is 2,200 feet higher than the Black Canyon Trail, an elevation gained in approximately 1 mile. A false summit 500 or so feet below the top could fool and disappoint you.

Back on the Black Canyon Trail itself, the path soon begins to descend. There are many ponds amid the large boulders. One of the largest ponds is **Potts Puddle,** which can shrink to nearly nothing in a dry summer. As it crosses Black Canyon Creek several times, the trail becomes gradually dimmer ("unimproved" is the local euphemism) but never disappears entirely. Eventually, it begins to become clearer, passes a junction with the Cow Creek Trail, and descends to Twin Owls.

Cow Creek Trailhead

One of the historic ranches in this area, McGraw Ranch was established before 1874. A century later, new owners began calling it Indian Head Ranch, but the name never caught on locally. Cow Creek Trailhead is located at the ranch site, at the end of the 2.3-mile unpaved McGraw Ranch Road, which leaves Devils Gulch Road 3.9 miles from downtown Estes Park.

The **North Boundary Trail** to lovely **West Creek Falls** cuts sharply uphill a few yards west of the ranch site. Ascend through a meadow to the spot where the trail crosses the lowest point on the ridge. It is very steep, eroded, and often sunny and hot.

From the ridge top, the trail zigzags steeply down through Rocky Mountain maple and Douglas-fir to West Creek, 1.4 miles from the trailhead. Cross the creek and turn left (west) at the trail intersection; the trail follows a gentle grade along the stream to West Creek Falls, which drops in two tiers through a rocky amphitheater. The trail to the right after the stream crossing follows the valley floor, eventually recrossing West Creek and circling back over the ridge to the ranch site.

The most popular hike from Cow Creek Trailhead is an easy 3 miles to **Bridal Veil Falls.** Head west on the Cow Creek Trail for slightly more than a mile to the Bridal Veil Falls Trail, which branches right. Passing through open montane zone vegetation, this trail can be hot at midday in midsummer. There are many lovely beaver ponds, though, along the trail as it follows Cow Creek, and Bridal Veil Falls ranks among the prettiest in the park.

Chapin Pass Routes

Chapin Pass is the back door to Mount Chapin, Mount Chiquita, and Ypsilon Mountain. Although the rugged, glacially carved east faces of these popular peaks are very visible and beautiful from the valleys around Estes Park, the unglaciated, less precipitous western slopes rising above Chapin Pass offer the easiest routes to the top. Beyond Ypsilon you can continue to Desolation Peaks, Flatiron Mountain, or Fairchild Mountain. Chapin Pass is the highest point on the **Chapin Creek Trail**.

The easiest way to Chapin Pass is to drive to a small parking area by the side of the unpaved Old Fall River Road about 6.5 miles from its beginning at the western end of Horseshoe Park. Old Fall River Road is one-way uphill; after the hike you will have to continue on to Trail Ridge Road at Fall River Pass. (Overnight parking is prohibited at the parking area below Chapin Pass.) From the parking area, follow the road for a few yards to the spot where the Chapin Creek Trail starts on the right (northern) side. Then follow the trail a short distance straight uphill to Chapin Pass.

If the Old Fall River Road is not yet open for the season and you are determined to hike through Chapin Pass, you must drive over Trail Ridge Road to Fall River Pass and begin there. Walk down the Old Fall River Road nearly to tree line. There you should angle off to the left and follow the ridgeline downhill to Chapin Pass, thus avoiding having to ascend to the pass from farther down the road.

Beginning at Fall River Pass adds almost 3 miles to the hike. It means that the final part of your trip, when you are tired, will be an ascent above tree line to reach your car. Furthermore, lightning-filled clouds may roll some excitement your way, forcing a retreat below tree line prior to climbing again toward Fall River Pass. (See the section on lightning in the Introduction.)

To climb **Mount Chapin, Mount Chiquita,** and **Ypsilon Mountain,** head east from Chapin Pass on a faint ("unimproved") path that branches off the main trail. The branch trail soon climbs out of the trees, cuts around the southern flank of a hill on the ridge, and disappears amid rocks and tundra. Do not fret if you miss the path; once above tree line, it is a simple, steep trudge up the ridge to Chapin, the rounded summit farthest to the right.

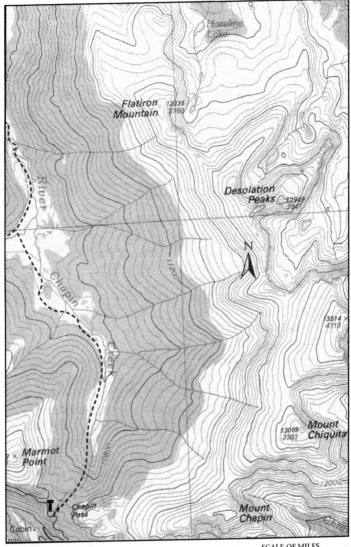

Hazeline Lake

Flatiron Mountain 12335 3760

River

Chapin

Creek

Desolation Peaks 12949 3947

N

13514 × 4119

Marmot Point

10,800

11,200

13069 3383

Mount Chiquita

Cabin

Chapin Pass

Mount Chapin

12000

Chi

Chapin Pass Routes

SCALE OF MILES
0   1

Ascending this ridge to Chapin seems like a steeper and harder climb than either Chiquita or Ypsilon. Many hikers bypass Mount Chapin and head directly for these two higher peaks via the saddle between Chapin and Chiquita. By so doing, they miss seeing good views down onto rock spires that rise from Chapin's rugged southern side. As you approach the top, bypass Chapin's western summit and head for the taller eastern one.

From Chapin, descend about 400 feet to the Chapin-Chiquita saddle, then ascend 1,000 feet to the top of Chiquita. You walk about a mile from summit to summit. The grade is not terribly steep; only the 13,000-foot elevation may pose minor problems. Chiquita is the easiest "thirteener" to climb in Rocky Mountain National Park.

If you are pressed for time or have a more distant goal, you can skip Chiquita and head straight for Ypsilon, a mile farther on. From the top of the snow-filled gullies that form a Y on the east face of Ypsilon, there is a spectacular view straight down to Spectacle Lakes, more than 2,000 feet below. Since you are likely to see this view in the morning, the sun probably will be glaring off the water. A polarizing filter over the lens will eliminate the glare from photos.

Beyond Ypsilon the going gets tougher. **Desolation Peaks** are located 2 rugged miles of ridge clambering and cirque skirting north of Ypsilon. It is a similar 1.5 miles beyond Desolation to **Flatiron Mountain.**

Fairchild Mountain, northeast of Ypsilon, is usually climbed from Lawn Lake (see Trails North of Horseshoe Park). But Fairchild can be reached also from Ypsilon, a route that necessitates losing and regaining 1,000 feet of elevation over a couple of very steep and rough miles. If you plan to go to so much trouble, you might as well descend Fairchild via Lawn Lake and arrange for transportation at the trailhead in Horseshoe Park.

Back at Chapin Pass, a route descends very quickly to the marshy drainage of Chapin Creek. You will probably reach the valley floor in less than twenty minutes; we will refrain from guessing how long it will take to climb back out. This unmaintained 3-mile route is followed mainly by backpackers on their way to somewhere else via the Poudre River Trail (see Trails from Milner Pass in the Trail Ridge Road chapter). Your chances of seeing elk along Chapin Creek or the Poudre River are excellent.

Moraine Park

Their easy accessibility and great beauty have made the trails west of Moraine Park very popular since before the national park was established. The two main trailheads, for Fern Lake and Cub Lake, are situated within a mile of each other on an unpaved road west of Moraine Park Campground. The proximity of the trailheads and a connecting link between their trails make a circle hike reasonably simple.

To reach the trailheads, turn onto the Bear Lake Road 0.2 mile west of the Beaver Meadows Entrance to the park, or 2.7 miles south of the junction of US 34 and US 36 on Deer Ridge. Follow the Bear Lake Road for 1.2 miles over a ridge to Moraine Park. A few yards past Moraine Park Museum, a paved road branches right toward Moraine Park Campground.

Follow this road for a half mile and turn left on the still-paved road to the trailheads. (If you reach Moraine Park Campground, you have missed the turn.) After 1.2 miles the pavement ends. The parking area for Cub Lake Trailhead is a mile ahead on the right. The Fern Lake Trailhead and its parking lot are located a mile up the valley, at the end of the road.

Three-tenths of a mile west of the Cub Lake Trailhead is another parking lot and the bus stop for Bear Lake Shuttle. When this free mass transit runs in the summer, hikers going from one of the trailheads near Bear Lake to Moraine Park can hop on a bus and return to their cars. Check with the National Park Service for detailed bus schedules.

Fern Lake Trail System

From Fern Lake Trailhead, the path meanders for 1.5 miles along the Big Thompson River to **The Pool.** Because this stretch of trail is relatively flat and easy to walk, many hikers hurry along it. Of course, they get hot and sweaty in the process and blame the trail for being too warm and dull. Such hikers should travel at a

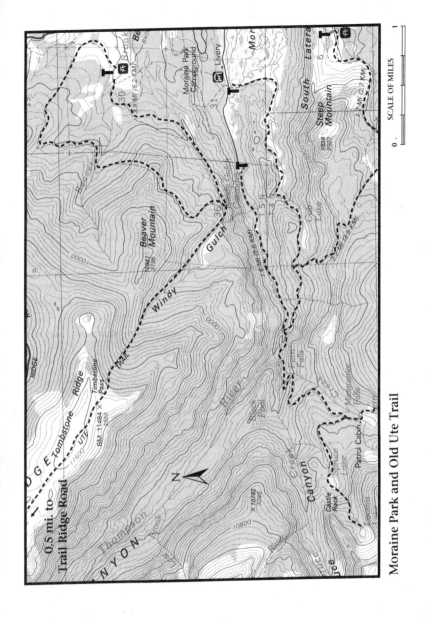

Moraine Park and Old Ute Trail

0   SCALE OF MILES   1

more comfortable pace and take time to see the many interesting features that make the trip to The Pool such a joy for an alert and observant hiker.

A little more than a mile from the trailhead, Fern Lake Trail winds beneath **Arch Rocks.** It is tempting to think that these giant monoliths were put there by a retreating glacier, but they more likely fell from the cliffs after the glaciers melted. One house-sized chunk crashed nearby in the winter of 1992–93. The best place from which to photograph the entire configuration of Arch Rocks is along or in the river a few hundred feet to the west. Afternoon sunshine, if available, is the best.

The trail crosses the Big Thompson River on a substantial log bridge at The Pool, where water swirling between steep stone walls has formed a pool in the rock. Past the bridge, the path divides. The left-hand branch passes along the valley floor through a meadow that is in the process of reverting to pine. As you begin to climb along a north-facing slope, thick forest closes in. Less than a half mile from The Pool, a lovely brook flowing down Mount Wuh intersects the trail through a patch of Rocky Mountain maple. Farther on there are views of Stones Peak to the west, but you will get better photographic composition of the mountain from Cub Lake. The trail levels out, and a path to Mill Creek Basin branches to the right about a mile from The Pool. It is easier to walk this 1.5-mile path from the other direction (see Hollowell Park Trails in the Bear Lake Road chapter). The trail to Cub Lake leads straight ahead and reaches the lake after 0.3 mile (see Cub Lake Trail). Back at The Pool, the Fern Lake Trail runs straight ahead from the Cub Lake Trail junction. Circling around open south-facing slopes, the trail to Fern Lake soon climbs along the side of a gully and enters deep subalpine woods. After crossing Fern Creek, you ascend a rather noisy ridge between the roarings of Spruce and Fern Creeks.

Continuing on the somewhat steep slope parallel to Spruce Creek, watch for brownie lady's-slipper orchids (*Cypripedium fasciculatum*) blooming in July at trailside. The path zigzags along a fairly level grade. As you curve up the hillside, the roar of **Fern Falls** announces its presence before you see it.

After climbing 480 feet in the mile from The Pool, you will probably be ready to cool off in the spray from the falls. Because Fern Falls is surrounded by dense woods of Engelmann spruce and subalpine fir, the best light for photography hits the falls in midday, when most hikers arrive.

Past the falls, the trail climbs rather steeply again, away from the creek, and the immediate rise in temperature and reduction of noise are always surprising.

A switchback brings you more or less parallel to Fern Creek, but you cannot see it until just after the junction with the Spruce Lake Trail (see below). Crossing Fern Creek at the outlet of Fern Lake, you walk onto the open shoreline for a fine view of Notchtop Mountain and the Little Matterhorn, which rise beyond subalpine forest on the other side of the lake.

For the best photographic effect, back up a bit to include lodgepoles or spruce as a frame for your picture. If you think the near shoreline looks slightly overtrampled, find a position where bushes in the foreground will block it out. A few yards farther along the shore, you can take similarly composed photos of Stones Peak and an unnamed neighboring summit to the right. (Avoid tramping areas that the Park Service is trying to revegetate on the site of old Fern Lake Lodge, which has been removed.)

Leaving Fern Lake, the path crosses a boulder field and climbs through classic subalpine forest. Shade- and moisture-loving flowers such as various species of pyrola are common along the mile of trail between Fern and Odessa Lakes (see Odessa Lake Trail in the Bear Lake Trailhead chapter).

Spruce Lake Trail begins back in the open forest amid moss-covered rocks just before you reach Fern Lake. The unimproved 0.8-mile path climbs at an easy grade, then drops through glacier-deposited boulders to cross an outlet creek and enter the marshy meadows that surround **Spruce Lake.** Convenient sitting rocks are somewhat difficult to appropriate at the lake; the best ones are partly submerged. Stones Peak rises massively beyond the lake. Even more spectacular are the chimneylike spires of Castle Rock, which loom directly overhead.

To reach **Loomis Lake,** continue around the north shore of Spruce Lake. Follow a path up the drainage into the amphitheater containing Loomis Lake. Dramatic craggy cliffs rise on three sides of this emerald tarn.

Spruce Lake is also the best starting point for climbing **Stones Peak**. Head north from the lake over the thickly forested low ridge below Castle Rock. On the other side of the ridge you'll find **Spruce Canyon,** which contains Spruce Creek. Follow the drainage upstream to tree line and a huge cirque between Sprague Mountain and Stones Peak. Choked with downed trees and very steep, Spruce Canyon presents very tough hiking. Pick the least steep route past **Hourglass Lake** and on up to a glacial shelf. Via the very steep slope to the right of an unnamed pool on this shelf, climb to the low point on the ridge that connects Sprague and Stones. Then turn right and climb the ridge to the summit of Stones Peak.

The top offers the best possible view of Sprague Glacier and the tarn into which it descends. South of you lies impressive Rainbow Lake. To the west, you look down on the crags of Hayden Spire rising from Lonesome Lake. (For an alternative route up Stones Peak, see Flattop Mountain Trail System in the Bear Lake Trailhead chapter.)

Cub Lake Trail

The Cub Lake Trail is known for its variety of wildflowers. It is also an excellent trail for bird-watching. The variety of both flowers and birds is created by many different types of habitats through which the trail passes in 2.3 miles. For driving instructions to the trailhead, see the beginning of this chapter. If both parking areas are full, please do not park on the side of the road. Additional parking is available only 0.3 mile beyond the Club Lake Trailhead parking lot.

From the trailhead, you cross a footbridge that spans old swampy beaver workings. In the wet meadowland beyond, the trail is lined with willows and thinleaf alder. Watch for various species of warblers, particularly yellow, Macgillivray's, and yellow-rumped (Audubon's). Just past the third bridge (this one crosses the Big Thompson River), watch for pink shooting stars growing at streamside, especially from late June through mid-July.

The trail continues amid water-loving shrubs that obviously have been browsed in winter by elk. Before long you arrive at a mixed grove of ponderosa pine and Douglas-fir. There are large, glacially scoured rocks to the right (west) and white-barked aspens to the east (left). This is a good area in which to watch for warbling vireos and western tanagers.

Soon a short uphill section of trail climbs over bare, rounded, glacially scoured bedrock. Large boulders—glacial erratics—perch isolated on the bedrock where the glacier left them 13,000 years ago. Views to the east show a long, forested, even-topped ridge of unsorted rock dumped by the glacier along its edge. That is the classic lateral moraine for which Moraine Park was named.

Yellow-bellied marmots appear among the glacial erratics at trailside. These larger cousins of the eastern woodchuck are especially appealing in early summer, when the young animals scamper about after emerging from their mothers' hibernation dens.

Pause at a large round erratic sitting right in the middle of the trail. If you feel beneath the rock, you will perceive at once the difference between the glacially polished surface protected by the erratic and the rough bedrock elsewhere, exposed to weathering for thousands of years.

From bedrock the trail descends to more wet meadow and reaches a horse trail that follows the lateral moraine. Look for elk tracks in the wet soil.

Bear right at the trail junction and follow the edge of the meadow in a westerly direction. The path is nearly level, with ponderosa-covered hillsides on the right and a series of old beaver ponds on the left. Although beaver sightings are unlikely, you may see a muskrat cutting a V in the water.

The scarce and spectacular wood lily grows by the ponds in late June or early July. Picking any wildflowers in national parks is, of course, both illegal and wrong; picking one of these rare blossoms would be an especially grievous offense.

Past the old beaver ponds, the trail begins a series of switchbacks uphill through aspens. Rather steep in places, it levels a short way before you reach the lake.

Cub Lake is very shallow. It is an excellent habitat for beautiful yellow pond lilies and for leeches whose mouth parts are unable to penetrate human skin. From the eastern end, you can shoot a good photo of Stones Peak with the lily-covered water in the foreground. A short telephoto lens would be helpful in composing the picture.

The path runs west along the north shore of the lake. At the western end, it passes through a small area of lodgepole pines that burned in a forest fire in 1972. Then the trail arrives at a junction with trails from The Pool (see page 63) and Mill Creek Basin (see Hollowell Park Trails in the Bear Lake Road chapter).

Mule deer doe and fawn

Bear Lake Road

Bear Lake Road provides access to one of the most popular areas in the park. Various problems have come about as a result of this popularity. The most obvious, if not the most serious, is awful automobile congestion—the epitome of what a national park experience should not be.

The National Park Service is striving heroically to deal with traffic congestion, but it is a complex problem because of the lay of the land and the distances involved. A mass transit system is the only way to save visitors from the soul-destroying battle against traffic jams on Bear Lake Road.

In summer only, a bus route begins at a parking lot on an old gravel pit across Bear Lake Road from Glacier Basin Campground, 4.8 miles from the beginning of the road near the park's Beaver Meadows Entrance (see Bear Lake Shuttle Bus Service, page 24.) Freed from their cars, visitors to Bear Lake and other points along the road can catch a free bus ride and save both fuel and incredible wear and tear on their nerves. For up-to-date details about the system, you should check with the National Park Service.

Perhaps more than everyone else, hikers benefit from a mass transit system. We hikers and backpackers tend to be more upset by traffic problems than other park visitors. Part of the reason we walk into the backcountry is to escape infernal automobiles. It is menacing to have them snapping and growling and roaring and lunging after us right at the trailhead. Buses do much to ease our jangled nerves.

More important is the increased flexibility they provide. With a mass transit system in operation, we can start at one trailhead and end up at another. Buses make possible the very desirable one-way hikes that otherwise pose logistical problems. As a result, hikers are distributed more evenly instead of being concentrated at two or three trailheads.

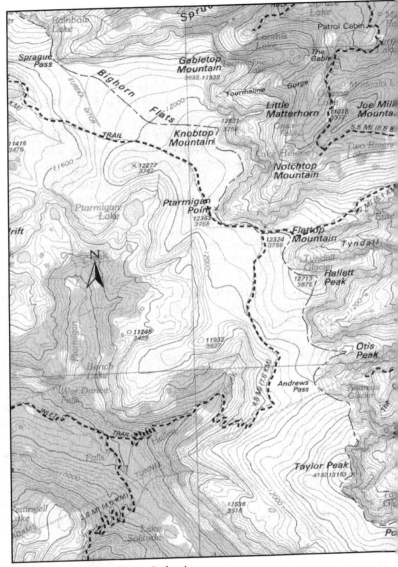

Bear Lake Road and Bear Lake Area

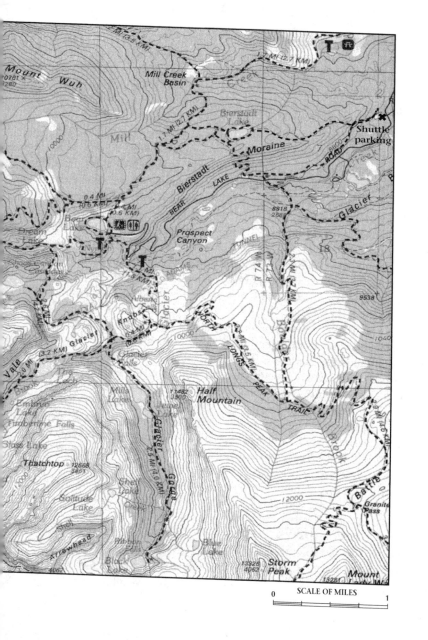

Mount Wuh
10701 X
1260

Mill Creek Basin

1.7 MI (2.7 KM)

Bierstadt Lake

Mill

Moraine

BIERSTADT LAKE

Shuttle parking

10000

Glacier

Creek

18

BEAR LAKE

Prospect Canyon

8818 2588

TUNNEL

Bear Lake

R 74 W   R 73 W

Dream Lake

0.4 MI (0.6 KM)

.4 MI (0.6 KM)

.3 MI (.5 KM)

9538

1040

Alberta Knobs
0.4 MI

GLACIER

Glacier Falls

NORTH LONGS PEAK

BLACK

Glacier

10000

.2 MI (3.5 KM)

Vale
.0 MI (3.2 KM)

The Loch

Mills Lake

11482 3500

Half Mountain

TRAIL

Brook

Emerald Lake

Jewel Lake

Timberline Falls

Bass Lake

Thatchtop 12668 3861

GLACIER GORGE

2.5 MI (4.0 KM)

.9 MI (.6 KM)

Shelf Lake

Battle

Solitude Lake

Shelf Creek

Granite Pass

Arrowhead

Ribbon Falls

4062

Black Lake

Blue Lake

13326 4062

Storm Peak

Mount

13281

0   SCALE OF MILES   1

Hollowell Park Trails

Hollowell Park Trailhead is reached by a short road that leaves Bear Lake Road 3.5 miles from Beaver Meadows. Turn right (west) and drive a few hundred yards to a parking area. From there a broad, clear trail runs up Mill Creek Valley for 1.6 miles to **Mill Creek Basin.**

The most notable features of this easy, pleasant walk probably are the stands of aspens and recent beaver workings along Mill Creek. The area was used for timber cutting and sawing in the 1880s, and the aspens and lodgepole pines may be a result of that clearing operation. These are the trees that begin to grow in places cleared by fire or lumbering.

Additionally, Mill Creek Basin is an excellent place to look for hawks. The broad, bushy flats of Hollowell Park provide the birds with good rodent hunting. The aspens and cliffs along Mill Creek offer well-watered nesting sites. Hence, this relatively small area gives hawks the essentials needed by all wildlife: food, water, and shelter.

From Mill Creek Basin a trail leads left (south) up the side of Bierstadt Moraine to **Bierstadt Lake,** a mile away. Most hikers reach Bierstadt Lake from Bierstadt Lake Trailhead or Bear Lake because those trails are shorter and more scenic (see Bierstadt Lake Trail in this chapter, and Flattop Mountain Trail System in the Bear Lake Trailhead chapter).

A right (north) turn in Mill Creek Basin takes you over the ridge between well-named **Steep Mountain** and **Mount Wuh.** The trail is a 1.5-mile link with the trails west of Moraine Park, especially the ones to Cub Lake. It is more easily walked from south to north than north to south, but it is not hiked much because there are easier and more interesting ways to Cub Lake (see Cub Lake Trail in the Moraine Park chapter).

Boulder Brook and Storm Pass Trails

The trailhead for the Boulder Brook and Storm Pass Trails is situated on Bear Lake Road 6.4 miles from Beaver Meadows, on the left (south) side immediately before the Bierstadt Lake Trailhead. The junctions of trails a short way south of the road are so complex that they defy verbal description. One trail dodges swamps for 1.5 miles to Sprague Lake and Glacier Basin Campground. Another intersects it after approximately paralleling Glacier Creek and the road the entire distance from Bear Lake. The Storm Pass Trail leaves the Glacier Creek Trail a half mile from the road. The Boulder Brook Trail cuts across this tangled web, heading due south and straight up Boulder Brook. Numerous short spur trails complete the confusion by connecting the trails in various ways. To sort all this out, refer to the map and pray that signs are in place.

These trails tend to be used mainly by horse riders, but the Boulder Brook and Storm Pass Trails, at least, attract some hikers as well.

The **Boulder Brook Trail** is fairly easy to follow. Just stay on the path that always seems to head uphill. Past the junctions, the trail stays close to Boulder Brook, a small stream bordered by aspens. Eventually, you arrive at an area that is still very open because of the forest fire of 1900. Amid many rocks, scraggly trees struggle for life where fire burned even the organic humus of the old forest floor.

Boulder Brook and its trail meet the North Longs Peak Trail (see page 88) 2.5 miles from the road. The Boulder Brook Trail may be best reserved for fall hiking, when the aspens have turned yellow, but it serves as a useful link between Longs Peak and Bear Lake Road throughout the hiking season.

The **Storm Pass Trail** strikes uphill from the Glacier Creek Trail a half mile from Bear Lake Road. Following an easy grade through thick woods, the trail winds to the top of a ridge and drops down a bit to marshland at the head of **Wind River,** 2.5 miles from the starting point. Beaver activity is obvious here, where aspen and willow dominate.

An unimproved trail leads 2.2 miles down the northwestern side of Wind River to a road just above the East Portal of Adams

Tunnel, a key link in the Big Thompson Irrigation Project. (The road is closed to public vehicles, however, at the east end of the East Portal lake.) Beyond Wind River, the Storm Pass Trail winds uphill through heavy forest for 1.7 miles to Storm Pass, southwest of Estes Cone (see Storm Pass Trail to Estes Cone in the East Edge Chapter).

Bierstadt Lake Trail

Bierstadt Lake Trailhead is located on Bear Lake Road 6.4 miles from Beaver Meadows. The starting point and parking area are on the right (north) side of the road immediately past the Boulder Brook–Storm Pass Trailhead.

The 1.4-mile trail to Bierstadt Lake zigzags up the south side of Bierstadt Moraine. A forest fire in 1900 cleared the area, which was reforested by quaking aspen. In summer this climb, a sunny one, can be rather hot. In fall, however, when days are cool and the aspens are yellow, the trail is a magical delight. Its views of the Front Range framed by aspens are hard to beat at any time of year.

On top of the moraine, lodgepole pines take over from quaking aspens. The grade levels, and the trail has been built up over marshy areas in a few places.

Bierstadt Lake is a short way to the right at a trail junction. Left leads to Bear Lake. There are many junctions in this vicinity; rely on signs to guide the way to Bierstadt or Bear Lakes or Hollowell Park. A trail circles Bierstadt Lake. The view of Longs Peak from the northwest shore likely will be your choice for photos. A trail from the east end of the lake descends to the shuttle parking lot and to a trail that parallels Bear Lake Road back to the Bierstadt Trailhead.

The ideal route to Bierstadt begins at Bear Lake. The trail is only 0.2 mile longer from there and is much easier to walk. You then can walk down the Bierstadt Lake Trail to Bear Lake Road to meet a shuttle bus or other prearranged transportation.

Broad-tailed hummingbird and Colorado blue columbine

Glacier Gorge Trail System

The second most heavily used trail system in Rocky Mountain National Park is based at Glacier Gorge Junction on the Bear Lake Road. Lately the little parking lot there inside a switchback has been full before midmorning. The case for car pooling or taking the bus cannot be made too strongly. It often is necessary for a driver to drop his fellow hikers at Glacier Gorge Junction and continue on 0.7 mile farther to the much larger and often full parking lot at Bear Lake. Use caution when walking from the parking lot across Bear Lake Road to the trailhead.

A 0.4-mile path near the beginning of the Dream Lake Trail (see Dream Lake Trail System in the Bear Lake Trailhead chapter) connects Bear Lake and Glacier Gorge Junction. We had not set foot on this connecting path until the parking problem exploded; we have used it often since. Looking on the bright side, the awesome traffic tangle forced us to discover this well-flowered, pleasant little stroll; you might want to walk it just for fun. A horse trail connects the east end of the Bear Lake parking area with the path linking Bear Lake and Glacier Gorge Junction.

The first part of the trail system leads upstream on Glacier Creek to **Alberta Falls,** 0.6 mile from Glacier Gorge Junction. The falls are pretty and among the most accessible in the national park. The extensive beaver workings, narrow gorge to peer into, classic whitewater stream to photograph, and abundant golden-mantled ground squirrels attract many people to the trail to Alberta Falls. Only limited parking prevents the crowds from rivaling the teeming throngs at Bear Lake.

On the other hand, the mountain vistas from this section of trail, although good compared with most places, are only fair compared with many other spots in Rocky Mountain National Park. A forest fire in 1900 cleared the area of shade, and the forest has been slow to grow back on such dry land where even the humus soil was destroyed by fire. The trail can get very warm.

A normal-length lens will do quite well for photographing Alberta Falls. The slopes of Half Mountain in the background add little to the picture; you may want to lower your sights and include more of Glacier Creek flowing below the falls. Use aspen trunks and branches as a frame in the photo.

Unfortunately, you will find that many aspen trunks have been scarred by hikers' carvings. The soft white bark seems to invite this kind of vandalism, and because Alberta Falls is an easy destination, the carvers concentrate there. It behooves all of us to put a stop to any further desecration. If you see someone of any age engaged in this activity, do not stone him and dump his body in the river. Rather, use your friendliest persuasion to educate him in proper backcountry behavior and good stewardship. Nearly everyone will respond positively, if somewhat sheepishly, to such an approach. A common stuttering response will be to ask whether you live in Colorado, as if that makes any difference in a national park.

Past Alberta Falls, the trail winds uphill on a gradual grade through more rocky land slowly recovering from the forest fire. The cliffs of Glacier Knobs appear to the right of the path, and then you reach the junction of the North Longs Peak Trail (see page 88). A short way past the junction, the Glacier Gorge Trail levels and even descends a bit above Glacier Creek, at the base of the southern side of Glacier Knobs. You may see pikas or marmots in the rock fields alongside the trail.

The trail descends into a bowl 1.9 miles from the trailhead, where there is a pleasant grove of subalpine woods spared by the 1900 fire. In this bowl, Loch Vale and Glacier Gorge come together, and there is a major parting of the ways. The trail to the right is a mile-long spur to the trail to **Lake Haiyaha** (see Dream Lake Trail System in the Bear Lake Trailhead chapter). The trail to the left leads into Glacier Gorge (see page 83). The trail in the middle leads uphill into Loch Vale.

Loch Vale Trail has a romantic euphony that must appeal to people, for this path tends to be used more than the Glacier Gorge Trail. Few hikers who opt for Loch Vale are disappointed. At first the path climbs gradually on an open slope above Icy Brook. Less than a half mile past the junction, you can get a good view of the brook cutting through a narrow gorge, with Taylor Peak just visible over the trees at the top of the gorge.

Switchbacks take you up the mountainside to the level of **The Loch,** one of the most photographed lakes in the park. With rugged peaks in the background, Taylor Glacier and other snowfields accenting the cliffs, and a rocky shoreline made picturesque by limber pines, The Loch presents a limitless number of photographic opportunities. Capturing fully the beauty of this spot is an impossible challenge, but it is fun to try.

The broad cliff that dominates the western end of The Loch is the Cathedral Wall, a popular playground for technical rock climbers. To the right of it you can see Andrews Glacier peering over a forested ridge of Otis Peak.

To hike to **Andrews Tarn,** at the base of the glacier, follow a trail around the right (northern) side of The Loch. Beyond The Loch, the path parallels Icy Brook through subalpine forests to a trail junction 0.9 mile from The Loch's eastern end. The trail going left from the junction leads to Timberline Falls, Lake of Glass, and Sky Pond. The heavily used trail going right leads to Andrews Tarn and the glacier. As glaciers in this vicinity go, Tyndall Glacier is more spectacular and easier to reach, via the Flattop Trail (see Flattop Mountain Trail System in the Bear Lake Trailhead chapter).

There are, however, plenty of other attractions on the way to Andrews Glacier. Andrews Creek presents many scenic spots while flowing through the subalpine woods below the glacier. The valley walls are decked with magnificent rock spires, the most obvious being the **Sharkstooth,** to the south. It was sculpted by a predecessor of Andrews Glacier.

Another notable feature is a large rock mass that dominates the center of the valley beyond tree line. It consists of glacial rubble dumped there by melting ice. The trail winds up the right-hand side of the mass to a shelf on which sits Andrews Tarn. Interesting chunks of ice may be floating in the lake, and the tundra flowers growing around the tarn are lovely.

The Andrews Glacier path is a logical route for ascending Taylor and Powell Peaks and a deservedly popular route for descending from Flattop Mountain, Hallett Peak, and Otis Peak (see Flattop Mountain Trail System in the Bear Lake Trailhead chapter). If your hiking time is limited and your goals are less ambitious than Taylor Peak, you would do well to choose the left-hand turn at the junction beyond The Loch and head for **Timberline Falls** and **Lake of Glass.** (The U.S. Board of Geographic Names perversely calls this tarn Glass Lake; everyone else calls it the more euphonious Lake of Glass.)

From The Loch you may have seen the three-tiered cascade of well-named Timberline Falls, hanging from ledges below and to the left of Taylor Glacier, and perhaps glimpsed the falls through trees near the trail junction. Then the falls are out of sight as you follow a fairly distinct trail through the forest to reach them. The path avoids marshes, skirts large boulders and probably snowbanks, and arrives at the edge of the catch basin at the foot of the falls.

At any time Timberline Falls must rank among the finest in the park. In early summer, when the flow of Icy Brook has sculpted winter's deep snowdrifts around it, the cascade is unexcelled in beauty. The trick is to predict when the sculpture will be just right.

Climb steeply beside Timberline Falls and then over the edge of the bedrock basin containing Lake of Glass, 4.2 miles from Glacier Gorge Junction. Looking back down the valley gives a nice perspective on The Loch and Loch Vale. Lake of Glass is a spectacular tarn surrounded by rock and tundra. Taylor Peak and Taylor Glacier, together with unnamed 12,000-foot precipices, form a dramatic semicircular wall around the lake.

Lake of Glass rarely lives up to its name, however; stiff breezes usually ripple its surface. Your best bet for catching a photo actually displaying a mirror reflection is to arrive just after sunrise, before convection currents in the air begin to take effect.

Twice as large as Lake of Glass, **Sky Pond** can be found 0.4 mile upstream in a similar rock basin. Scoured out by the predecessor of Taylor Glacier, Sky Pond sits below the vertical east face

Elephanthead (little red elephant)

of Taylor Peak. A spectacular view missed by many hikers is gained by making your way around the rocks to the left (south) of the lake's outlet to the southwestern shore. From this point, you can see three dramatic spires much favored by technical rock climbers: the Sharkstooth on the left, the needle of Petit Grepon in the center, and the Sabre on the right.

Between the two lakes, a bog to the left of the path produces masses of marsh marigolds just after the snow melts. If you caught the sculpture at Timberline Falls, you probably have timed the hike correctly for the flowers as well. Photos of masses of flowers rarely work, but these flowers have large enough blooms and burst forth from the water in sufficient abundance to make photos successful. Shoot from a low perspective; a wideangle lens helps.

Back at the major trail intersection located 1.9 miles from Glacier Gorge Junction, the short stretch of the **Glacier Gorge Trail** to Icy Brook is a good spot to watch for birds. Ruby-crowned kinglets, mountain chickadees, and gray jays are easy to find. More secretive is the uncommon orange-crowned warbler. Excellent clumps of Colorado blue columbine bloom near the stream in July.

Past the crossing of Icy Brook, the trail zigzags through spruce and fir forest to bare bedrock, where there are isolated glacial erratics, boulders deposited by the final retreating tongue of ice. The trail disappears, so make a note of where you hit the bedrock. On their return, hikers commonly walk all the way to the end of the rock, whereas the trail is located only about two-thirds of the way down. People who have made this error in the past have tended to cut back to the trail, off the rock, and have worn another path, which creates erosion. If you goof on the return, retrace your steps rather than cutting through.

At the top of the bedrock "pavement," picturesque limber pines have grown from remarkably little soil. These fine trees make good frames for pictures of the square, flat-topped tower of Longs Peak, which lies ahead, but later you will find even better composition for Longs Peak photos at Mills Lake.

The trail crosses Glacier Creek and passes through a marshy area that displays fine examples of subalpine flowers. The extra water could cause a steep place immediately ahead to be rather slick; be careful and be ready to grab an aspen trunk for support.

Past the marshy area, the path again disappears on bedrock. Watch for cairns to mark the way to **Mills Lake,** 2.5 miles from the trailhead. Mills is considered by many to be the prettiest lake in the park. We think such praise is too extravagant in the face of Lake Nanita and Chasm and Spectacle Lakes, yet Mills is undeniably grand.

The best light for photography at Mills occurs in early evening; the weather usually cooperates. Frame Longs Peak with limber pines on the left, and include glacial erratics on the bedrock shoreline for foreground interest. You might even get a reflection if the water lies still in shoreside pools. If the huge bowl of Glacier Gorge is shadowed by the 13,000-foot peaks to the right, be sure to expose your film for the light on Longs, the Keyboard of the Winds, and Pagoda Mountain, not the much darker slopes below.

The Glacier Gorge Trail follows the eastern shore of Mills for a half mile to the almost adjacent **Jewel Lake.** Jewel is about as marshy as Mills is rocky. The best picture is from the lake's outlet; a wide-angle lens may help to capture the gracefully bent shapes of marsh grass in the foreground.

The trail continues past Jewel, built up above bogs in some places, paralleling Glacier Creek through wet and flowery woods. The woods eventually open to reveal **Ribbon Falls** rushing over rock slabs above a lush meadow filled with senecios, tall chiming bells, and bistort. A short way past the crest of the falls you arrive at **Black Lake,** 4.7 miles from the trailhead. Make your way for a few yards to the left over boulders along the shore, then traverse through the woods to reach the lakeshore again at one of three inlet streams.

The sheer face of a glacial shelf rises above Black Lake, and the even more sheer east face of McHenry's Peak rises above the shelf. There are appropriate trees on the shore to frame the scene, but getting it all in with a normal-length lens is a little tight. A wide-angle lens will be welcome.

A trail of sorts heads steeply up the inlet stream to level out on the shelf. There it degenerates to an occasional cairn and then disappears completely. Rock slabs extend everywhere. The trick is to navigate from one to the other without getting caught in krummholz. A left turn from the spot where the inlet creek bends right will take you over a crest to the rock basin containing **Blue Lake,** three-quarters of a mile from Black.

If your destination is **Green Lake,** bend right with the stream. Cross it to the south, which soon becomes its western side. Following the creek, navigate across rock slabs at an easy grade to Green Lake, a mile from Black. A short distance beyond Green is **Italy Lake,** whose unofficial name derived from its maplike shape when viewed from Longs Peak.

To ascend **Pagoda Mountain,** start climbing from the left side of Green Lake, bypassing Italy. The route is obvious: straight uphill over loose rock and slabs to the notch at the end of the Keyboard of the Winds. It is also fraught with all the frustrations of scrambling over loose rock and is very tiresome. From the notch, climb west, scrambling with hands and feet over fairly solid rock to the summit. The top of Pagoda, just as pointed as it looks from below, is an interesting place with room for two or three climbers on the very summit. Anybody else has to cling to the sides.

To reach **Frozen Lake,** the largest of the tarns scoured in the rock above Black Lake, curve west from Green Lake's outlet stream. Hike over slabs below The Spearhead, a sheer and pointed pyramid. Frozen Lake sits on the first shelf immediately to the west of The Spearhead.

Frozen is a well-named tarn that rarely, if ever, is completely free of ice. The glacier that gouged out Frozen Lake cut deeply; the tarn is boxed in and confined by rock walls. Hence, it is best photographed not from the water level but from the rocks above, and with a wide-angle lens to include **Stone Man Pass** and **McHenrys Peak.**

McHenrys Peak is climbed via Stone Man Pass, whose name came from a man-shaped pillar located above the pass to the east. From Frozen Lake, circle the base of a ridge below the Stone Man to a narrow gully below the pass. The gully, of course, is full of treacherous, tiresome, and trying loose rock. Constant alertness is necessary to keep from kicking rock onto climbers below and to watch for rock falling from above. Early in summer, snow fills the gully, and it is possible to slip into an uncontrolled crashing slide.

Many people reach the gully directly by climbing a shorter and steeper route from Black Lake. From the lake's outlet, they circle right through the timber on the northern shore to climb steeply from the northwestern side of the lake to a shelf below the base of Arrowhead. They then follow this shelf to the base of the gully.

The gully is mercifully short, though not as short as you wish. From the pass, immediately bear right and traverse slightly upward for several hundred yards. Look for cairns, and begin a careful ascent of the steeply pitched ledges. Climb diagonally left to a break in the ridgeline.

Before descending into a second gully, located beyond this ridge, turn around and take a photo of Longs Peak from an unusual angle, using the rocks around the break in the ridge for a frame.

This gully is the route to the top, but it can be snow filled and create uncontrolled slides ending in injury on rocks. It is best to climb late in the summer or to carry an ice ax and know how to use it. Crampons strapped to your boots may also be useful.

McHenrys has the reputation of being the hardest nontechnical climb in the park. That probably is an exaggeration. Several peaks in Wild Basin, for instance, are harder by virtue of longer approaches. McHenrys does require a considerable expenditure of energy, however, and it is worth it. The views from the summit are spectacular in all directions. West to

Ptarmigan Mountain above North Inlet is very appealing, and the view straight down to Black Lake rivals that from the top of Longs down to Chasm Lake.

It is very difficult to get a photo of Black Lake from McHenrys that conveys a sense of the true distance down, because all the granite slabs extending from the summit to the lake are the same color and tone. Lack of intervening reference points in the wide-open landscape above the lake adds to the problem. Nevertheless, if a passing cloud throws a shadow on the lake, or better (and luckier) yet, between the lake and the peak, the resulting contrast will break up the sameness and result in a much more gut-grabbing photo. Good luck; it is a long way back to try again.

Thatchtop is an isolated mountain that sits between Loch Vale and Glacier Gorge. Its position makes it a superb viewing platform for spectacular peaks. The same glaciers that created the scenery also whacked off the sides of Thatchtop, however, so it is a fairly steep, if uncomplicated, climb from both Glacier Gorge and Loch Vale. And the tundra slopes between the glacier level and the summit are none too flat.

To climb Thatchtop from the Glacier Gorge Trail, turn right from the trail onto a path across a meadow about a mile past the lower end of Jewel Lake. Cross Glacier Creek here, below the spot where Shelf Creek flows into Glacier Creek. Staying north of Shelf Creek, climb along a faint track marked by occasional cairns and blocked first by downed timber then by rock ledges. All in all, it is an interesting half-mile scramble up to **Shelf Lake.** The hardest part now behind, follow the creek upstream to **Solitude Lake.** Perched on steps between Thatchtop and Arrowhead, these lakes are very beautiful and certainly worthwhile goals themselves. Marvelous cascades connect the two lakes.

From Solitude it is a steep trudge straight to the summit of Thatchtop. Descent can be via Loch Vale, following cairns from the summit along the tundra to the top of a famous, steep gully shaped like an S. This gully leads down between cliffs to the Loch Vale Trail. If you miss the cairns, line up your path of descent with the Bear Lake parking area, a tactic that should also bring you to the krummholz-choked head of the gully.

The S-shaped gully is the more direct route of ascent—3.5 miles as compared to 5.5 miles via Shelf and Solitude Lakes. To hike it in the opposite direction, leave the Loch Vale Trail at the first switchback past the major trail intersection located 1.9 miles from Glacier Gorge Junction. Cross Icy Brook and follow a faint track to the base of the gully.

The **North Longs Peak Trail** branches left from the Glacier Gorge Trail east of Glacier Knobs, 1.4 miles from Glacier Gorge Junction. This trail is 2.6 miles longer to Granite Pass than the trail from Longs Peak Ranger Station (see the Longs Peak and Nearby Goals chapter). In our opinion, an extra 2.6 miles is the last thing you need when climbing Longs Peak. On the other hand, for those who can work out the vehicular logistics of widely separated trailheads, descent by the North Longs Peak Trail is an interesting and worthwhile conclusion to the climb. The trail is well laid out with moderate grades for most of its length. It is in excellent condition and easy to walk.

From the trail junction, the North Longs Peak Trail starts out encouragingly by going downhill. But reason correctly informs you that most trails do not run downhill all the way to the top. Soon you cross a bridge over Glacier Creek at a spot where it is confined narrowly between two steep rock walls. Past the bridge, there is no downhill.

An interesting occurrence that happens now and then on this trail comes about as the result of shortcutting switchbacks. (Shortcutting, of course, is a very bad practice that inflicts significant harm on the landscape by encouraging erosion and trail disintegration.) Hikers inclined to cutting switchbacks come striding down the Glacier Gorge Trail from The Loch or Mills Lake and see the North Longs Peak Trail below them. Such folks generally were not too observant on the way up and have forgotten about the North Longs Peak Trail, if they ever noticed it in the first place. They cut straight down to the trail below them and keep heading downhill—in exactly the wrong direction. Some realize their error when they reach the bridge over Glacier Creek; others do not catch on until they have climbed for a while. Incredible as it seems, an occasional hiker climbs a considerable distance on the trail to Longs Peak and never realizes what has happened. Often he has run ahead of his hiking companions, who miss him only after they arrive at Glacier Gorge Junction.

By then the rangers have to be called to sort out the mess. Sometimes the missing hiker is found on Bear Lake Road, having wandered there via the Boulder Brook Trail. Sometimes he turns up the next day near Longs Peak Ranger Station, having climbed all the way over the flank of Battle Mountain and down the other side. He usually has spent a dangerous night in misery and is in less than great shape when found. After such an experience, he repents of cutting switchbacks—until the next time.

The North Longs Peak Trail is the route followed by climbers headed for **Half Mountain.** Although it is possible to climb straight up to the summit after crossing the bridge across Glacier Creek, a barrier of large boulders discourages use of that route. Actually, it is far better to take a less direct route and follow the trail around to the eastern side of the mountain to a point almost 3 miles from the trailhead. This enables you to gain a good deal of altitude on the trail. Leaving the trail at last, you strike uphill through subalpine forest, which very soon gives way to limber pines. Pick the least steep way to the top for a magnificent view of Glacier Gorge. A bonus of the climb up Half Mountain is the abundance of very photogenic limber pines, some still standing as scorched skeletons of trees killed in the 1900 forest fire.

You are doing well if you can find your way down Half Mountain to the trail by exactly the same route you went up. Of course, it would be highly unethical and irresponsible backcountry stewardship to mark your uphill climb on trees and rocks. Besides, there is no assurance that the uphill route will be better than the downhill route.

Back on the North Longs Peak Trail, walking 3.6 miles from Glacier Gorge Junction brings you to a junction with the Boulder Brook Trail. The scraggly forest of limber pines is very open. A series of switchbacks eases you up the mountain by moderate grades to tree line.

Above the trees the grade steepens, and the tundra seems to stretch on forever. It is only about 1.5 miles to Granite Pass, 6.8 miles from Glacier Gorge Junction, but the "forever" aspect stems from the fact that it is another 1.7 miles of tundra to the Boulder Field (see the Longs Peak and Nearby Goals chapter).

Bear Lake Trailhead

Bear Lake is Rocky Mountain National Park's most popular trailhead. As you walk a few yards from the multiacre parking lot to the lake, you will see more people at any time of the day or year than at any other spot in the park. In summer, a free mass transit system connects Bear Lake with a parking area across the road from Glacier Basin Campground, 4.8 miles from the beginning of Bear Lake Road, west of the Beaver Meadows Entrance to the park (see "Bear Lake Shuttle Bus Service," page 24.) Buses relieve the soul-trying, gas-guzzling traffic jams and provide many advantages to hikers. Check with the National Park Service for details about the system's operation.

Bear Lake teems not only with people but with people-habituated Clark's nutcrackers, gray and Steller's jays, chipmunks, golden-mantled ground squirrels, and red squirrels (chickarees). Feeding the animals is against park regulations and can lead to trouble for you or for the next person who happens by and does not pay the peanut toll. The rodents reputedly bite. Additionally, fleas carrying bubonic plague (black death, which once killed 25 percent of Europe's population) have been found on rodents in the park. Human infection by this disease in Colorado is extremely rare, but it never hurts to be wary.

Dream Lake Trail System

A left (south) turn at Bear Lake (there are signs to point the way) starts you on the trail to Nymph, Dream, Haiyaha, and Emerald Lakes and Pool of Jade. It is one of the most beautiful trails in the park and, for most of the distance, one of the easiest. Of course, it is also the most heavily used.

The first half mile of trail to **Nymph Lake** has been paved because ordinary rock and dirt could not stand the pounding of so many feet. Although unnatural, the asphalt does prevent unacceptable erosion. You can avoid the crowds by starting your hike at six o'clock in the morning.

With an early start, you should arrive at Nymph Lake before the day's breezes begin to ripple the pond's surface. A wide-angle lens will be useful to capture the reflection of Hallett Peak and Flattop Mountain (anything but flat from here) among the still-shadowed lily pads on the surface of Nymph. Take your light reading off the sky, or your meter will be fooled by the foreground shadows and cause you to overexpose the peaks.

As you walk a bit farther around the edge of Nymph, a normal-focal-length lens will be best to photograph Thatchtop Mountain dramatically framed by burned limber pines. Longs Peak looks good from a bit farther up the hill, where it is framed by living lodgepole pines and subalpine fir. The patterns in upturned tree roots around Nymph also make good subjects.

After you leave Nymph Lake, the asphalt runs out, but the feet of thousands of hikers have beaten a trail that differs little from pavement. The path between Nymph and Dream Lakes is very picturesque, bordered with bright subalpine wildflowers and leading into magnificent views of Longs Peak above Glacier Gorge. About 0.1 mile downstream from **Dream Lake,** the trail divides. The left-hand branch crosses Tyndall Creek and heads toward Lake Haiyaha (see page 93). The right-hand fork continues on to Dream, 1.1 miles from Bear Lake.

Dream is the park's most photographed lake that is inaccessible by car. Photos of the lake with Hallett towering on the left and Flattop on the right should include limber pines in the foreground. A wide-angle lens will help.

Continuing along Dream's right (northern) shore, the trail follows the valley for 0.8 mile up to **Emerald Lake.** A few places along the way are steep, and occasional photography stops are usually welcome. One good place is at a long, banded slab of bedrock smoothed by glaciers and thousands of tramping feet. Tyndall Creek tumbles across the steep rock on the left. The moisture makes possible a belt of green, including some ferns, in large cracks in the slab where soil has accumulated. Walk over the rock for a few yards to the left of the trail to compose a photo of this wild garden with the very rugged spires of Flattop rising in the background.

Forest and trail end at Emerald Lake, where casual hikers are left behind by determined rock scramblers. The 1.5-mile stretch up Tyndall Gorge to **Pool of Jade** is tough and interesting. Making your way around the south side of Emerald, you face a steep series of shelves. (Do not try to follow Tyndall Creek, which flows from Pool of Jade to Emerald Lake.) As you stumble over and around loose rock of all sizes, you begin to believe that the next level grassy area must hold the pool. You are wrong many times before you are right. Pool of Jade is a good destination for those who want to feel as though they have hiked somewhere remote but do not want to pound many miles of trail in a long approach.

Past the bridge downstream from Dream Lake, the trail to **Lake Haiyaha** climbs in a series of switchbacks through dense subalpine forest where snow usually covers the trail until July. After the path crosses onto a sunny southern exposure, you get good views of Nymph, Bear, and other lakes down the valley. Just ahead, dramatic views of Longs Peak towering above Glacier Gorge are framed by dead limber pines. A normal-length lens is satisfactory.

Heading down through limber pines, the trail reaches Lake Haiyaha a mile from Dream Lake. In June a stretch of trail near the lake may be under water, forcing a detour over the big boulders that surround the lake. **Haiyaha** is said to be an Indian word meaning "big rocks."

At the spot where the trail hits the lake stands a very striking limber pine that we have had trouble photographing adequately. Likewise, photos of the lake with Hallett above are disappointing compared with those from Nymph and Dream Lakes. But from the other side of Haiyaha, a short telephoto shot of Longs Peak turns out well in the afternoon, given a benevolent cloud arrangement.

About a quarter mile before reaching Haiyaha, the trail branches left to meet the Glacier Gorge Trail System (see the

Bear Lake Road chapter). The mile-long link between the two trail systems is quite charming. Although its views are relatively unspectacular, the path passes through wild gardens of midsummer flowers and rushing water. On this stretch of trail, we are particularly conscientious about picking up litter, scattering remains of illegal campfires, staying on the path, and educating the unenlightened about ethical wilderness behavior.

Flattop Mountain Trail System

A right turn at Bear Lake takes hikers a short way along a paved lakeshore path until the unpaved Flattop Mountain Trail departs uphill to the right. (Signs at appropriate places point out both of these right-hand turns.) Climbing through quaking aspens, the trail divides after less than a half mile.

The right-hand branch runs along the top of Bierstadt Moraine through pleasant woods to **Bierstadt Lake.** This route to the lake is easier and cooler, although 0.2 mile longer, than the path from the Bierstadt Lake Trailhead. If you intend to start at one trailhead and end at another, sanity dictates starting at Bear Lake (see Bierstadt Lake Trail in the Bear Lake Road chapter). A trail connects the east end of Bierstadt Lake with the shuttle parking areas.

Before it reaches Bierstadt Lake, the trail divides again; the left-hand path runs down to beaver ponds in **Mill Creek Basin.** A spur trail links the Mill Creek Trail with Bierstadt Lake so that no backtracking is necessary if you wish to descend into the basin directly from the lake. Once in the basin, the trail follows Mill Creek (named for a sawmill that operated there from 1877 to 1880) for a short way before branching yet again. The right-hand fork passes through Hollowell Park to Bear Lake Road. The left-hand fork crosses the creek and winds over the ridge between Mount Wuh and Steep Mountain. After about 1.5 miles, it arrives at the Cub Lake Trail (see the Moraine Park chapter).

Back at the first trail junction, after leaving Bear Lake, a switchback left turn takes hikers along the more heavily traveled trail to **Flattop Mountain.** On a warm south-facing slope, it climbs somewhat steeply above Bear Lake. It soon levels off, however, passing through Engelmann spruce and subalpine fir that are growing back after the 1900 forest fire.

A little less than a mile from Bear Lake, the trail forks. Continuing on the lower path, to the right, you reach Odessa Gorge (see page 100). The trail to the left zigzags uphill through fir and spruce, which seem not to cast as much cooling shade as they should. Dream Lake Overlook is a good rest stop just below tree line, with limber pines to frame vistas of Longs Peak rising above Glacier Gorge and of the ever dramatic Hallett Peak. The view of Dream Lake itself is more interesting than photogenic.

Above tree line you arrive at another overlook, this time of Emerald Lake, 1,300 feet below. Ahead are nearly 1.5 miles of moderately steep walking to the top of the mountain. Just up the trail from Emerald Lake Overlook, be sure to notice and reflect upon a sign that warns of the dangers of hiking above tree line in stormy weather. Lightning is the biggest danger, but this sign was inspired by hikers walking over a precipice in a blinding snowstorm, with fatal results.

Watch closely for two species of interesting alpine wildlife that are common on the tundra. Pikas—round-eared, rabbitlike little creatures—are active but well camouflaged. Their loud sharp squeaks are heard more often than the animals are seen. Ptarmigan (high-altitude grouse) also blend in with their background and materialize suddenly underfoot, only to scamper away.

Shortly before you top out on Flattop, you receive fine views to the south of Hallett Peak's true summit and Tyndall Glacier. Most hikers do not bother trying to find the true summit of appropriately named Flattop. It is a broad uplifted plain that usually serves as a route to more dramatic goals. Among the best is **Hallett Peak,** easily reached by crossing the tundra at the head of Tyndall Glacier. Then, as you begin to climb, boulders replace tundra. Pick your own best route over the rocks; the way is short but steep, and the summit is very nice.

Otis Peak, the next mountain south of Hallett, is climbed in much the same way en route to **Andrews Glacier.** Many hikers descend via the glacier into Loch Vale for a circle trip back to Bear Lake (see Glacier Gorge Trail System in the Bear Lake Road chapter). Sliding down the glacier is fun, but dangerous crevasses can open late in the season. Also, icy conditions have led to an out-of-control slide with a sudden, fatal stop on the rocks at the foot of the glacier. It is best to check with the National Park Service about the current state of Andrews Glacier before planning to slide down.

Taylor Peak rises south of Andrews Glacier and is a rough climb if Hallett and Otis are included along the way. But you can skirt those two peaks by staying on the broad tundra slopes west of their summits, more or less level with Flattop's summit. Otherwise, from the head of Andrews Glacier, pick your way over the rocks to the top of Taylor. The ascent is harder than the ascent of Hallett, but the view of Longs Peak and Loch Vale is well worth it. Taylor is sometimes climbed via Loch Vale by ascending Andrews Glacier; this route is 2 miles shorter than the route via Flattop (see Glacier Gorge Trail System in the Bear Lake Road chapter).

It is fairly simple to follow the ridge from Taylor Peak along the Continental Divide to **Powell Peak.** But peak bagging beyond Powell changes from hiking to technical climbing. McHenrys Notch, a 300-foot-deep cut in the divide, is a significant barrier between Powell and McHenrys Peak, which climbers usually ascend from Glacier Gorge (see Glacier Gorge Trail System in the Bear Lake Road chapter).

On the summit of Flattop, the trail forks at a pair of 8-foot cairns. The North Inlet Trail to the left is the shortest way to Grand Lake, at the park's southwest corner (see page 99). The **Tonahutu Creek Trail,** to the right, is an older route to the same goal, first walked by Native Americans. This path follows the Continental Divide to an overlook above Odessa Gorge, then runs northwest around Ptarmigan Point and begins to descend the western slope.

Notchtop, Knobtop, and **Gabletop Mountains** are climbed by striking northeast from the Tonahutu Creek Trail as it begins to go downhill. Proceed carefully on the tundra, stepping on rocks rather than plants whenever possible. The walking is easy and pleasant; the mountains' gentle west faces contrast dramatically with the cliffs on their heavily glaciated east faces.

A round-trip to Bear Lake can be made by descending from the Tonahutu Creek Trail to Odessa Lake via Tourmaline Gorge, a steep gully on the northern side of the Little Matterhorn knife ridge (see page 100). Be careful on the rocks above Tourmaline Lake. Below the lake, be clever picking your trackless way through the trees to the trail at Odessa Lake.

The Tonahutu Creek Trail misses good views of **Ptarmigan Lake** dramatically set at the foot of Snowdrift Peak, but a short downhill detour to the left of the trail below Ptarmigan Point takes you to an overlook at the edge of the cirque containing the lake. Again, tread lightly on the tundra.

Rather than retracing your steps all the way back up to the spot where you left the trail, walk north, heading gradually uphill to meet the trail as it descends east of an unnamed high point above marshy **Bighorn Flats.** There is a slight chance of spotting bighorn sheep there, but your best bet is on the glaciated cliffs surrounding this uplifted plain. Anywhere you might go looking for sheep would be out of the way and a long shot.

In 1902 the **Eureka Ditch** was dug across Bighorn Flats to divert westward-flowing water to Spruce Canyon, on the thirsty eastern slope. In essence it moves the Continental Divide slightly west. The ditch does not intersect the trail, and there are no significant landmarks to indicate where to leave the trail to find it. You have to watch your map, plot your position on it, and aim through the marshes by dead reckoning.

The ditch looks similar to a natural stream. It is probably not worth the bother to locate unless you have a particular interest in the history of water diversion projects or are headed for **Sprague Glacier, Sprague Mountain,** or **Stones Peak.** To reach the glacier, follow Eureka Ditch to Sprague Pass, at the head of Spruce Canyon. From there hike north up a tundra slope to the top of Sprague Glacier, one of the most remote glaciers in the park.

To climb Stones Peak, walk uphill from the top of Sprague Glacier to Sprague Mountain. A ridge extends northeast from Sprague Mountain to Stones Peak. You must follow it carefully down to the base of Stones, then regain 800 feet of elevation. Retracing your steps to Bear Lake means a round-trip hike of more than 20 tough miles. It all must be done in one day, for there are no campsites along the way.

Afternoon storms and lightning sometimes catch hikers when they have many miles more to go above tree line. At such times it may be advisable to descend into Spruce Canyon, bushwhack through its thick forest to Spruce Lake, and exit via the Fern Lake Trail. Better yet, take two days and climb Stones via Spruce Canyon in the first place (see Fern Lake Trail System in Moraine Park chapter).

West of Bighorn Flats, the Tonahutu Creek Trail descends between a few tall cairns through lovely flowered meadows. It then turns sharply right (snow cover could make the way vague in spots, necessitating a bit of casting about) to the head of a very steep, beautiful valley. An impressive bit of trail construction leads you easily across a sunny (south-facing) but precipitous valley wall through enchanting subalpine meadows and forests.

The surroundings would be even more enchanting if you were not so tired by this time. Getting a permit to camp in this area is a good idea. Camping will give you time for a side trip to **Haynach Lakes** via a faint trail heading upstream to the right at the spot where the main trail cuts sharply left across a boulder-strewn tributary to Tonahutu Creek. A sign warns that hiking above tree line in stormy weather can be fatal.

The tributary does not extend all the way to Haynach Lakes. There is a short steep climb at the end of it to the bench on which the lakes sit, looking very striking below Nakai Peak. The route up the drainage is easy, although somewhat marshy.

If you are determined to hike the Tonahutu Creek Trail and return to civilization in only one day, you can grind out the rest of the miles past Granite Falls to Big Meadows. Granite Falls is easy to miss if you are trail weary. *Tonahutu* is Arapaho for "big meadows," and they are big to the point of seeming interminable. The trail is excellent, however, always skirting the bogs and staying just within the forest shade.

At Big Meadows, two trails join Tonahutu at different points: a spur from the Onahu Creek Trail, and the Green Mountain Trail (see the Trail Ridge Road chapter). The easiest route to civilization is 1.8 miles along the Green Mountain Trail to Trail Ridge Road. It is a pleasant, wide subalpine trail and much preferable to the hot 4.4 miles of lodgepole pines along the Tonahutu Creek Trail to Grand Lake (see the Grand Lake chapter).

The **North Inlet Trail,** which is the left-hand fork at the trail junction on the summit of Flattop, is widely praised for the quality of its scenery, trail construction, and campsites. Leaving the junction, it descends between tall cairns over tundra slopes west of Hallett and Otis Peaks. Tundra flowers clinging to windy Flattop are spectacular in July and early August. The display becomes even more outstanding as you drop down a series of switchbacks along the steep valley wall at the head of Hallett Creek drainage. Spreading all the way to tree line is one of the most outstanding wildflower displays in the park.

Down in the valley the trail passes through an alpine setting of glaciated cliffs and snowbanks. A fairly level stretch through fine subalpine forest is followed by a series of switchbacks affording grand views of cascades along Hallett Creek. Soon after the trail leaves the switchbacks and creek, a cutoff to the left leads uphill to Lakes Nokoni and Nanita (see North Inlet Trail in the Grand Lake chapter).

Below the cutoff, the trail winds its way through the woods and meadows along North Inlet, so named because the creek flows into the Grand Lake on the north shore. When the trail branches again, take the left-hand fork, which leads down to Cascade Falls.

(The right-hand fork eventually rejoins the left.) The water fall is best photographed by climbing to the rocks below.

The trail from Cascade Falls to Grand Lake is easy and frequently used. Maps show a road to Summerland Park, located this side of Grand Lake, but this access to private land in the park is not open to vehicles. You have to walk 1.2 miles more to reach the trailhead (see North Inlet Trail in the Grand Lake chapter).

Odessa Lake Trail

Among the most popular hikes in the park is the hike to Odessa Lake, from which many people continue to Fern Lake and then to prearranged transportation at Moraine Park (see Fern Lake Trail System in the Moraine Park chapter). From Bear Lake, you travel uphill on the Flattop Trail for 0.9 mile to the trail junction. The left-hand fork goes to Flattop Mountain (see page 95); take the right-hand fork. The path now is easy and level. Thus, after a short, moderately steep climb at Bear Lake, the trail has only a slight up or down grade until it reaches **Odessa Gorge,** about 3 miles from Bear. Hikers can take a very short side trip on a fishermen's path to **Lake Helene** at the head of the gorge, east of Notchtop Mountain, and then retrace their steps to the main trail.

The Odessa Lake Trail now slants down the valley wall with views of Grace Falls hanging on the opposite wall, across the gorge. Crossing snowbanks (until mid-July), the path passes below Odessa Lake and eventually arrives at a trail junction. The trail straight ahead goes to Fern Lake (see the Moraine Park chapter). The Odessa Trail makes a switchback left turn and crosses Fern Creek, then heads upstream along a narrow gorge to reach **Odessa Lake.** The outlet is the best spot for photos; a wide-angle lens may be helpful but is not essential. The most dramatic peaks rising above Odessa Lake are Notchtop Mountain and the Little Matterhorn. Notchtop can be climbed from Flattop Mountain (see page 95).

One route up the **Little Matterhorn** begins from a trail that follows the west shore of Odessa. Leave the trail at the spot where a stream flows into the lake, about a quarter of the lake's length from the outlet. Head upstream, picking whatever route seems easiest through dense forest, into **Tourmaline Gorge.** Past tree line on the open tundra is **Tourmaline Lake.** Stay south of the lake and climb the steep slope to the top of the Little Matterhorn ridge. As you may have noticed while hiking to Odessa Lake, the Little Matterhorn really is a sharp ridge extending east from the Continental Divide at Knobtop.

Some climbers reach the ridge top from Lake Helene by traversing the bases of Notchtop and Knobtop west of Grace Falls. From the south base of the Little Matterhorn ridge, climb straight up to the ridge top. This route eliminates the loss in elevation between Lakes Helene and Odessa.

To reach the summit of the Little Matterhorn, follow the top of the ridge eastward, keeping to the north (left) side. There are a couple of places that are easy to traverse but very exposed to long drops. The final 4 feet to the tiny summit is extremely exposed, so some folks are content to place their elbows rather than their feet on the very top.

Overall, the hike up the Little Matterhorn is short, thrilling, beautiful, and not particularly difficult. But it is also steep and windy, and climbers have been killed on the way.

Yellow-bellied marmot

Longs Peak and Nearby Goals

We huddled, cold and fuzzy headed, in the utterly dark parking lot at Longs Peak Ranger Station. Pulling ourselves from bed at 1:00 A.M., we had driven 7.5 miles south of Estes Park on Colorado Highway 7 to a sign indicating a right turn for the Longs Peak Area. After a mile, we turned left into trailhead parking.

Sensing our sleepy reluctance to begin climbing Longs Peak, our leader threw on his pack, jammed his alpine hat on his head, and proclaimed to the peaks, "I feel the call of nature." Inspired, we grabbed our assorted equipment and tramped off gallantly behind him—right into a nearby comfort station.

So began our first climb of Longs. Many others followed as we, in turn, led various people up the mountain. It is a great peak, the highest in the park (14,255 feet; it shrank a foot in the last U.S. Geological Survey calculations), both photogenic and fun. Longs teaches climbers that fun is the best reason to climb—not because the mountains are there, not for an elevated ego trip, not to prove some profound "truth" about the nature of man.

To make the climb more fun, we now sleep late and usually leave at 4:00 A.M. Nevertheless, we are still groggy as we begin hiking up the steep, dark **Longs Peak Trail.** Flashlights illumine dimly apprehended ranks of lodgepole pines, varied by white aspen trunks, near the turnoff to Eugenia Mine (see page 111). Occasionally, the babble of Alpine Brook disturbs our half-slumber as we somnambulate near the stream. At **Goblins Forest,** 1.2 miles up the trail, twisted limber pines pass vaguely into and out of sight.

We really awaken only when we cross Alpine Brook, and LIGHT-NING HAZARD in bright orange letters jumps out through the flashlight beams in predawn darkness. Less dramatic letters explain what to do if lightning threatens and static electricity causes your hair to stand on end.

As we continue uphill to tree line, deformed and stunted trees appear to be battered climbers in the dim light. They struggle constantly toward the heights while storms, jealous of their un-shared control, fight to hold the forest back.

Above tree line, the trail climbs below Mills Moraine toward Chasm Lake (see page 109). At the junction of the Longs Peak Trail with the spur to Chasm Lake are opportunities for spectac-ular photography when alpenglow radiates red, orange, and gold in succession from the dramatic East Face of Longs.

The Longs Peak Trail circles the base of Mount Lady Wash-ington toward the junction with the North Longs Peak Trail (see Glacier Gorge Trail System in the Bear Lake Road chapter) and Granite Pass. From the pass, a series of switchbacks climbs to a giant jumble of rocks called the **Boulder Field,** beyond which there is no trail, only rock scrambles.

Here the real climb begins as the flat top of Longs, 1,500 feet above, catches early morning sun. Dramatic patterns of light and dark spreading across the peak's north face tempt use of a wide-angle lens, but a normal-focal-length lens produces more striking results.

Formerly, the route to the top was via the North Face. Wire cables used to be bolted to the steepest rock to help climbers ascend straight up from the Boulder Field. The National Park Service removed the cables in 1973 as part of a program to elim-inate as many man-made contrivances as possible from the wil-derness.

We ascend Longs by a less direct but easier route, through an oval gap in the ridge between Longs and Storm Peak. This gap is called the **Keyhole** and, with two large ledges overhanging it on each side, actually looks like its name.

Clambering over the huge chunks of granite that glaciers and weather have carved from the peak entails gasping for more oxy-gen than the thin air holds. The Keyhole, rather than the sum-mit, becomes the immediate goal. On the other side are rest, food, and magnificent views to the north into Glacier Gorge.

Just below the Keyhole, near the ridge line, a stone hut materializes. Built from the same granite as the mountain, the beehive-shaped memorial blends inconspicuously with the ridge. A sobering bronze tablet set into the cabin's wall commemorates Agnes Wolcott Vaille, "a Colorado mountaineer conquered by winter after scaling the precipice, January 12, 1925, and one who lost his life in an effort to save her, Herbert Sortland."

Agnes Vaille and Walter Kiener had made the first winter ascent of the difficult East Face. Twenty-five hours of climbing so exhausted Ms. Vaille that she was unable to descend to shelter from the storms and subzero temperatures. Kiener had to leave her on the North Face and go for help. By the time he and another rescuer could return, she had died. Meanwhile, Herbert Sortland, another member of the rescue party, could not continue in the adverse weather. He turned back, lost his way, broke a hip, and froze to death a short way from the safety of Longs Peak Inn. As for Kiener, frostbite took all but one of his fingertips, all his toes, and part of his left foot.

As of this writing, fifty-seven people have died on Longs. One accidentally shot himself. Some fell or were hit by falling rocks. One person simply disappeared.

From the tragedy and gloom of the Agnes Vaille hut, we pass through the Keyhole into the joy and light of Glacier Gorge. Before us, three 13,000-foot peaks west of Longs—Pagoda Mountain, Chiefs Head, and McHenrys Peak—form a huge amphitheater at the head of the valley. They sparkle with streams of melting snow, which feed many lakes below. Most of the lakes lie in the cold shadow of Longs until midmorning. Some are frozen; others reflect snow and sky.

After a bite of breakfast at the Keyhole, we have to go down to go up. The route, marked by yellow and red bull's-eyes painted on rocks, descends into the Trough, a long, steep gully filled with loose stones. Here it is important for climbers to stay close together and catch kicked-loose rocks before they build up dangerous momentum. If one gets away, yelling "Rock!" is the normal warning. Slick snow and ice add further hazards, especially in early summer, when ice axes and ropes are necessary protection in unmelted places.

When we finally leave the seemingly interminable Trough, our reward is traversing a section less arduous and more interesting: the cliffs on the West Face. Here we cross the Narrows, a ledge that looks worse than it really is. In some places it is wide enough to walk two abreast, although the long drop straight down certainly discourages such a practice.

As we reach the other end of the Narrows, we see far below a large black rock shaped like and named the Black Hearse. But now is no time for ill omens. We are at the base of the **Homestretch**, a long, steep, smooth slab of granite that ends on the summit of Longs. The thin air at 14,000 feet is supplemented by the nearness of success. We finally arrive!

In good weather we spend a couple of hours on top, resting, eating lunch, photographing marmots and the view, meandering around (the summit covers several acres), and gazing 2,000 feet down the East Face into Chasm Lake. As soon as storm clouds appear in the west, prudence demands a descent.

Although it is possible to walk down the very steep Homestretch, many hikers find that the seat of their pants serves as a convenient brake. This is one of the few places where you can see someone hiking while sitting down. Once we pass the Narrows and are back in the Trough, the view of Glacier Gorge, now brimful with sunshine, is spectacular. The distraction of the view and fatigue make falling rocks and slipping even more hazardous than earlier. It always is a relief to reach the Keyhole and the Boulder Field.

The trail is the same one we traveled on the ascent, yet it seems like a new path. At dawn we missed the tiny tundra flowers growing close to the ground. The wind, snow, and cold of the mountaintops have failed to deter or distress the little rose crown, moss campion, and alpine forget-me-not. Their colors are more brilliant, their blooms more profuse, and their beauty

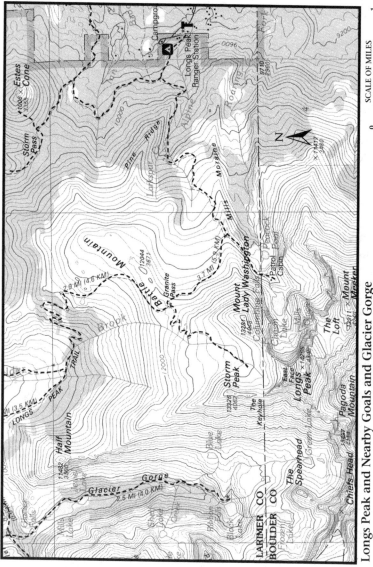

Longs Peak and Nearby Goals and Glacier Gorge

SCALE OF MILES

0   1

greater than that of the big flowers living in relative ease below tree line.

Difficult to see among the flowers and rocks is the little farmer of the tundra—the round-eared, rabbitlike pika. Pikas keep busy harvesting alpine plants to dry in piles for their winter food supply, but they often pause to pipe shrill barks at hikers passing through their hay fields.

We find it difficult to pass by the various tundra flora and fauna without closer examination and picture taking. When lightning-filled clouds begin to roll in, we must push on toward the safety of tree line. We cannot hurry much, however, because feet heavy with fatigue are hard to lift over the rocks that reach up to trip us. Rain is usually popping on ponchos before the day ends.

That sound and the sound of boots thudding monotonously on the trail discourage conversation. Each climber has his own thoughts. Some imagine a big dinner; those who are finishing their first ascent of Longs have more elevated visions. For many, Longs is a high point in their lives. They will always remember it as a great effort and as great fun.

Storm Peak and Mount Lady Washington sit on either side of the Boulder Field as 13,000-foot buttresses of Longs. They tend to be overlooked in the excitement about their 14,000-foot neighbor. Storm and Lady Washington are uncomplicated to climb and provide fine vantage points for photographers.

The top of **Storm Peak** is reached by a right turn and a steep climb from Boulder Field. Pick the easiest way over the boulders, avoiding snowbanks and the steepest rock. Rest often. The view from the summit gives a unique perspective of the North Face of Longs and of the summits and cirques above Glacier Gorge.

People in a hurry and feeling vigorous can boulder-hop up the east slope of **Mount Lady Washington** from the Longs Peak Trail at some point west of the Chasm Lake Trail junction. An easier but longer route heads left from the trail just as it levels above the switchbacks between Granite Pass and the Boulder Field. On this western side of Lady Washington, the trail is 1,000 feet nearer the summit than on the eastern side. Also, the slope is less steep on the west. Traversing Lady Washington up the western slope and down the eastern one is a favorite route.

From the top of Lady Washington, the view of the East Face of Longs is unsurpassed. For portrait purposes, the East Face makes an excellent background to frame a head-and-upper-torso shot of one or several climbers. The view of Mount Meeker also can be exciting early in the morning when Meeker's rugged slope is accented by the low angle of the rising sun's rays. Do not expect much of a view of Chasm Lake, though. Half the lake is hidden by a rocky bulge on Lady Washington's south slope.

The hike to **Chasm Lake** has infected more than one person with a permanent passion for mountaineering. This trip offers great variety and exciting scenery in return for 4.2 miles of moderate effort. Of course, it is very popular, and the lake is often crowded. It is seen in its best light and greatest isolation by hikers who leave the trailhead at the same time they would leave for Longs.

The Chasm Lake Trail branches off the main trail to Longs Peak at the base of Mount Lady Washington. From the vicinity of the trail junction, the view into Roaring Fork drainage with the East Face of Longs towering above is hard to beat. Peacock Pool stares up like the "eyes" in peacock tail feathers, and Columbine Falls hangs as a white accent below the precipice. Climb the rocks a few feet above the trail to include the path and fellow hikers in your picture. A normal-focal-length lens is perfect.

During much of the summer, the trail crosses a snowbank. Some care is necessary there; a slip could mean an uncontrolled slide far down to rocks and serious injury. Beyond the snowbank, Colorado blue columbine, the state flower, blooms abundantly among the rocks above Columbine Falls. We probably need not say that picking wildflowers, especially the state flower, is punished by public hanging on the steps of the state capitol and a $500 fine. Coloradans tend to be fussy on this point.

Just above the falls, a lush alpine meadow boasts a flower-lined stream, yellow-bellied marmots, which are easily photographed, and a picturesque hut. The hut (locked) is a National Park Service storage building for rescue equipment, which is used with unpleasant frequency when hikers or technical rock climbers get into trouble on the East Face, one of the country's most famous and heavily used rock-climbing areas. Foresighted folks tuck a pair of binoculars, for watching climbers, into their packs.

The lake itself is a short scramble from the meadow onto the rocky edge of a deep glacier-scoured basin. From behind the stone hut, follow a path up a short gully to a small shelf. Head left from there across a few yards of tundra and rock, then turn right for the last short pull to the lake.

Part of Chasm Lake's beauty may derive from the fact that it hides from hikers approaching from below. Suddenly the lake becomes visible, a large tarn in a setting of unexcelled drama. High crags tower on all sides, but every eye locks on the huge sheer East Face rising straight up for nearly a half mile. It is difficult to realize how far Longs rises above the lake unless climbers on its summit present tiny silhouettes against the sky. Sudden comprehension of the overwhelming massiveness of the scene can induce momentary dizziness in first-time visitors.

Maybe dizziness causes mental lapses. The Park Service reports that an extraordinary amount of trash is left around Chasm Lake. In gratitude for admittance to this sanctuary, visitors would do well to help clean up and carry out such a mess left by insensitive hikers. (Longs Peak rangers also asked that we urge hikers to keep trash out of the four high-tech solar privies that have been installed around the mountain. Perhaps you thought being a backcountry ranger was a glamorous job.)

Predawn arrival at Chasm Lake can provide an opportunity for magnificent alpenglow photos. Trying to capture the mood and beauty without a wide-angle lens is a certain road to frustration and disappointment. Chasm Lake and the top of Longs can just barely be squeezed into the format of a 35mm camera with a normal lens, but the result is unsatisfactory. With a wide-angle, the East Face and its colorful reflection on the lake's surface, unrippled in the still, early morning air, can appear together in one outstanding photograph.

In Rocky Mountain National Park, **Mount Meeker** is second in elevation only to Longs. For experienced hikers in good shape, Meeker's summit is two or three hours of steep hiking from Chasm Lake. As on Longs, hikers face the hazards of falling or being hit by falling rocks. Fatigue increases these dangers because your mind will fail before your body, making you careless. Make a conscious effort to stay alert.

The most popular route up Meeker begins at the stone cabin in the meadow below Chasm Lake. From the hut, head south along the stream to the left of the prominent rock wall called the Ships Prow. Climb toward the cliffs on the right side of Meeker, following a faint path. Eventually, a 160-foot cliff and waterfall will prevent you from hiking straight up. Near the bottom of the falls, the route turns left along a ledge around the cliff. This ledge is narrow in places, with exposure to long falls. Falling rocks here also are hazards.

The route up the cliff cuts back to the right, leading hikers to the **Loft,** a broad saddle between Longs and Meeker. Cairns, which are easy to spot on the way down, mark critical points along the route. Be sure to watch for them to prevent getting off-route and ending up on some sheer cliff that requires technical climbing skill and equipment.

Above the ledges and waterfall, the faint path disappears altogether in fields of rocks. Pick out whatever seems the best way to the west (nearest and highest) summit of Meeker. The most direct route, straight up the nearest ridge, provides some protection from high winds. However, the direct route is more laborious and not as scenic as climbing more to the right onto less steep sections of the Loft and circling around to a ridge that reaches the summit from the west. (For a description of another route up Meeker, see Sandbeach Lake Trail System in the Wild Basin chapter.)

Eugenia Mine, dating from 1905, now consists of scraps of mining machinery, and several piles of mine tailings. The Rocky

Mountain National Park area is as poor in exploitable minerals as it is rich in scenery. Local mining efforts fortunately were failures, sparing the scenery the scars of boom and bust.

To reach the mine, leave the main trail up Longs at a right fork a half mile from Longs Peak Ranger Station. After following fairly level terrain through aspens, the path undulates moderately through various evergreens for almost a mile to Inn Brook and the mine. It forks at the ruins of a once sturdy cabin that used to house the operator of Eugenia Mine and his family. The left-hand fork leads a few hundred feet uphill to several mine workings. The trail to the right of the cabin passes through pleasant Moore Park and joins the Storm Pass Trail (see the East Edge chapter).

East Edge

For many years, having to pass through private land complicated hikers' access to trails leading to very worthwhile destinations on the southeast edge of Rocky Mountain National Park. In 1990, two nonprofit organizations, the Conservation Fund and the Rocky Mountain National Park Associates, solicited donations to buy private land around Lily Lake near mile marker 6 south of Estes Park along Colorado Highway 7. They gave the land to the national park, and converted a gift shop already on the property into an information center. In 1998, a further acquisition of eighteen acres for the park in the vicinity of the visitor center increased the manageability of the area for park visitation. In 2000, the National Park Service bought the water rights to Lily Lake to guarantee the lake's aesthetic and recreational benefits.

Three enjoyable trails—(Twin Sisters Peaks, Storm Pass, and Homer Rouse)—radiate from Lily Lake. A wheelchair-accessible trail completed in 1997 with privately donated funds circles Lily Lake. The increasingly popular Lily Mountain Trail begins along not-so-wide shoulders of Colorado Highway 7 in Roosevelt National Forest 0.4 mile downhill from Lily Lake, somewhat ominously at the site of an emergency telephone.

Twin Sisters Peaks

The Twin Sisters Trailhead perches in thick lodgepole pine forest 0.4 mile up an unpaved road from the left side of the Lily Lake Visitor Center parking lot. Using switchbacks, the trail maintains a reasonably gentle grade for about 3 miles to tree line. Hikers who are climbing Twin Sisters to condition themselves for higher climbs may become winded, but they can hide this fact by claiming to stop to enjoy the fine views of Longs Peak across the Tahosa Valley.

Above tree line, more switchbacks lead to a rocky tundra meadow between two summits of Twin Sisters. The lower western

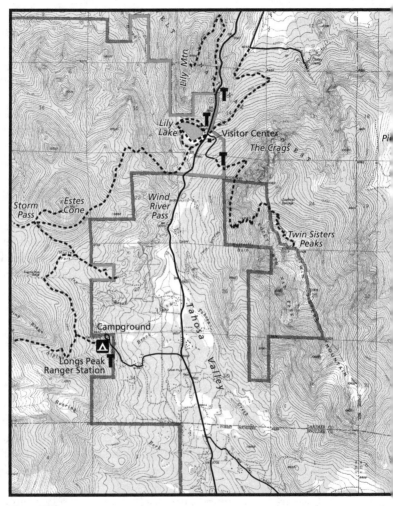

East Edge

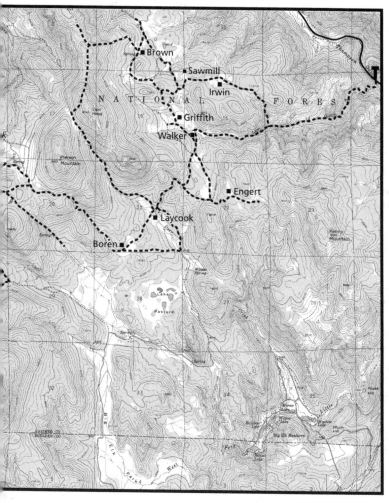

summit attracts the most visitation. A trail still leads to the site of a fire lookout that stood here until 1977, when the National Park Service removed it because it was no longer necessary for wildfire control. The view remains as ample testimony to why the lookout stood on this spot. A stone hut housing a radio repeater used by various government agencies sits below the western summit. The eastern summit, 15 feet higher, provides good views of the foothills of the Rockies and the megalopolis spreading between Colorado Springs and Fort Collins.

Lodgepole pines along the lower part of the Twin Sisters Trail grow there because fire destroyed denser forest and created room for sun-loving lodgepoles. Similarly, in 1929, a fire destroyed a stand of lodgepoles on the west flank of the peaks, allowing quaking aspens to replace the pines. The stand of aspens is called the Butterfly Burn. The supposed butterfly shape is rather vague, but the butterfly colors appear beautifully above the Tahosa Valley in September, when these trees are among the first in the area to turn red and yellow.

About 2.7 miles from the trailhead, at the top of a low point on the ridge north of the summits, some maps show a feature called Lookout Springs about a quarter mile east of the trail. This spring was once a drinking water source, but we doubt its purity and recommend that you skip sampling it and instead carry your own water.

To help fight the heat of a summer day, you may want to put a three-quarters-full water bottle in the freezer the evening before your hike. It will contain a lump of ice when transferred to your pack. Carried next to your back, the ice will absorb heat generated by hiking and melt into cold drinking water. Thus the bottle will cool you on the outside as well as the inside.

A better solution is to climb Twin Sisters not on a hot summer day but on a cool summer night. The trail is clear enough to hike by starlight, and a full moon is magic if you can arrange it. A flashlight is worth its weight in confidence.

Starting well before dawn (camping is forbidden on Twin

Sisters), you should arrive on the ridge top in time to witness sunrise above the plains, shining with reservoirs. Here a short telephoto lens can be very helpful to photographers; be sure to include silhouettes of some limber pines in the foreground.

Few early morning hikers who arrive on top of Twin Sisters 3.9 miles from the trailhead are eager to leave; they have literally all day. Yet there is much to experience on the easy return. Pikas squeak their alarms from the invisibility of their near perfect camouflage among the rocks. Also finding shelter among the rocks is dwarf blue columbine. This rare alpine flower is only a few inches tall with stubby curved spurs, an obvious relative of the popular blue columbine, state flower of Colorado. Additional interesting photos of limber pines present themselves on the way down.

The limber pines are dramatic in shape because of winter wind that blasts Twin Sisters. Winter hikers bold enough to face this bombardment (100 miles per hour is not unusual) at least will not be hampered by much snow, which the wind blows away. There is more snow below tree line in winter, but it often is so hard-packed that snowshoes usually are not needed. The winter trail to Twin Sisters begins just above the Lily Lake Visitor Center, adding 0.4 mile of walking on the closed unpaved road to the summer trailhead. Leashed dogs may hike on the closed road, but not in adjoining forest or on the trail beyond the summer trailhead.

Storm Pass Trail to Estes Cone

Once, while leading a group of hikers to Chasm Lake, we informed them of a lecture to be given that evening by a man who had climbed Longs Peak more than fifty times. "Fifty times!" exclaimed one panting hiker. "Why, any reasonable man would have stopped at thirty."

Relatively few climbers can claim such a record on the park's tallest peak. Fewer yet may be able to match *our* record on the park's ninety-fourth tallest peak: One summer we climbed Estes Cone more than a dozen times. Why? Because it is strategically located. Although not very high (11,006 feet), it is a good vantage point from which to photograph taller peaks, especially Mount Meeker. Among the bare rocks at Estes Cone's top hide rare dwarf columbine, and photogenic limber pines grow on the slopes below the summit.

We always climb Estes Cone by way of **Storm Pass.** You can hike to Storm Pass from Longs Peak Campground, 2.6 miles away via Eugenia Mine (see the Longs Peak and Nearby Goals chapter) from Bear Lake Road, 3.75 miles away on the Boulder Brook and Storm Pass Trails (see the Bear Lake Road chapter).

But the most interesting route to Storm Pass is the 3-mile trail from Lily Lake. From the parking lot at the east end of Lily Lake, hikers head left along a wheelchair-accessible trail that follows an old road around the south side of the lake. This easy walking turns to a rather steep path where the Storm Pass Trail branches left to cross the Aspen Brook drainage. A separate trail branches north descending along Aspen Brook to a private road. This road is not open to public use and is gated where it meets Tunnel Road (Larimer County Road 69B) near the YMCA of the Rockies.

The Storm Pass Trail climbs from Aspen Brook over the east flank of Estes Cone to where spectacular views provide an excuse to rest on trailside rocks. On this sunny south-facing slope, lodgepole pines cast little shade, and the trail can be warm in summer. If you plan to continue over Storm Pass, you will feel an obvious drop in temperature when you reach the north-facing slope. Of course, you will be walking mostly downhill, which will have something to do with the perceived drop in temperature.

If you are headed to the top of **Estes Cone,** however, pines and warmth predominate for the 0.7 mile from Storm Pass to the summit. From a classic limber pine grove in Storm Pass, follow the path that runs uphill to the right (east). Keep alert to the view on the left through the pines; the first example of Estes Cone's strategic position is a unique perspective of Specimen Mountain straight down Forest Canyon. The trail first runs clear and certain, zigzagging up the steep slopes, then it degenerates to cairns and then not much of anything.

The terrain guides you to a spot where a bit of rock scrambling is necessary. Avoid trampling rare dwarf columbine growing among the rocks. The top of this climb is a false summit, but it is easier and more fun to go over the rocks than around them. Next you must descend into a gully and then climb to the cone's summit on the east side of the mountain.

The panoramas are excellent in all directions from the top of Estes Cone, especially if you started before dawn. Such an early beginning has the dual advantage of cool temperatures on the way up and the best light for summit photographs. Normal and short telephoto lenses are the most useful on this hike, plus close-up equipment for flowers.

Lily Lake Trail

A wheelchair-accessible path circles Lily Lake, traversing sunny slopes of Lily Mountain to the right of the parking lot off Colorado Highway 7 and penetrating a mixed forest of Douglas-fir and ponderosa pine on the left (south) shore. The lakeshore path varies little from the 8,927-foot elevation at the east edge of the lake. A detour path climbs steeply from the right side of the lake, taking rock climbers near the dramatic slabs on Lily Mountain before descending again to the main trail. Another detour leaves the lakeshore on the south side, taking walkers through elk-chewed quaking aspen groves and lodgepole pines. Both paths on the south shore are wheelchair accessible.

The able-bodied can circle Lily Lake in fifteen minutes or circle it twice in thirty. The able-minded, however, take much longer for there is much to see along this path. It may be the easiest place in the national park to find a varied collection of woody plants. You can buy several botanical guides to identify these trees, shrubs, and ground covers at the Lily Lake Visitor Center.

With a mixture of habitats, Lily Lake is also a good place for summer bird-watching. Most of the ducks are mallards, which feed by dabbling in the shallows with their tails in the air. Those that dive below the water are less common ring-necked ducks.

Red-tailed hawk

Homer Rouse Trail

Named for a former superintendent of Rocky Mountain National Park, this Larimer County Trail outside of park boundaries commemorates Rouse's significant volunteer service to the Estes Park community outside of his national park duties. This route begins at the parking lot in front of the Lily Lake Visitor Center and proceeds down an unpaved road about 400 yards to historic **Baldpate Inn.** On the National Register of Historic Places, this privately owned lodge dates from 1917 and recalls a less hurried era of park visitation. Its unique key collection and display of old photos supplement the interest inherent in the log building itself. The route continues past the inn and its parking area.

Some Baldpate photos show views of the inn's vicinity taken from the old road that climbed from the valley of Fish Creek to Lily Lake. Long abandoned by vehicles after the blasting of Colorado Highway 7 through spectacular cuts on Lily Mountain, this old road is now the Homer Rouse Trail. Trees have grown to block most of the views displayed in the historic photos. Nonetheless, you still can see spectacular scenery, especially The Crags on the north side of Twin Sisters. The road grade is reasonably gentle on the knees of those headed downhill and on the lungs of those climbing up from Fish Creek. A detour path through the woods near the bottom takes hikers away from the old road to avoid private homes.

To drive to the lower end of the Homer Rouse Trail, turn left from CO 7 at a curve a bit less than a half mile south of Marys Lake Road. This turn onto Fish Creek Way is hard to see. After 0.3 mile, continue straight on an unpaved road at the bottom of the hill where Fish Creek bends left. Drive another 0.6 mile to where the road turns sharply left. The road straight ahead is the bottom of the Homer Rouse Trail. Lily Lake is less than 2 miles ahead and less than 700 feet above.

We usually want to hike a bit farther, the ranch land south of Fish Creek is very pretty, and we are a bit unsure about where to park where the trail actually begins. Therefore, we often park somewhere along the shoulder of the paved road and walk the scenic half mile to the trailhead. Intermittent streams that flow across the Homer Rouse Trail can create fall-inducing patches of ice in winter. Because the entire trail is outside the national park, canine companions can accompany human hikers; it is best to keep the dogs leashed.

Lily Mountain Trail (Roosevelt National Forest)

Lily Mountain is the easiest mountain in this book, yet it offers a genuine climbing experience. As such, it is an excellent first climb for children whose parents want them to acquire a taste for mountaineering. It is also popular with visitors who want to hike with dogs. Keep the dogs leashed.

To reach the trailhead, drive south of Estes Park on Colorado Highway 7 to a point 2.4 miles south of Marys Lake Road (just before mile marker 6). At present, you park on the shoulder of the highway. There is not much room, which somewhat limits the number of people hiking the trail at one time. Additionally, it is easy to err and drive on uphill past the trailhead. Watch for three major road cuts as the highway climbs the valley wall; the trail begins on the right-hand (west) side just past the third big cut.

The USDA Forest Service has considered building a parking area nearby. If it has been established by the time you read this, the trailhead should be easy to find. The parking area would allow more people on Lily Mountain simultaneously. Opinions doubtless will vary as to whether that would be a good thing.

The first part of the trail follows a very gentle grade, slightly rising and falling parallel to the road. The slope is partially forested and dotted with interesting rock outcrops. Eventually the way begins to veer left, more steeply uphill and away from the highway. At this point another trail continues straight ahead, dropping downhill. This is but one example of several branching paths that might lure you from the main trail. Ignore the right-hand fork and follow the clearer path to the left. After a series of short switchbacks, yet another false trail leads downhill. Bear left again, and climb a few more yards to the ridge top. Turning left, follow the trail south along the ridgeline toward the summit.

Before you reach the top, the trail becomes less distinct and then fades away. Here you get to practice the challenge of route finding. Climb a few yards to the right, then cut left directly for the summit. Clambering over the rocks for the last few yards should be easy and fun.

From the top there is a good view of Twin Sisters, to the south over a bump on Lily. Panning to the right from there you'll see Meadow and St. Vrain Mountains, the Longs Peak group, the Front Range, and, away to the north, the Mummy Range. The extensive red-roofed buildings of the YMCA of the Rockies lie below, in the northwest. In the valley to the northeast, ranch land and residences extend along Fish Creek to Estes Park and Lake Estes. All in all, the summit of Lily Mountain is a pleasant, satisfying sort of place, well worth the effort it takes to get there.

Homestead Meadows (Roosevelt National Forest)

The **Lion Gulch Trail** to Homestead Meadows has become popular since 1978, when the Forest Service purchased land on which sit ruins of ranches established in the late 1880s and early 1890s. Staying well below 9,000 feet, this system of trails is free of snow most of the year. It is a favorite of horseback riders and hikers who want to enjoy canine company but cannot take their dogs on national park trails.

The trailhead is on the south side of US 36, 8 miles east of Estes Park and 13 miles west of Lyons. From the highway, the trail drops to cross the Little Thompson River, then climbs into **Lion Gulch,** following a tributary brook along an easy grade. The brook in Lion Gulch originates on the slopes of a 9,740-foot prominence called Lion Head. Although mountain lions still roam the area occasionally, the chances of spotting one are extremely slight.

Lion Gulch opens into **Homestead Meadows** 2.5 miles from the trailhead. Here begins a series of loop trails that lead past the ruins of eight old homesites and various other buildings. Many sections of trail follow old wagon roads that served these home-sites. Other sections of trail were laid·out to avoid crossing private property contained within the national forest. Hikers should heed closure signs to avoid trespassing.

Forest Service signs also will guide you around the loops. The interpretive signs have pictures and information about the people who lived in and "proved up" each site. Homestead Meadows is on the National Register of Historic Places. It should go without saying that all ruins should be left exactly as found; no part of them should be removed as a souvenir.

Upon emerging from Lion Gulch, the first homestead you will encounter is the Walker Homestead. The buildings of Homestead Meadows were constructed mostly of timber cut on the site. Lumbering was a major source of income here for several years, and wood from this area was used in Allenspark and Meeker Park.

Beyond Walker Homestead, a left turn leads, after another 1.3 miles, to the Engert Homestead. A right turn takes you a half mile along the road to the Griffith Homestead, then another 2.3 miles to the Irvin Homestead and an abandoned sawmill. Whether you go right or left on the Sawmill Loop, there are other loops and trails that will take you to the other five sites. The 3-mile hike from US 36 to the Walker and Griffith Homesteads has a gradual elevation gain from 7,360 feet to 8,400 feet.

The trail southwest to the Boren Homestead continues 2.5 miles beyond Homestead Meadows to **Pierson Park,** on the east side of Twin Sisters Peaks. At Pierson Park, a right turn (north) along Road 119.2 (passable only by four-wheel-drive vehicles) eventually leads through residential developments on the out-skirts of Estes Park. A left turn (south) follows four-wheel-drive Road 119.1 through former logging areas to Cabin Creek Road, off Colorado Highway 7 near Meeker Park. Road and trail maps are available from the USDA Forest Service, 161 Second Street, Estes Park, CO 80517; (970) 586–3440 (limited hours during non-summer months).

Wild Basin

In late summer of 1978, a large and well-publicized forest fire swept through Wild Basin, causing a good deal of distress among nearby residents. Backcountry travelers feared that one of the park's finest hiking areas would be destroyed. Fortunately, such was not the case. Most hikers will notice signs of the fire in only a few places; Wild Basin trails and destinations remain lovely. Trailhead parking is limited; car pooling and arriving early are advisable.

To reach the Wild Basin trails, drive south from Estes Park on Colorado Highway 7 for more than 11 miles through the village of Meeker Park to a large sign indicating Wild Basin. Turn right and follow the paved road a few hundred yards to the Wild Basin entrance station located on an unpaved road to the right. (The Sandbeach Lake Trailhead is to the right of the station.) The road extends 2 miles to Wild Basin Ranger Station.

Beyond the entrance station, the road turns left and passes over the dam that forms **Copeland Lake.** Copeland Lake is a good place to photograph Copeland Mountain. Early in the morning, the massive, round-topped peak often is reflected by the still waters of the lake, as long as the city of Longmont, which owns the lake, has not drawn off the water for use down on the plains.

Past Copeland Lake, much of the road is one car wide and dusty. If you arrive before 9:00 A.M., you probably will not meet anyone leaving. Driving out will be more difficult later in the day because of increased traffic. Really, the road is perfect—passable in any passenger car without damage to car or occupants, but discouraging to folks who just want a nice place to take a drive. Park at the end of the road, at the ranger station.

Ouzel Falls Trail System

The Ouzel Falls Trail System begins at a bridge across Hunters Creek, south of the picnic area at the end of the road. A mere 0.3 mile of easy, pleasant trail brings you to **Copeland Falls,** a somewhat sudden drop in North St. Vrain Creek. It is a pretty spot and

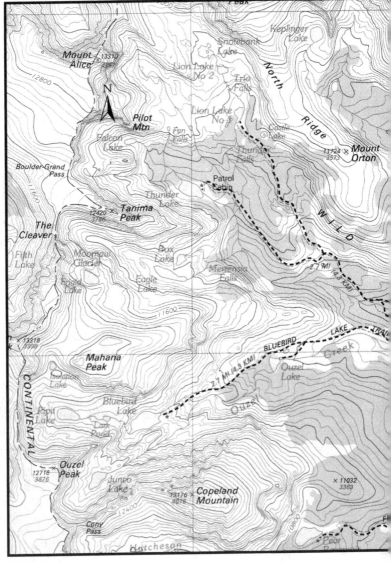

Wild Basin

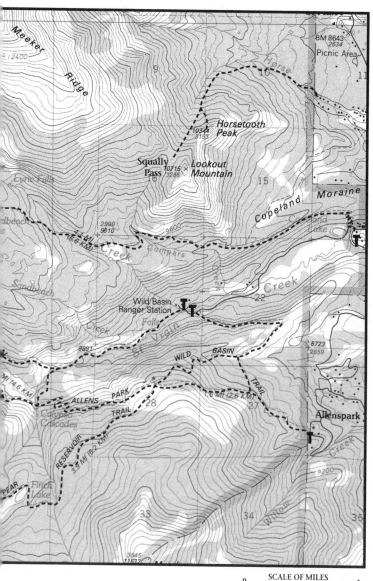

Meaker Ridge

BM 8643
2634
Picnic Area

12400

Horse

9

10

11

Horsetooth
Peak

10344
3153

Lynic Falls

Squally
Pass
6

10716
3266
×
Lookout
Mountain

15

Copeland
Moraine

Sandbeach

2990
9810
16.6 KM

9600

Coopers

Creek

Copeland
Lake

Sandbeach

Creek

Creek

22

Wild Basin
Ranger Station

Falls

8723
2659

MI (4.6 KM)

8891

St. Vrain

WILD

BASIN

ALLENS

PARK

TRAIL

28

TRAIL

1.6 MI (2.6 KM)

27

Allenspark

Copeland
Cascades

RESERVOIR

3.9 MI (6.2 KM)

Creek

9200

PEAR

Finch
Lake

33

34

Willow

35

3545
11532

0   SCALE OF MILES   1

well worth a picture, but no more spectacular than several unnamed places along the creek, which the trail follows for the next mile. A detour left of the main trail hugs the creek bank for a short way upstream to one such picturesque spot, unofficially called Upper Copeland Falls. Be sure to stay on the detour or the main trail; do not trample through the narrow, flowery meadow between the two.

A little more than a mile from Copeland Falls, you cross North St. Vrain Creek on a substantial log bridge. Just before the bridge, a path to the right to backcountry campsites extends up North St. Vrain Creek as a shortcut to the Thunder Lake Trail. It bypasses the very scenic Calypso Cascades and Ouzel Falls, but also could be used as a return route from these destinations (see page 133).

Ascending beyond the bridge, you may notice some spot burns of the Ouzel Fire. Where the path bends left, you can walk straight ahead onto a large boulder and look down on the confluence of North St. Vrain Creek on the right and Cony Creek on the left. The trail continues through the subalpine forest along Cony Creek to **Calypso Cascades.** Named for the little pink calypso orchids that bloom nearby in July, this outstanding whitewater scene is best photographed (oddly enough) at the time when most hikers arrive, toward midday. Overcast skies can help reduce light contrast between the white water and dark woods.

There is a trail junction at Calypso Cascades. The trail to the left is the Allens Park Trail (see page 142). Take the trail to the right for **Ouzel Falls,** crossing Cony Creek via two bridges. Remnants of spot burns from the 1978 fire are much more common beyond Calypso Cascades. Watch for deer or elk grazing on shrubs or flowers that sprout up in these burned areas. Climbing through a couple of wide switchbacks, you will see through the trees Mount Meeker and Longs Peak to the north. Meeker gives the false impression of being the taller of the two because it is closer.

Past the switchbacks, begin to listen for the sound of Ouzel Falls, which ranks among the most spectacular in the park. From

Water ouzel (dipper)

the trail's bridge across Ouzel Creek it is possible to see the falls, but the best view is obtained by climbing up the hill just before reaching the bridge. There are worn paths of a sort weaving in and out. None is better than another, all are informal, and the very slick rocks can cause a tumble anywhere. The falls can be photographed from many different angles with normal or wide-angle lenses.

After crossing Ouzel Creek on the bridge, the trail circles below the ridge from which Ouzel Falls drops, reaching a spot where there is another view of Longs and Meeker. At 0.4 mile from the falls, you arrive at another trail junction. The Thunder Lake Trail goes right (see page 133), and the Bluebird Lake Trail goes left.

The **Bluebird Lake Trail** climbs steeply south from the junction to the crest of a moraine. Once on top, you are where the 1978 Ouzel Fire raged at its hottest, killing everything. Before the fire, most of the trees were lodgepole pines. Adapted to grow in burned areas, lodgepole almost certainly will be the tree species that will reestablish the forest. Views to the right to Tanima Peak and Mount Alice were not visible before the fire cleared the trees.

Beyond the area of complete deforestation, 1.3 miles after the previous junction, you reach the spur trail to **Ouzel Lake.** The Ouzel Fire began with a lightning strike near this lake, but damage along the trail and lakeshore was relatively light. Ouzel and Manaha Peaks are the most photogenic mountains seen from the lake and are best pictured from the northern shore.

Ouzel Lake is dominated by the imposing bulk of **Copeland Mountain.** To climb Copeland, cross the lake's outlet and fight your way through a half mile of heavy subalpine forest to the top of a tree-covered ridge. Bear right there, following the ridge southwest for a half mile to tree line. From tree line it is a tiresome tundra trudge past innumerable discouraging false summits to the top of the massive mountain. Copeland is the tallest peak on the southern side of Wild Basin, and the view from the top is spectacular.

The Bluebird Lake Trail continues past the Ouzel Lake spur

for a half mile to **Chickadee Pond,** passing through an area that was heavily burned. Past Chickadee Pond the trail traverses a small boulder field and passes through subalpine forest. The forest is followed by subalpine meadows, where yellow snow lilies bloom in late June. A small waterfall tumbles into this garden all summer. The path runs through rocks and back into trees and ever increasing flowers to a meadow 5.6 miles from the trailhead. In a marshy area where the trail crosses Ouzel Creek, look for tiny white bog orchids among the many wildflowers. Often, too, there is an ice cave upstream at the foot of a gully where the creek has carved its way through a deep snowdrift.

After crossing Ouzel Creek, the path steepens dramatically while climbing parallel to the stream, which is out of sight on the opposite side of a narrow ridge. The beaten track frequently disappears on bedrock or under snow, so it may be necessary to search for cairns.

In 1988 Rocky Mountain National Park bought three reservoirs—Bluebird Lake, Pear Reservoir, and Sandbeach Lake—from the city of Longmont. Dams impounding these reservoirs were dismantled, and the water dropped to its natural levels in those lakes. The massive concrete dam at Bluebird Lake, 6 lung-popping miles from the nearest road, was the most difficult to remove, a major engineering feat. Here the dam's removal affected the view less than at the other two lakes because Bluebird's shore is mostly naked rock anyway. The best view of the lake and of Ouzel Peak rising out of the water is from the southern shore, over and around various rock outcrops.

The trail ends at the lake. To reach higher goals, cross the creek on rocks at the outlet, scramble with hands and feet up steep rock on the other side, and keep climbing to the north. After you have gained about 200 feet in elevation above the lake, bear to your left (west) across slabs of rock and tundra. Where the drainage becomes wider and less steep you find **Lark Pond.** West from there it is an easy meander to **Pipit Lake,** about a mile from Bluebird.

Pipit is bleak, despite a rim of bistort and avens. Isolation and Ouzel Peaks, stark rock towers, rise on either side. Between them is a barren pass, which looks almost as though the glacier that sculpted it melted only yesterday. Few patches of green soften the harsh landscape.

Clambering up to the pass for closer examination, however, reveals that life has taken hold. Patches of tundra are vibrant with the color of alpine flowers, delicate yet rugged. From the top of the pass, a left-hand (south) turn heads along the ridge top for the summit of **Ouzel Peak.** At first the ridge is narrow and nearly as steep on the west side as on the side you ascended. This is the line of the Continental Divide. Climb along the west side of the ridge, crossing rocks and tundra below the crest. Eventually, you walk above the area of glacial action onto a broad slope leading to the top of Ouzel. The view is magnificent, of course; you look down into Wild Basin and Paradise Park Research Natural Area.

A walk of an additional mile along the tundra, on the Continental Divide, takes you to **Ogalalla Peak.** Halfway there you'll bypass Cony Pass, a route of descent to either Junco Lake, south of Bluebird, or Cony Lake, in the Finch Lake Trail System (see page 140).

A right-hand turn from the pass between Ouzel and Isolation Peaks leads north along the Continental Divide to **Isolation Peak.** It is a steep trudge along the narrow ridge past five false summits to the true summit. Because Isolation is higher than nearby Mahana and Ouzel Peaks, the view from there is superior. From Isolation, the prospect south to Indian Peaks is unobstructed. (Isolation's altitude is 13,118 feet, 200 feet less than the number recorded on the 1987 USGS map of Rocky Mountain National Park.)

A preferred route of descent is via the broad saddle between Isolation and Mahana Peaks. From the saddle, you can descend directly to **Eagle Lake** or take a side jaunt to **Frigid Lake.** The direct route is to walk north downhill to a broad shelf below the saddle, follow a border of alpine willows to the edge of the shelf, and drop down to Eagle Lake. For the side trip to Frigid Lake, circle downhill from the saddle along the base of Isolation, and cross snow to the lake. To go from Frigid to Eagle, make your way down to the broad shelf and follow the route described above. You can circle Eagle Lake on the southern (right) shore, descend to Box Lake, and exit via the Thunder Lake Trail (see below).

Rather than climbing north and west from Bluebird to Pipit Lake, you can contour south from the Bluebird outlet and ascend the ridge between Bluebird and the outlet stream from Junco Lake. Junco Lake is three-quarters of a mile from Bluebird's outlet. From Junco it is a rough half mile uphill to Cony Pass, which is situated south of Junco between a ridge of Copeland Mountain and the Continental Divide. From Cony Pass you can drop down to Cony Lake and exit via Finch Lake (see Finch Lake Trail System).

Back at the Bluebird–Thunder Lake junction, you can continue straight ahead along an easy grade on the **Thunder Lake Trail.** Cross a bridge over North St. Vrain Creek 0.4 mile from the junction, after which the shortcut trail comes in from downstream. Follow the main trail through a tight switchback and up steepening grades. At 1.3 miles from the bridge there is a junction with the Lion Lakes Trail, which goes to the right (see page 134).

Take the left-hand (lower) fork, and continue on through a set of switchbacks and limber pines struggling amid rocks. Then subalpine fir and Engelmann spruce enclose the trail, and the grade becomes less steep. Soon a faint path strikes downhill to the left toward Box and Eagle Lakes (see page 136). Continuing on the level, you cross a large stream, then a smaller one, and at last reach the top of a wooded slope above Thunder Lake.

Descend with the trail to a meadow at the eastern end of the lake, 6.8 miles from the Wild Basin Trailhead. The meadow is marshy in spots; on close inspection, stalks of pink blossoms growing there turn out to be elephant heads, or little red elephants. A log patrol cabin at Thunder Lake is kept locked, but its long eaves give shelter from afternoon showers. Slosh east through the meadow to get damp feet and a good photo of the cabin, lake, and Boulder–Grand Pass with the peaks in the background.

To reach **Boulder–Grand Pass,** follow a trail around the northern (right) shore of Thunder Lake. Two streams feed the lake from the west. The first one (northernmost) comes from **Falcon Lake,** about three-quarters of a mile away and more than 580 feet higher than Thunder Lake. The second stream flows from **Lake of Many Winds,** a boulder-bordered pond immediately below the pass. Cross both streams, then, avoiding marshes, climb through woods and rocks to the vicinity of Lake of Many Winds. Circle it on the left and, staying to the right of a prominent snowfield, scramble slowly up loose rock to the pass.

Broad tundra extends downhill from Boulder–Grand Pass toward as fine a string of paternoster lakes as ever a glacier carved (see East Inlet Trail in the Grand Lake chapter). A left turn at the pass presents an uncomplicated ascent over tundra to the top of **Tanima Peak.** Hikers turning right at the pass have a much longer ridge-top journey to the summit of Mount Alice. Most people climb Alice from Lion Lakes and descend via Boulder–Grand Pass.

Leaving the Thunder Lake Trail at 4.8 miles from the Wild Basin Trailhead, the **Lion Lakes Trail** climbs straight up the hill for about 100 rocky yards. The grade then becomes more reasonable as the trail snakes through large boulders and levels on a crest. After a descent into subalpine forest, which gets your hopes up, the trail again shoots steeply uphill. Steepness is followed by moderation and steepness and moderation and swamp.

At the marshy area, the trail becomes faint while the mosquitoes become strong. Of course, this would be the best spot for photographing majestic Mount Alice, to the west. A little pond here is usually still and provides a more dependable reflecting surface for Alice than does **Lion Lake No. 1** a few yards farther ahead.

It is very pleasant to sit a spell on relatively soft and dry meadows by the shore of Lion Lake No. 1, but there is much to lure you on. A short walk along the northeastern shore presents good views of Tanima Peak rising behind a small rock- and tree-covered ridge. Very lush meadows border the stream between Lion Lake No. 1 and **Trio Falls.** Immediately beyond the falls is **Lion Lake No. 2,** which may have more snow on its shore than **Snowbank Lake,** a short way farther up the drainage.

From Snowbank you can veer left to the top of a ridge leading uphill to the saddle between Mount Alice and Chiefs Head Peak, to the north. Very fine photos of the east face of Alice are available from the ridge. Having hiking companions in the foreground of your pictures helps give an idea of the immensity of this sheer rock wall. From the saddle, there is an interesting northern view looking down on Lake Powell in its cirque below McHenry Peak. Chiefs Head is seldom climbed from this saddle because there is a shorter way to get there (see page 137).

To reach the summit of **Mount Alice,** turn left at the saddle and descend for a short distance along the Continental Divide on rocks that look more difficult to pass over than they really are. The route is easiest on the right-hand (western) side of the ridge. Actually, the rocks are quite interesting and definitely should be included as a frame for a photo of the North Inlet valley, to the west. A little ridge-top notch at the bottom of the descent is a cozy, pleasant place, carpeted with patches of tundra.

From the notch, it takes a certain amount of will to begin the very steep ascent, over boulders, of the final long slope to Alice's summit. Again, the route is less awful than it appears. As you approach the top, bear to the right (west) to avoid a false summit on the left (east). From the summit, the bulk of Chiefs Head Peak diminishes the drama of Longs Peak and Pagoda Mountain; Mount Meeker, on the other hand, looks singularly pointed.

There is well over a mile of downhill tundra walking to Boulder–Grand Pass from the top of Alice. The alpine flowers can be magnificent. Half sliding down loose pebbles past Lake of Many Winds leads to glacier lilies and Thunder Lake, the goal of your lengthy descent. But unless you have a camp there, it is a long 7 miles out to the trailhead. After a fine climb like Alice, you will have a lot to think about on the way.

The fisherman's path to **Box** and **Eagle Lakes** leaves the Thunder Lake Trail a little more than a half mile before Thunder Lake. Descending through subalpine forest and meadows, the path disappears in the vicinity of North St. Vrain Creek. You should keep going in the same general direction through narrow, slanting meadows lying between cliff and forest, then climb a steep, narrow gorge that levels off to a marsh. Skirt the marsh on the left, and climb through flowered subalpine meadows, following the brook that flows from Box Lake, a basin carved from solid rock by glaciers.

Eagle Lake was similarly carved in a shelf 70 feet higher than Box Lake. To reach Eagle, climb up the rocks on the left-hand (southern) side of Box. Make your way through the least dense krummholz to the edge of the lake.

More trails in the krummholz along the northern shore take you to Eagle's outlet stream. There, in early September, we found the largest arctic gentian we have seen. From the same spot you can take a good photo of Mount Meeker, featuring Box Lake in the lower part of the frame.

The most unusual sight at Eagle Lake appears a few yards downstream from the outlet: a tunnel. Big enough to walk into, with dynamite-fractured rock at its mouth and on the floor, it leads straight through the granite back toward Eagle Lake. It evidently was intended to provide a means of draining the lake when water was needed on the plains. Fortunately, the tunnel remains unfinished, and Eagle Lake undrained.

Peak baggers may want to add **Mahana Peak** to their list by climbing it from Eagle Lake, even though Mahana is bounded on three sides by taller peaks. Make your way around the eastern end of Eagle Lake, and climb by the least steep route over rocks to the shelf overhead. Follow the border of alpine willows uphill to a broad expanse below the Mahana-Isolation saddle. From there you can turn right to **Frigid Lake,** which sits below the base of Eagles Beak, nearly a mile's hike from Eagle Lake, or you can climb on to Mahana, more than 1.2 miles from Eagle Lake. Head first for the broad easy saddle, because an attempt to cut straight up the peak could lead to a bothersome false summit. The true top is on the right (southwest) side of Mahana.

Sandbeach Lake Trail System

The Sandbeach Lake Trailhead lies at the eastern end of the unpaved road leading into Wild Basin. (For driving instructions to this point, see the beginning of this chapter.) From the lake, the trail ascends steeply through sunny woods on Copeland Moraine. Eventually, you reach a ridge top after a short set of switchbacks. Here a trail from Meeker Park comes in on the right, 1.2 miles from the trailhead.

Continue climbing straight ahead at a steady rate for 1.1 miles to the crossing of Campers Creek. Exactly 1 mile farther on you cross Hunters Creek. After almost another mile of steady uphill hiking, you arrive at **Sandbeach Lake,** 4.2 miles from the trailhead.

If this description of the hike to Sandbeach Lake has failed to stir your interest, it may be because until you reach the lake the trail is not terribly fascinating. The lake itself is pretty, with the high peaks in southern Wild Basin rising beyond, somewhat subdued by distance. Removal of its dam allowed the water to drop to its natural level, revealing the sand beach that the reservoir had covered when it was full. Sandbeach Lake serves as a jumping-off point for the three highest mountains in Rocky Mountain National Park—Longs Peak, Mount Meeker, and Chiefs Head Peak—plus the difficult Pagoda Peak.

The actual point of departure for all these summits lies a short way back up the trail, before it reaches the lake. At the point where the trail turns southwest and begins to descend to the lake, climbers must strike off through the woods. The first step in climbing **Chiefs Head Peak** is to climb **Mount Orton.** From the trail, keep walking northwest, in the same direction the trail was heading before it turned toward the lake. Then bear a little to the left to cross a rivulet that flows into the lake, and climb out

Fairyslipper (calypso) orchids

of the trees onto a ridge above the lake. Keep heading uphill until you reach the top of Orton, a jumble of rocks on the eastern end of a crest leading to Chiefs Head.

Mount Orton is not particularly high, but you will notice before you reach the top that it is strategically located. The Orton Ridge (also called North Ridge) juts into Wild Basin from the surrounding mountain wall, providing a relatively convenient platform from which to view the entire basin.

From the top of Orton, which you can bypass easily on the right, it is an uncomplicated hike over tundra to the summit of Chiefs Head. The way becomes steeper at the end, naturally. Nearby peaks such as Mount Alice, McHenrys Peak, Pagoda Mountain, Mount Meeker, and Longs Peak fill the panorama with grandeur.

The Wild Basin route up **Mount Meeker** (see the Longs Peak and Nearby Goals chapter for an alternate route) leaves the Sandbeach Trail as it begins to descend to Sandbeach Lake. Bear to the right and cross Hunters Creek. Ascend the gully on the south side of Meeker, keeping to the left of Dragons Egg Rock, which stands out obtrusively in the middle of the gully. As you draw even with the rock, bear left to climb Meeker's southwestern ridge. The final stretch along the ridge to the summit is steep but uncomplicated.

Pagoda Mountain usually is climbed from Glacier Gorge (see the Bear Lake Road chapter), but if you are in Wild Basin and get the urge to do Pagoda, leave the Sandbeach Trail as it turns down to the lake. Keep walking in the same direction the trail was heading, into the valley between Mounts Meeker and Orton.

Cross Hunters Creek, and pick your way up the valley until you can turn right without scaling cliffs. Climb up the steep valley between Meeker and Pagoda to masses of loose rock (scree) at the base of Longs Peak. Scramble up this scree toward the cliffs on the right-hand side. Keep climbing the right-hand side of a huge cirque in the southeast face of Pagoda to the lowest point in the saddle between Longs and Pagoda. Long after you have grown thoroughly sick of loose rock, you will reach the saddle and turn left toward the summit. The terrain will guide you below the crest of the ridge to the very small summit of Pagoda, which is just as pointed as a mountaintop should be.

To climb **Longs Peak** by the difficult route of the first ascent back in 1868, follow the above route (from the Sandbeach Trail to Pagoda) as far as the scree slopes at the base of Longs. Then look up for the Notch on the right-hand side of the peak, and a wall to the right of it. Climb up the fan of loose rock farthest to the right, below the wall. When the fan narrows, bear left and follow a diagonal ledge to the left. This becomes a gully (filled with loose rock, what else?), which eventually takes you to a small shelf below the vertical columns—the Palisades—to the right of the Notch.

On ledges to the left of the gully, traverse a few hundred feet across cliffs, then climb diagonally left to the base of the Homestretch. Follow the red-and-yellow painted bull's-eyes up the 45 degree slope to the summit.

This route up Longs was discovered by L. W. Keplinger, who scouted it for explorer John Wesley Powell. Nearby **Keplinger Lake** commemorates the intrepid scout. To reach the lake, climb Mount Orton. If you wish, you can bypass the top of Orton and contour along its northern slope to Hunters Creek. The traverse will necessitate some steep sidehill walking and perhaps a slight loss in elevation, but it will keep you out of dense krummholz traps that require magic to pass through. Follow Hunters Creek upstream past large boulders to its source, Keplinger Lake. A cirque hangs dramatically over the lake on the southwest face of Pagoda.

Finch Lake Trail System

The Finch Lake Trailhead is located about 1,000 feet east of the bridge that crosses North St. Vrain Creek to Wild Basin Ranger Station. Look for an identification sign on the left-hand (south) side of the road. An even better starting point for a hike to Finch Lake is the Allens Park Trailhead (see page 142).

From the Finch Lake Trailhead, the trail climbs steadily eastward through heavy forest along a lateral moraine. The trees disappear at the top of the moraine where the path switchbacks toward the west, nearly a mile from the trailhead. The path passes on a level grade through aspens and lodgepole pines, then runs gradually downhill to an intersection with trails from Meadow Mountain Ranch (on the park's eastern border) and the little town of Allenspark.

Take the trail farthest right (north), continue through an aspen grove, and resume climbing via wide switchbacks. Visible to the north (right) across Wild Basin are Chiefs Head, Pagoda Mountain, and Mount Meeker. The bulk of Meeker hides all but a corner of Longs Peak.

Another intersection is reached 2.3 miles from the trailhead. For its mysterious power to baffle hikers, this spot is dubbed **Confusion Junction.** The trail on the right descends for 1.5 miles to Calypso Cascades (see Ouzel Falls Trail System), passing through 1978 burn areas as it approaches the cascades. The trail on the left starts out uphill but soon drops through thick woods to meet the Allens Park Trail, coming from the previous intersection. The Allens Park Trailhead is 1.6 miles from Confusion Junction.

Follow the middle path along a mostly moderate grade to **Finch Lake.** A quarter mile from the junction, the trail crosses a fire corridor for another quarter mile. After crossing several streams, the way leads over a small ridge and down to Finch Lake, 4.5 miles from the trailhead. Finch is often calm and reflects Copeland Mountain. The best photo may be had from just off trail on the eastern shore of the lake.

The trail goes around Finch Lake on the northern side. The 2 miles of uphill trail from Finch to **Pear Lake** are pretty but rather steep and sloppy in places. Snow there lasts far into the summer. When it finally does melt, excellent flower displays spring up in response to the abundant water.

The trail reaches Pear Lake at the best place for taking photos of the always dramatic Ouzel Peak. (In 1988 the Park Service bought Pear Lake from the city of Longmont and lowered the surface to its natural level; the resulting "bathtub ring" between reservoir and natural levels could cause some photo problems.) A sheer-faced ridge of Copeland Mountain will add a share of drama to the picture. Follow the path as it bears left along the southeastern shore. Among the rocks along the trail, roughly 100 yards past the lake, hide rare dwarf columbine.

The trail is not maintained beyond Pear Lake, but it is obvious nonetheless to the lowest of the **Hutcheson Lakes,** in the Cony Creek drainage. These lakes can be reached also via the Middle St. Vrain Trail System (see the Indian Peaks East of the Divide chapter).

Stay north of and higher than the lowest Hutcheson Lake, and continue up the drainage. The way is marshy in places and lined with krummholz in others. At the largest of the Hutcheson Lakes, the tree line setting is spectacular, with Ogalalla Peak rising in the background.

Cross the outlet of the largest Hutcheson Lake, and angle uphill on the left-hand (south) side. Follow Cony Creek upstream from where it tumbles over a cliff into the lake. Circle with the creek around a buttress jutting from the south, and walk across rocks and tundra to **Cony Lake.** Situated high above tree line, Cony Lake is devoid even of bushes. Its shore is more tundra than rock, and glacier-sculpted peaks rise directly from the water. The entire effect makes a very fine photo; you will want to use a wide-angle lens. Rocks or hiking companions in the foreground will add interest to the rather plain shoreline.

Allens Park Trail

The first problem with this pleasant alternative route into Wild Basin is figuring out whether Allens Park or Allenspark is the correct name. The first is the National Park Service/U.S. Geological Survey spelling; the second is the U.S. Postal Service spelling. This problem is best solved by ignoring it.

The trailhead itself is also a bit confusing because the parking is on private land dedicated as open space in a residential subdivision. The sign marking the trailhead is in the national park. If the rather small parking lot is full, do not park anywhere that blocks driveways or access to the subdivision water system.

To reach the trailhead, leave Colorado Highway 7 on Business Route 7 (Washington Street) into the town of Allenspark (spelled as one word because this street goes to the post office). A block from the highway, turn right on unpaved County Road 90. After 0.7 mile, bear left uphill on South Skinner Road. Drive 0.6 mile and turn right uphill on Meadow Mountain Drive for a few yards to the Allens Park Trail parking on the right.

The Allens Park Trail leads to two main destinations in Wild Basin. It meets the Ouzel Falls Trail System (see page 125) at Calypso Cascades 3 miles from the Allens Park Trailhead. This is 1.2 miles farther than the Ouzel Falls Trail, but it is less crowded. Although it lacks the streamside views of the Ouzel Falls Trail, the Allens Park Trail offers more spectacular mountain vistas opened by the 1978 forest fire. The same fire improved the habitat for mule deer, which are more common along the Allens Park Trail than on the Ouzel Falls Trail below Calypso Cascades.

The Allens Park Trail also intersects the Finch Lake Trail System at Confusion Junction (see page 141). Beginning at the Allens Park Trailhead makes for a shorter and easier hike to Finch, Pear, and Hutcheson Lakes via this meeting of trails with its mysterious power to befuddle hikers. (Allens Park Trailhead is 1.6 miles from Confusion Junction; Finch Lake Trailhead is 2.3 miles from Confusion Junction.)

Horsetooth Peak and Lookout Mountain

These small peaks provide good views into Wild Basin and are not frequently climbed. To reach their obscure trailhead, turn west from Colorado Highway 7 onto unpaved Road 113N in the middle of Meeker Park, opposite Meeker Park Lodge. Follow this rough lane for 0.6 mile, and park where you will not block the road or someone's driveway. Walk up the lane past private cabins, which should not be disturbed in any way. (There has been some objection to hikers in this area in the past.)

Soon after you enter the national park, the way branches. The left path crosses Horse Creek in the direction of the Sandbeach Lake Trail. Continue on the right fork to the next junction. This time go left and cross the creek. Climb the trail through a mile of pleasant woods to where a spur cuts to the left, heading up **Horsetooth Peak.** You may notice HT carved on a tree at this junction.

The best way up the final rock pitches to the summit on Horsetooth is a matter of opinion, but you probably will not want to approach it directly from the trail. Try circling left to scramble up from the northeast side of the peak. Be careful. Gravity works on Horsetooth just as it does on Longs Peak, and the rocks at the end of a fall are equally hard on both mountains.

The main trail continues up to a level area called **Squally Pass.** Here picturesque limber pines show the effects of wind. From the pass, the walk southeast to the top of **Lookout Mountain** is uncomplicated.

Trail Ridge Road

Climbing to 12,183 feet above sea level, Trail Ridge Road is the highest continuous highway in the United States. Because life zones of different kinds of plants vary with altitude, this highly scenic road passes through three different levels of life: the montane zone of ponderosa pine and Douglas-fir at the base of the road, the subalpine zone of thickly growing Engelmann spruce and subalpine fir, and the alpine zone above tree line.

Approximately 11 miles of the road's 44-mile length are above tree line; 3 miles run more than 12,000 feet above sea level. Only from late May or early June to approximately the latter part of October do wind and snow permit Trail Ridge to be open to motorized traffic. This easy access to broad, rolling expanses of alpine tundra completely unaltered by grazing livestock is an outstanding feature of Rocky Mountain National Park.

On the alpine tundra, the wind does not allow tree growth, and a tall plant is 6 inches high. During the short blooming season, however, alpine vistas of abundant wildflowers carpeting the tundra and snow-accented crags in the background are breathtaking. It is small surprise that many people want to get out of their cars to examine this unique environment more closely.

Unfortunately, tundra plants live constantly on the edge of death due to the bitter climate they must endure during most of the year. Trampling by thousands of feet near Trail Ridge Road can destroy a system of plants that could take centuries to grow back. Random walking, though, by a few park visitors has no significant effect.

Therefore, where large parking areas concentrate visitors on the tundra, the National Park Service has built hardened trails. Foot traffic is restricted to these trails in order that the surrounding tundra might be spared excessive wear. Thus, many people can observe from the trails what healthy tundra looks like. These tundra protection areas surround the short trails at Forest Canyon Overlook, Rock Cut, and Fall River Pass.

Away from these heavy-use areas, there is no restriction on where you may walk on the tundra. There are, however, suggestions about how to reduce walking impact on the plants. If a trail crosses the tundra, use that trail, thereby limiting wear to areas already sacrificed. If a trail is not available, walkers should spread out rather than follow one behind the other. Try to tread lightly and step from rock to rock when possible.

Old Ute Trail

Trail Ridge was so named because the Native Americans used it as a route across the mountains. Perhaps as long as 11,000 years ago, hunters of now extinct camels and long-horned bison followed the ridge from one hunting ground to another. During the last 8,000 years, native Americans used it to journey from Estes Park to Grand Lake. The most recent of these high-altitude travelers were bands of Utes and Arapaho, well over a century ago. They were accompanied by dogs, the beasts of burden with the longest history in the park. The dogs carried packs, rather similar to modern dog packs with the load hung on both sides. The dogs also dragged platforms, travois, which gouged parallel ruts across the tundra.

Tundra vegetation is very slow to heal; probably these ruts never did. Rather, they were obliterated as Utes and Arapaho hauled bigger travois with horses, introduced to North America by Europeans. Use of the trail, however, evidently decreased for a long enough time to allow the travois ruts to heal before wagon ruts came to mark the route used extensively by pioneers traversing the mountains. Early pioneers in the area saw no trace of Native American paths on Trail Ridge. Modern archaeologists, however, have discovered signs of Native American presence that the first explorers on the scene failed to notice. North of the road, the trail is only a trace, little used, and largely healed over.

The Utes' route began in Beaver Meadows, threaded through Windy Gulch to the present road's location just above tree line, followed the road's route across the tundra, descended from Gore Range Overlook to Forest Canyon Pass, then on down to Milner

Pass, and out to Grand Lake along the Kawuneeche Valley. The Ute Trail was identified in 1914 by aged Arapaho brought down to the area from Wyoming to convey to settlers how Native Americans had related themselves to these mountains. Many of their names for natural features are used in some form today.

Those working with the Arapaho to preserve this heritage understood their informants to say that the Old Ute Trail had been called the "Child's Trail" because it was so steep that children had to get off the horses and walk. Although there are places in Windy Gulch where this might have been true, this explanation seems dubious because the Ute Trail is the least steep of the three routes over the mountains in the national park. (Flattop Mountain and Fall River Pass were the others.) Perhaps the Arapaho were trying to convey to the whites that this was a trail used by their short (like children) enemies, the Utes.

A 6-mile stretch of the Old Ute Trail between Beaver Meadows and Trail Ridge Road is stilll used by walkers, both children and adults. On the way, it passes through a wide variety of plant communities, allowing hikers to experience nearly every type of environment in Rocky Mountain National Park. However, walking the full length of the trail usually involves some logistical complications, and it is helpful to have transportation available at both ends. You must shuttle cars between the two trailheads or find a cooperative driver to act as chauffeur. Of course, as on any other trail in Rocky Mountain National Park, there is much enjoyment to be had in walking for a mile or two along the Old Ute Trail from either trailhead and then walking back to your car.

The lower trailhead is in Upper Beaver Meadows. To reach it, drive past the park headquarters building on US 36 and into the park through the Beaver Meadows Entrance. Continue straight, bypassing the Bear Lake turnoff, to an unpaved road that meets US 36 from the left (west) at 0.7 mile from the Beaver Meadows Entrance. (If you are approaching from the opposite direction, the unpaved road is 2.7 miles south of where US 36 and US 34 join at Deer Ridge Junction.) Turn onto the unpaved road and drive 1.5 miles to the picnic area at the end of the road.

The Old Ute Trail begins on the south side of the parking lot, at a crossing of Beaver Brook. The way is very wide and obvious through a grassy meadow into an aspen grove. A fenced-in area is an elk "exclosure," an experiment to determine how vegetation reacts to protection from browsing elk herds. The difference in plant growth inside the exclosure is obvious. In early July, you might see some rare orange wood lilies in this vicinity, particularly inside the exclosure, where they receive extra protection from picking.

Soon a maintenance-vehicle track branches off to the right to a water filtration plant. Follow the path to the left to a trail junction. From the junction, the left-hand fork, which is used mainly by horse riders, extends for a mile to Moraine Park. The Old Ute Trail follows the right-hand fork toward **Windy Gulch Cascades,** a good destination just 2 miles from the lower trailhead for those who do not want to hassle with car shuttles to the upper trailhead.

At its base, the Old Ute Trail winds through classic—that is, open—montane zone forest of ponderosa pine, aspen, juniper, and Douglas-fir. About a mile from the trailhead (after passing a spur trail to the left that goes to Moraine Park), the path climbs a bit more steeply through thick Douglas-fir forest on the northern side of a lateral moraine, a rocky ridge dumped by a glacier.

Below an interesting rock prominence, the trail levels in a very narrow gulch. Aspens predominate at first, but soon Engelmann spruce and subalpine fir take their place in the forest. This delightful cool gulch is the result of the lateral moraine (on the left) having been dumped beside Beaver Mountain (on the right). Here and there to the left along the trail you can see faint spur paths where hikers have climbed to the ridgeline of the moraine to look down into Moraine Park.

The gulch is easy and comfortable to walk. It is filled with beautiful trees and flowers and seems to have a rather hidden, secret mood. But the unusual way in which it was formed probably contributes most to its special charm.

At the upper end of the gulch, the **Beaver Mountain Trail** branches right. An easy and very pleasant path, it passes through Douglas-fir, ponderosa pine, and grassy meadows, crossing Beaver Brook and several other aspen-filled drainages. The best vista comes about 0.7 mile from the Old Ute Trail. A view of Longs Peak opens up after you pass through a drainage and its aspen grove. Farther on, note how grasses are coming in after Douglas-fir beetles have killed the trees, allowing sun to reach the forest floor. This trail circles back to Beaver Meadows, forming a loop hike about 5 miles long. It is used also by horseback riders in summer; be sure to step well off the trail as they pass.

Beyond the Beaver Mountain Trail junction, the Old Ute Trail climbs onto a sunny south-facing slope. The grade moderates amid alder bushes and quaking aspens at a stream crossing. Another short steep stretch follows, then the trail levels again before descending slightly to the top of Windy Gulch Cascades.

The top of the cascades overlooks the Big Thompson River Valley. Standing on an open rock ledge and looking southwest up the drainage, you get excellent views of glacier-sculpted Notchtop, Knobtop, and Gabletop Mountains. The rounded green summit of Mount Wuh, on the opposite side of the valley, blocks views any farther south along the Continental Divide. But Longs Peak and its neighbors stand out well, defining the horizon to the southeast.

All in all, the view from this easily reached high point is quite good—despite the fact that you cannot see Windy Gulch Cascades. Here the wall of the valley is so steep that from the top of the cascades they are out of sight below.

A few steps from the viewpoint, the trail enters cool, charming woods where the stream flows from Windy Gulch, which is uphill from the cascades. This is a good spot to watch for dippers, stream-loving birds resembling large gray wrens, which do a funny bobbing dance on spray-splashed rocks.

Windy Gulch represents another interesting feature of glacial geology, a hanging valley. Water draining from Trail Ridge eroded the gulch; there has been no glacier between its walls. But a series of very large glaciers did move down the Big Thompson River Valley between 15,000 and 160,000 years ago. They broadened the valley floor and steepened the walls. The steepening left Windy Gulch and its tributary stream hanging 1,000 feet above the valley floor. Windy Gulch Cascades are the result of the stream's tumbling down the clifflike, glacier-carved valley wall.

A short walk through lodgepole pines leads to an opening unofficially called Ute Meadows. The Old Ute Trail skirts the northern edge of the meadow area, dodging old beaver-made marshes. Past Ute Meadows, the route climbs very steeply through picturesque limber pines to krummholz at tree line and then onto tundra.

Above the trees, the trail heads through **Timberline Pass** and levels on the south side of **Tombstone Ridge.** The 2-mile walk across tundra below the monolith-lined ridge will probably reveal many fine flowers and possibly a ptarmigan. The trail is easy to follow from cairn to cairn as it descends to Trail Ridge Road.

Most hikers who travel this end of the Old Ute Trail start at the upper trailhead (sometimes called Ute Crossing) on Trail Ridge, 2 miles west of Rainbow Curve or 0.8 mile east of Forest Canyon Overlook. Parking for a few cars is available at the trailhead and for more cars a short way up the road. Walking along the road from this parking area to the trail is the most dangerous part of the hike; be alert for traffic hazards.

Of course, hiking the whole length of the trail is easier from top to bottom, if you can arrange transportation at each end. Probably more commonly done is a short hike across the tundra approximately to tree line and then back to cars parked beside Trail Ridge Road. This tundra stretch of the Old Ute Trail is described here in detail as a typical example of walking the park's alpine zone.

Chipmunk and golden-mantled ground squirrel

Tundra Nature Walk (Alpine Zone)

Wind is the ever present, most important, least ignorable factor in the tundra environment. At its worst in the winter, it can rage at more than 200 miles per hour across the tundra. Even in summer you cannot walk far along the Trail Ridge without commenting, at least mentally, on the wind.

The higher you climb in the mountains, the faster the wind blows. The average wind speed increases also with height above the ground. When you begin to feel the chill and pressure of the wind on the Old Ute Trail, try lying down for a not-to-be-completely-understood-until-you-try-it lesson in how alpine plants survive by being small.

Plants are short on the tundra because the growing season is not long, because food for growth may be in short supply, and because hugging the ground provides protection from wind. Wind quite simply kills anything that dares to stand upright against it. Wind drastically increases the chill effect of temperature that is already quite cold. It sucks moisture from plant tissues at a time when it cannot be replaced because all water is locked up as ice. Winter winds that often howl between 100 and 200 miles per hour carry bits of gravel and ice, sandblasting anything that gets in the way.

But wind can be beneficial too. It scatters pollen and seeds of willows, sedges, and many other plants. It piles up snow in some places while sweeping other areas bare of snow's cover, moisture, and insulation. This action creates variety in the life of the tundra; some plants have adapted to heavy snow cover, while others live without protection of snow.

Hikers feel ambivalent about the wind. It is exciting, for it adds a touch of adventure and romance to mountaintop experiences. The best-known quotation from the writings of America's most famous conservationist, John Muir, states that on mountains, "the wind will blow its own freshness into you and the storms their energy."

Perhaps. But the wind also saps your energy if you have to walk into it. It chills your body and dries it out, compelling you to carry extra clothing and water. It "burns" exposed skin, brings tears to your eyes, and is more than an inconvenience to contact lens wearers. Although experienced mountaineers can predict what the wind will do, local variations caused by the shape of nearby terrain destroy the usefulness of such predictions.

With its habits subject to unpredictable whims, with its power to both benefit and harm, wind is more human than any other inanimate aspect of nature. It is not surprising that people throughout history have tended to think of the wind as a living force. In fact, the original New Testament Greek of the Bible uses the same word for both wind and spirit.

Not only does it seem living, wind even appears to be creative. It sculpts self-portraits out of the conifers that dare to face its fury at tree line. At 11,440 feet, the upper trailhead of the Old Ute Trail is only a short distance above tree line. In fact, a few stunted trees bunch together up the hill from the trailhead, on the other side of the road.

These are the skirmishers of the forest as it tries to advance its front line in the war between woods and wind for control of the heights. Although they do not look very magnificent, these dwarfed and battered krummholz trees are arboreal heroes.

Krummholz is a German word that translates aptly as "elfin-wood." These trees—usually Engelmann spruce, subalpine fir, or limber pine—sprout from seeds that blow up from tree line. The seeds land in some spot protected from the wind. After several years of growth in this sheltered outpost, a tree peeks above the level of its protection, usually a rock. Almost at once the wind kills the top of the tree by desiccating and sandblasting it. But lateral branches fill the protected area and take root where they touch the ground. Gradually, the krummholz expands its beachhead by growing into the shelter of its own increasing bulk.

There is, of course, a limit to how far this tactic can expand the tree's living space. The wind prunes off every shoot that extends into its blast. No gardener with active shears could be more zealous or thorough in shaping the krummholz into living sculpture.

Some trees may gain enough erect posture so that their trunks become windbreaks for branches growing on the lee side. All twigs on the windward side are killed, while the leeward branches are flung out like flags on a staff. This distinctive shape has earned the name the *banner tree*. Indeed, these trees are the forest's banners of defiance against the mighty wind.

After the trees establish their positions, they provide shelter for other forms of life. Wildlife, such as various birds, snowshoe hares, or even elk, find refuge from the wind under krummholz branches. Subalpine flowers can extend their range up a slope if their seeds chance to land within the krummholz sphere of influence. More often than not, however, hikers find that dense stands of krummholz are impassable barriers to walking.

Between patches of krummholz, there are large open areas of tundra where the wind continues to dominate. One animal affected by it only indirectly is the northern pocket gopher. The chance of seeing one of these subterranean burrowers lies somewhere between slim and zero, but along this trail, evidence of their activity is easy to find: long mounds of dirt, looking rather like a jumble of heavy rope cable.

In winter, when the soil is frozen, pocket gophers tunnel through the snow where it meets the ground. They dig up tundra plants to eat, and dump the dirt behind them in the snow tunnel. When the snow melts, the core of dirt remains to mark the route of the tunnel. These jumbled mounds of dirt are called gopher eskers.

A pocket gopher is difficult to flatter. A little larger than a rat, it has constantly prominent yellowish-orange incisors. Its eyes and ears are small; its tail is short and hairless; it has cheek pockets lined with hair that are open to the outside rather than the inside of the mouth. The critter is said to have a grouchy disposition and generally lives alone in unforested habitats at all elevations in the mountains. (In the montane zone, Richardson ground squirrels are hard to miss and often are incorrectly called gophers.)

As burrowers, pocket gophers have no peers in the Rockies.

Their strong, heavily clawed front limbs can dig through the rockiest soil. Their lips close behind their prominent front teeth, which they use to carry rocks and dirt. The burrow of a single gopher can be as long as 500 feet, running from 4 to 18 inches beneath the surface. This represents about three tons of excavated soil. Side tunnels and galleries are stuffed with roots and other plant parts stored for future gopher meals. Additional chambers are filled with feces or are used for nesting.

All this digging has a profound effect on the tundra. Pocket gophers are second only to the wind as a force creating diversity among tundra environments on Trail Ridge. Gophers churn up the soil and enrich it with their droppings. On the other hand, the mounds of dirt from their tunneling cover up and kill many plants besides the ones they eat. The dirt dries out and blows away, eventually leaving bare spots where soil rebuilding may take centuries. But before the erosion takes place, the disturbed soil nurtures for decades the most spectacular flower displays on the tundra. Relatively large-blossomed plants like alpine sunflower and many other colorful blooms grow thickly in these "gopher gardens."

Alpine sunflowers are practically impossible to miss along the Old Ute Trail. They boast the largest blossoms on the tundra, 2 to 4 inches in diameter. These blossoms are all the more prominent because every alpine sunflower always points its face to the east, a worshipper of the rising sun.

Most tundra flowers cannot spare the time or energy to produce such large blossoms in the six-week interval between winters at this elevation. Alpine sunflowers achieve relatively gargantuan blooms by growing only roots, leaves, and short stems for several years. When enough food is stored in a large taproot, a sunflower expends it all in a glorious splendor of flower and seeds, then the entire plant dies.

A massive display of alpine sunflowers may indicate that the previous summer was a good one for building food reserves. Additionally, large numbers of sunflowers indicate that the local soil is in transition. It contains much sand and gravel and a little organic material. Water drains away easily. The soil is still evolving, and decaying alpine sunflowers may contribute to the formation of rich humus that eventually will support different types of plants.

If not the largest, then by far the most common tundra flower along the Old Ute Trail is alpine avens. This diminutive member of the rose family grows in a wide range of habitats, although, like alpine sunflower, it prefers gopher-churned soil. Alpine avens, with its five-petaled yellow flowers, blooms throughout the short summer. The flowers mature to feathery seed heads, and ultimately the fernlike leaves color the autumn tundra red. Alpine avens tend to attract tiny black flies rather than bees to their nectar. Like many fly-pollinated flowers, these have scant scent.

Quite strong in fragrance is sky pilot, a flower with bell-shaped blossoms growing close together in a loose formation. Bright orange pollen contrasting with royal blue flowers may be sky pilot's main attraction for bees, but the skunklike aroma of the leaves certainly adds to the plant's distinctive lure.

When checking the aroma of tundra flowers, be careful. Donna once seriously injured herself while sampling the sweet fragrance of alpine wallflower along the Old Ute Trail. The injury came from a sedge. Sedges, a family of grasslike plants, make up the largest proportion of vegetable matter on the tundra. Easy to distinguish from grasses, most sedges are three-cornered and solid. Some grow erect and have sharp tips.

One of these pierced Donna's left eye as she crouched low to smell the wallflower. The injury was very painful and totally incapacitating. Had it occurred on a tundra slope far from any road, the accident could have been very serious indeed. As it was, Donna was bedridden for days. We still do not let a summer go by without stooping to smell an alpine wallflower. But the lesson has been well learned: To avoid injury in the mountains, it does not always pay to keep your eyes open.

Beautiful as they are, gopher gardens eventually are stripped away by the wind. Bare gravel then remains. But not only gophers denude patches of tundra vegetation. Road building causes damage beyond the edge of the pavement. Similarly, the waffle-stomper boots that keep hikers from falling on their faces also exact a considerable toll on tundra vegetation. Both these types of wear have made the tundra rather ragged right at the trailhead.

The damage, at the time of this writing, is healing. Cushions of moss campion and mats of white alpine phlox have pioneered the battered gravel and are preparing the way for other plants to follow. The classic shape of cushion plants is a flattened hemisphere. It presents the minimum possible amount of leaf surface exposure to wind and cold and the maximum possible exposure to sunlight for photosynthesis. Also, the low, streamlined profile is best suited for offering the least amount of resistance to the wind. The shape may be varied to suit particular conditions.

Moss campion (resembling but not truly a moss) is the most common and typical cushion plant. It also is one of the prettiest and fastest growing. Under relatively favorable conditions, it may grow to a half inch in diameter in five years. At ten years it begins to produce dainty pink blossoms; at twenty years blooms cover the cushion. At twenty-five years the cushion may be 7 inches in diameter.

Some of the cushions at the trailhead are being invaded by grasses and other flowers that have taken root in the little mounds of wind blown soil captured and hoarded underneath the cushions' many-branched stems. In another century or so, this area may have evolved from gravel to an alpine meadow densely carpeted with plants. If so, moss campion will have started the reclamation effort.

Of 157 species of flowering plants on Trail Ridge, moss campion probably arouses the most admiration. It invades sterile ground, bearing a pink banner of life. Although moss campion manages to survive the rigors of mountaintop living, it would die quickly if transplanted to a milder climate.

Similarly, the white-tailed ptarmigan is the toughest animal adapted to life above the trees. This small grouse is the only species in its clan to sport white feathers on the edges of its tail. In winter, the rest of the feathers also are white, providing perfect camouflage in the snow. The camouflage continues into summer: White plumage is replaced by mottled gray and brown feathers, which blend with the rocks protruding everywhere from the tundra.

Hikers rarely notice ptarmigan along the Old Ute Trail. Holding every feather still, the birds completely trust their protective coloration to disguise them as rocks. Sometimes, though, close approach will cause them to flush and run away. To have inanimate granite transformed into a scurrying bird is startling, no matter how many times the trick is repeated. After fleeing on foot, ptarmigan may take flight if they feel closely pursued.

The invisibility of a ptarmigan hen on her nest defies belief. She probably will expose her eggs to the elements only if she is actually touched. If she does not move, a passing hiker is more likely to hear her pounding heart than to see her. Finding a ptarmigan nest is a very rare privilege, even though they must be relatively common.

Spotting ptarmigan at any time of year is a thrill and joy to mountaineers, who seem to identify with the alpine birds. One similarity may be mountaineers' down jackets. Ptarmigan, too, use down, but they can control its insulating capacity by raising or flattening their feathers. Widespread toes are covered with feathers in winter to keep the birds' feet warm and to support them, just as snowshoes support humans. Mountain climbers may even recognize in ptarmigan a heroic stubbornness to survive and enjoy life on the high peaks.

At the trailhead, the coarse sand and gravel that moss campion is invading is mostly decomposed granite. Between 1,400 and 1,450 million years ago, molten rock beneath the earth's surface cooled slowly to granite, with large grains of quartz and feldspar. Uplifted by forces generated when North America drifted away from Europe some 50 to 70 million years ago, the granite emerged at the surface as eroision tripped away overlying sedimentary rock. The expansion of granite under high-altitude extremes of heat and cold, the expansion of ice in cracks, and the blasting by fierce winter winds are now tearing the granite apart. Fine bits of rock are blown away, leaving only larger bits of rock on the ground.

Look also for a dark boulder of schist, sparkling with bits of mica embedded in it. Among the oldest rocks in the national park, schist originally was laid down as sediment that was cemented into fine-grained rock. Eventually buried deep within the earth, this sedimentary rock was subjected to heat and pressure, which so changed its structure that it became metamorphic rock with almost no resemblance to its original composition.

The Old Ute Trail climbs a slight rise as it departs from Trail Ridge Road, giving hikers a good view to the right into Forest Canyon. Headwaters of the Big Thompson River, the canyon originally was cut in a V-shape by water erosion after the most recent uplift of the Rockies, about 28 million years ago. Glaciers 1,000 to 1,500 feet thick flowed down the valley during past ice ages, steepening its walls and broadening its floor to create a U-shape.

The most recent glacial period began to abate about 15,000 years ago. Perhaps we are in an interglacial time at present. The valley below may once again fill with a moving tongue of ice.

Probably the most striking thing about the awesome view across the valley is the contrast between the broad, rounded slopes of Terra Tomah Mountain and the jagged precipices along Hayden Gorge. The gorge is to the left of Terra Tomah and culminates in the fanglike tower of Hayden Spire. The relatively gentle tundra slopes of Terra Tomah, like the rolling highlands of Trail Ridge, have never been glaciated. They are the remnants of hills eroded into their present configuration between 28 and 65 million years ago, before they were raised 6,000 feet to their present heights. The vertical, ragged rock below the tundra was sculpted by moving belts of glacial ice.

During the Ice Age, deep snowdrifts did occur in areas on Trail Ridge that were protected from the wind, which swept most of the ridge clear of snow. The abundant snow that fell on the ridge ended up in the valleys below, piling ever higher as more

Young bighorn

accumulated in winter than melted in summer. When it piled up to approximately 100 feet, the ice crystals at the bottom were compressed and transformed by the great weight of snow on top. The ice at the bottom began to ooze downhill in response to gravity. A glacier was born.

The climate of that glacial era was a good deal more frigid than today's. Frost heaves—the expansion and contraction of the ground from successive freezing and thawing—tilted rocks on edge. On steep slopes, gravity pulled rock debris downhill, shaping the slopes in a descending flowing pattern. Abundant water from thawing ground and melting snow completely saturated the ground, so that large sections of soggy soil began to slide downhill. The process, called solifluction, formed terraces on the slopes below the Old Ute Trail, some of which catch water and form marshes.

As the Old Ute Trail climbs around a shoulder of Trail Ridge, the road is out of sight and hikers are treated to a view of Longs Peak, a blocky, flat-topped tower rising obviously higher than surrounding peaks. At 14,255 feet, Longs is the tallest peak in Rocky Mountain National Park.

Where Longs drops temporarily out of sight behind a hill, look west down Forest Canyon to a view of the Never Summer Range. The name of these mountains is a tranlastion from the Arapaho *Ni-che-be-chii*, and was probably inspired by the number of perpetual snowbanks that deck their eastern slopes. Prevailing westerly winds sweep the snow from western slopes and pile it on the eastern slopes. In summer the resulting huge drifts never disappear completely before winter returns to replenish them.

Walking past a ridge-top jumble of rocks, which probably are home to yellow-bellied marmots (large woodchuck cousins) and pikas (small, short-eared rabbits, nearly invisible but often identified by their high-pitched bark), hikers receive a good view of the Mummy Range to the left. Beyond some hardy krummholz hiding behind rocks, the ridge to the right breaks to provide another opportunity to look into Forest Canyon.

This break also permits wind to rush through from the west. Because the same volume of air that has been howling across unobstructed space must pass through this constricted area in the same amount of time, the wind must blow faster. A wind scarp, where even cushion plants can achieve scant hold on the gravelly ground, testifies to the bitter gales that scour this stretch of trail in the winter.

Just beyond the wind gap, however, the turf of a well-developed mountain meadow contrasts with the sterile gravel of the scarp. Here rock polygons demonstrate how the expansion and contraction of the ground by freezing and thawing sorts the rocks into patterns amid lush plants.

As the trail begins to descend toward the head of Windy Gulch, hikers notice a tor in the middle of Timberline Pass. A tor is a mass of broken rock. Such formations usually overlie unbroken bedrock. They are formed either by freezing and thawing of exposed rock or by the disintegrating effects of groundwater before erosion of overlying rock uncovers the tors. Such formations are common along the Old Ute Trail.

Below the tor is tree line in Windy Gulch. Farther below is a good view into Moraine Park, named for a lateral moraine along the south edge of the meadowland. This moraine was deposited by the glacier that spilled out of Forest Canyon.

In the cracks of the tor live marmots and the many flowers that feed them: Colorado blue columbine, bushy cinquefoil, sky pilot and the similar cream-colored honey polemonium, blue chiming bells, harebell, yarrow, thistle, sorrel, gooseberry, and many more. Here the flowers of the tundra mix with those of the subalpine zone in a rich floral climax to your tundra nature walk.

Deer Mountain Trail

Oddly enough, there are quite a few mule deer on Deer Mountain. You also might see a fairly uncommon flower. But virtually certain is an enjoyable view of dramatic peaks. The hike is more comfortable if you carry a quart of water per person, because the trail is sunny and dry.

The Deer Mountain Trailhead is at Deer Ridge Junction, where US 34 and US 36 join inside Rocky Mountain National Park. Park your car somewhere along the wide road shoulders, and begin hiking uphill east of the road junction.

The trail proceeds along a level grade in an open parklike stand of mature ponderosa pines. Be sure at this point to bear right; do not get off on a trail that drops downhill into Horseshoe Park and Aspenglen Campground.

As you begin to climb gradually to the east, notice the wildflowers typical of open montane zone forest: wild geranium, Indian paintbrush, penstemon, miners candle, harebell, sulphur flower, and wallflower. The less common Britton's skullcap can be recognized by its blue-purple blossoms, each of which has a protruding lip shaped like a cap. A member of the mint family, Britton's skullcap's leaves grow opposite each other on a 4- to 6-inch-tall square stem.

Quaking aspens soon begin to appear at trailside, their white bark scarred black by nibbling elk. The aspens frame lovely vistas of Longs Peak and other high mountains along the Front Range. Closer by are lateral moraines—glacial ridges—bordering Moraine Park and Beaver Meadows.

From the view of Longs Peak and the Front Range, the trail zigzags to the left to a view dominated by Ypsilon Mountain, in the Mummy Range. Ypsilon is named for vertical snow-filled gullies that form a Y on its face. For the first 2 miles, the path maintains a fairly moderate grade by following switchbacks, which take you from the view on one side of Deer Mountain to the view on the other.

Eventually, you reach a broad level area on Deer Mountain, where limber pines and aspens block long vistas. The natural tendency of limber pine to drama, especially in death, is obvious here. Forest fires have left enough picturesque twisted snags of burned pine to keep photographic artists busy for days. Despite its relatively low altitude, Deer Mountain seems to be a preferred target for lightning, which probably started the fires. Remember this when thunderheads start to build; a hasty retreat back down the mountain would be wise.

For more than a half mile, the trail meanders up and down on the mountain until you suspect that you are headed down the other side toward Estes Park. About the time your suspicion matures to certainty, you reach a trail junction where a spur branches sharply south (right) to the summit. The final few yards to the top are steeper than most hikers like, but the reward is a good view in nearly every direction.

Beyond the junction, the trail zigzags downhill to the east in the same fashion by which it climbed. Following this path across the park boundary will lead you to mazes of horse trails, roads, homes, and eventually an ice-cream cone in downtown Estes Park.

Abandoned Road

A 4-mile tundra hike on the west end of Trail Ridge follows the old route used by auto traffic between 1918 and 1932, which was abandoned when Trail Ridge Road opened between Milner and Fall River Passes. The ideal way to walk this section is to park one car near the Continental Divide sign at the southwestern end of Poudre Lake (Milner Pass) and hike down to it from Fall River Pass. The return to Fall River Pass from midway down at Forest Canyon Pass is not terribly steep, however.

Park at the large parking lot serving the Fall River Pass Store and Alpine Visitor Center. Bear left to locate traces of the old road, still scantily revegetated after well over a half century. Gravel quarries and borrow pits along the abandoned, unpaved road look as though the road machinery left only yesterday. Here is one of the best places in the national park to see moss campion and other cushion plants massing their forces to begin the centuries-long process of tundra repair. (See page 157 for more about moss campion.)

About 2.5 miles from Fall River Pass, the old road levels in Forest Canyon Pass. Looking southeast down Forest Canyon of the Big Thompson River conveys the impression that Estes Cone sits at the end of the canyon. Actually, that small peak is situated several valleys beyond the mouth of Forest Canyon, just north of Longs Peak. From Estes Cone, it appears that Specimen Mountain sits at the northwestern end of the canyon, which, as you can see from this pass, is equally untrue.

Although Forest Canyon is not quite as long as it appears, 15,000 years ago it did contain the longest glacier—13 miles—on the east side of the park. The canyon's U-shape, which is quite noticeable from Forest Canyon Pass, is typical of valleys carved by ice 1,000 to 1,500 feet thick. Today, the steep walls of this trackless canyon help make it the national park's most difficult wilderness to penetrate (see Gorge Lakes, page 169).

A short and very gentle uphill walk from Forest Canyon Pass takes you to trees: genuine, erect, undistorted Engelmann spruce and subalpine fir. You have left the tundra behind. Your trail now traverses the subalpine zone, where wind is a friend, for it piles up precious water in reservoirs of snow stolen from the alpine zone. The old road is a wide aisle enclosed by spruce and fir. Smaller spruce and fir are making a good beginning toward reforesting the road itself.

The path is built up over bogs in openings that explode with the colors of lush subalpine flowers after the snow melts. Where it passes through forest, the old road becomes more and more overgrown by trees the lower you go. In a few spots, it and the invading trees are totally obliterated by what appear to be annual avalanche runs.

Yet the trail remains clear as it follows the route of the old automobile road. Poudre Lake and Trail Ridge Road appear through the trees below. The trail continues on, eventually leaving the old highway, passing a trail south to Mount Ida, and descending in easy switchbacks to the parking lot at the south end of Poudre Lake.

Trails from Milner Pass

Milner Pass is a low point on the Continental Divide. From Poudre Lake, on the east side of the pass, the Cache la Poudre River flows into the Mississippi River drainage. Beaver Creek, on the west side, flows into the Colorado River drainage. The pass is the focal point of several trails.

The **Poudre River Trail** begins on the west side of Trail Ridge Road, just north of Poudre Lake. The path passes up and down through subalpine woods but soon drops into willows along the river and is very sloppy. Occasionally, it loses itself in a maze of elk trails. The chances of seeing deer and elk in the valley are excellent.

The valley widens a bit, and the trail dries out considerably 5.6 miles downstream, where Chapin Creek and the Chapin Creek path join the Poudre River and its trail from the right. From this point on, the Poudre River Trail is much easier to walk, avoiding beaver swamps and willow thickets. Running north, it follows an easy grade for 3.4 miles to a junction with the Mummy Pass Trail (see the Mummy Range chapter).

The trail to **The Crater,** on Specimen Mountain, is the most popular trail beginning at Poudre Lake. Parking space at The Crater Trailhead is situated on the west side of Trail Ridge Road at roughly the midpoint of the lake. The damp meadow beside the parking area can be very colorful with subalpine flowers in July and August.

Most of **Specimen Mountain** has been given special preservation status as a research natural area. The entire mountain is closed to hiking each spring and early summer for Park Service wildlife management purposes. Hiking above The Crater on Specimen is prohibited at all times to protect wildlife and to allow healing of foot traffic wear and tear on the tundra. Descending into The Crater also is forbidden, for the sake of wildlife. Signs delineate the boundaries. On heavily used tundra where hiking is permitted around The Crater and on Shipler Mountain, please walk as lightly as possible.

The trail up to The Crater climbs steeply through mature subalpine forest to tree line. At the forest's upper edge there are classic banner trees as well as Colorado blue columbine and Indian paintbrush. Well onto the tundra, a mile from the trailhead, you arrive at the edge of The Crater at a higher point on the Continental Divide. This area was named in the belief that it was the eroded crater of a long-extinct volcano of Specimen Mountain. Subsequent geological study, however, established that The Crater is merely an erosional feature shaped by ice and water. Additional investigation showed that Specimen Mountain is not a volcano, extinct or otherwise. Rather, it is formed of ash and other volcanic material from an eruption that took place elsewhere, perhaps in the Never Summer Range.

The mountain itself was named for the variety of interesting rock specimens deposited by volcanic eruptions. Of course, collecting specimens is strictly forbidden in a national park.

The top of **Shipler Mountain** is an easy 1.5 miles from The Crater. To reach Shipler, head left (south) from The Crater to follow the contour around the east side of the ridge. Once around the large bump south of The Crater, descend slightly into an open saddle bordered by krummholz. Bear right out of the saddle to bypass another bump on the ridge. Past the second bump, climb directly to the top of Shipler. The view of the Never Summer Range from the summit is similar to that from The Crater or the summit of Specimen. Additionally, Shipler offers unique perspectives of The Crater and of the Kawuneeche Valley. Remember, stay out of The Crater.

The **Mount Ida Trail** begins at Milner Pass at the south end of Poudre Lake. For 1.5 miles the trail climbs through subalpine forest, filled with Jacob's ladder wildflowers, to a junction with the abandoned road route to Fall River Pass (see page 164). Turning right (south) at the junction, the Mount Ida Trail continues zigzagging up frequently damp terrain to the tundra. Above the trees, the trail was laid out by wildlife and does not switchback. It climbs steadily along the south side of the Continental Divide, avoiding bumps atop the ridge.

Somewhat less than 3 miles from the trail junction, the beaten path gives out near the ridgeline at the base of the final push to the top—almost. A false summit is disappointing, but the true peak is only a short distance beyond. Like Milner Pass, about 4.5 miles away, Ida's summit is on the Continental Divide.

The view from the top of Ida is well worth the moderately tiring walk it takes to get there. The Never Summers are fine to the west, but even more dramatic, scattered among rugged precipices, are Gorge Lakes, hundreds of feet straight down from your boots. Less rugged but nevertheless grand is the view to the southwest of Julian Lake, Big Meadows, and Lake Granby.

From Ida you can descend steep and rocky slopes to Timber Lake and the 4.8-mile path to Trail Ridge Road at Timber Creek Trailhead. Arrange for vehicular transportation back to Milner Pass. Timber Lake is also a common route of ascent for Ida (see Timber Lake Trail, page 170).

From the saddle southeast of Ida, on the divide, it is a relatively easy descent to Azure Lake and other Gorge Lakes. Climbing back out is another matter.

Another possibility is to hike southeast from the saddle, climbing or skirting **Chief Cheley Peak,** to look down on Highest Lake, highest of the Gorge Lakes. To reach **Cracktop,** circle around the top of the cirque containing Highest Lake and head northeast toward the summit of **Mount Julian.** Cracktop is the last bump before you reach the ragged knife ridge that leads from the divide to Julian. Continuing the half mile to Julian necessitates finding a way around the huge boulders blocking the rugged ridgeline. Use extreme caution and try to stay on the less cliffy side, away from Gorge Lakes.

Three-quarters of a mile past Julian, at the end of the ridge, is **Terra Tomah Mountain.** It is an uncomplicated walk, but after Ida, Cracktop, and Julian, the up-and-down trudge to Terra Tomah is wearing, and once there, you retrace your steps. The only alternative is to descend into Forest Canyon, which is a good deal harder to traverse than the peaks.

Gorge Lakes are the nine tarns and scattering of unnamed pools on the other side of Forest Canyon when viewed from Rock Cut, on Trail Ridge Road. Because Gorge Lakes are so visible and in such a dramatic setting, many hikers are struck with a desire to visit them. But there is no trail, and they are difficult to reach.

The longest route, which crosses the least difficult terrain, follows the abandoned road from Milner Pass to Forest Canyon Pass. If you can work out transportation, begin at Fall River Pass and end the hike at Milner Pass.

At Forest Canyon Pass, leave the old road and climb to the south along the side of the long ridge leading up to Mount Ida. From Forest Canyon Pass, it is 4 miles of up-and-down hiking with some unavoidable marsh sloshing to reach a ridge overlooking lovely meadows in the vicinity of Love Lake. Then continue to **Arrowhead Lake,** the largest of the Gorge Lakes and one of the closest. From Arrowhead the uphill terrain to **Inkwell** and **Doughnut Lakes** is not terribly steep. Reaching the higher lakes involves steep climbing over rock ledges.

The trail that approaches closest to Gorge Lakes is a trail to Timber Lake (see Timber Lake Trail). From Timber Lake, it is less than a mile as the raven flies to **Azure Lake,** among the highest Gorge Lakes. That would be fine if you could fly 1,800 feet up and over Mount Ida and down 980 feet to Azure. Alas, to follow this route, mere hikers must climb Mount Ida twice in one day. The terrain is steep and arduous, but it is not as difficult as the shortest (by idiomatic bird flight) route to the lakes, which is not recommended. It drops from a parking area east of Rock Cut into Forest Canyon, struggles through dense subalpine forest, fords the Big Thompson River, and fights uphill through more thick woods and marsh to **Little Rock Lake** and **Rock Lake.** These are not the most scenic of the Gorge Lakes, and returning to Trail Ridge is much harder than the descent. This route combines most of the problems of the other two and throws in some of its own. It is a challenge.

Timber Lake Trail

The Timber Lake Trail is advocated by some hikers as the best route up Mount Ida, despite the fact that the route from Milner Pass is 1.5 miles shorter and has 1,750 feet less elevation gain. Nonetheless, the route to Timber Lake is an interesting hike, worth doing on its own merits.

The parking area for **Timber Lake Trailhead** is located on the east side of Trail Ridge Road, 9.6 miles north of the Grand Lake Entrance to the national park and 10.7 miles southwest of Fall River Pass. From the trailhead, Timber Lake Trail heads east across a level meadow, then cuts right through open woods to cross Beaver Creek on a substantial bridge. Past the crossing, the trail climbs fairly steeply along the flank of Jackstraw Mountain. Still close enough to Trail Ridge Road so you can hear the traffic, the trail is enclosed by dense stands of lodgepole pines.

A few miles from the trailhead and 400 feet above the valley floor, the path begins to parallel Timber Creek, going upstream. Then the grade is gentle until you arrive at the junction of the Timber Lake and Long Meadows Trails, 3.1 miles from the trailhead. Here, where a tributary flows into Timber Creek, the landscape is filled with moisture-loving flowers: marsh marigold, senecio, tall chiming bells, Parry's primrose.

The **Long Meadows Trail** crosses the creek a few yards south of the junction, then climbs steeply to moderate its grade parallel to the creek, going downstream along the south valley wall. But after 0.6 mile, the path disappears in the marshes of Long Meadows. It reappears 1.5 miles later at the southern end of Long Meadows and proceeds very obscurely for another 1.5 miles to meet the Onahu Creek Trail. The least swampy way to traverse Long Meadows is anybody's guess. The Park Service terms Long Meadows a "cross-country experience."

Back on the Timber Lake Trail, the grade steepens past the junction and climbs through a series of very short switchbacks. Finally you emerge into a meadow at the base of Jackstraw Mountain. Wetland subalpine flowers—paintbrush, king's crown (roseroot), tall chiming bells—line both sides of the trail as it parallels Timber Creek through the meadow.

The trail reenters pleasant subalpine forest but soon leaves again to wind across a very rocky area. A final set of switchbacks takes you to the marshy land around the outlet of **Timber Lake.** The northern shore of the lake bears some trees, but the southern end has only rock, some tundra, and snowfields that last far into summer.

Timber Lake is not as spectacular as many lakes in the park; no sheer cliffs rise above it. But the terrain is rugged enough to hide the summit of **Mount Ida.** To climb Ida, head up not terribly steep tundra to a low point on the ridge south of the lake. From this saddle it is an uncomplicated walk to the summit.

From this saddle you can also go to **Julian Lake,** about a mile southeast of Timber Lake, although most hikers merely view Julian from the summit of Ida. Julian can be reached also via an unmaintained path from the lower (south) section of the Long Meadows Trail, which also is rather vague in places.

Jackstraw Mountain is an easy climb from the flowery meadow you encountered on the way to Timber Lake. Various game trails, typically quite steep but short, lead up to the broad summit. Jackstraw was named for the view of its fire-cleared slopes as seen from Trail Ridge Road. Had the namers seen the massive spread of elk excrement on top of the peak, the name chosen might have been even more colorful.

Trails from Never Summer Ranch

Never Summer Ranch became part of Rocky Mountain National Park in 1975, providing access for hikers to Mount Stratus and Green Knoll. The parking area for Never Summer Ranch lies (well marked) on the west side of Trail Ridge Road, 7.2 miles north of the Grand Lake Entrance to the park and 13.1 miles southwest of Fall River Pass. From the parking area, you walk to the homestead along an unpaved road that is closed to public vehicles.

At the homestead, continue walking until you reach a fork in the road. Take the right-hand fork, which is a service road for the Grand Ditch, a water diversion project in the Never Summer Range that supplies the populous but dry plains east of the Rockies. Follow the road uphill to the level of the ditch, about 3 miles of walking from the parking area.

The grade flattens beside the ditch, which you must cross—somehow. If water is low, perhaps you can scrounge some remnants of an old bridge and rebuild a temporary one. Or you could try leaping or wading the very cold water. From the other side, a faint path takes off straight uphill through the trees several dozen yards north of where you first encounter the ditch. Blazes on the trees as well as the track on the ground make the path uncomplicated to follow, but very steep, up **Green Knoll.**

If the water is too high to improvise a ditch crossing, walk south along the road that follows the ditch. Before too long you will come to a point where the ditch is covered by rock and dirt. Cross at the easiest place. Do not try to head back to the trail. Rather, climb directly up the mountain by the best route you can find. Perhaps you will hit the trail as it zigzags its way to tree line.

Where you reach tree line, either on or off the trail, follow the least steep route over the tundra to the top of the Green Knoll, or skirt the top to hit the ridge between Green Knoll and Mount Stratus. We recommend climbing all the way up Green Knoll, less than 5 miles from Trail Ridge Road. This mountain is not high but is well situated for excellent views of the Colorado River drainage all the way north to La Poudre Pass.

Prior to the opening of access through Never Summer Ranch, **Mount Stratus** was one of the most remote summits in the Never Summer Range. The narrow ridge, covered with loose rock, between Mount Stratus and Green Knoll now offers a readily accessible and exciting route to Stratus. There is some exposure to falling as you scramble up the ridge. Be careful here; do not cause rocks or your body to bombard folks exploring in

Red Gulch, on the north side of the ridge. From Stratus, if the weather is holding fair, you can scramble down and back up over rocks to either **Mount Nimbus** to the north, or **Baker Mountain** to the south.

Very tempting is a descent west into Baker Gulch (see below). Be warned: There is not one solid rock on the whole long slope down to tree line in the gulch. It will take you longer than you think to get down. The walk out through Baker Gulch is lovely, but the walk back along the ditch below the east slopes of Baker Mountain is not very exciting. You may enjoy this roundabout return route once; you probably will not do it twice.

Baker Gulch Trail System
(Arapaho National Forest)

The Baker Gulch Trail is the easiest approach to a lake or peak in the Never Summer Range. Baker Gulch has felt the heavy hand of man, but the area remains beautiful and well worth visiting. Leashed dogs are allowed on this trail.

Access to the Baker Gulch Trail begins at a picnic area on the west side of Trail Ridge Road, 6.4 miles north of the Grand Lake Entrance to the park and 13.9 miles southwest of Fall River Pass. From the picnic area, an unpaved road extends west for three-quarters of a mile, nearly to the boundary of Arapaho National Forest. Because this road may be closed to public vehicles during the summer, you should park at the picnic area and walk along the road.

From the picnic area, the unpaved road crosses the Colorado River and meadows in the Kawuneeche Valley. As meadow gives way to forest, the road divides. Take the right-hand fork, which bends around to the beginning of the Baker Gulch Trail, just short of the national forest boundary.

Once inside the national forest, the trail runs upstream on a ridge above the creek flowing down Baker Gulch. Lodgepole

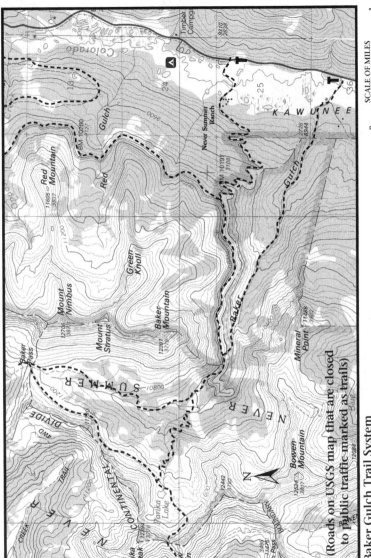

(Roads on USGS map that are closed to public traffic marked as trails)

Baker Gulch Trail System

SCALE OF MILES

0   1

pines block all distant views until you reach clearings created by beavers about 1.5 miles from the forest boundary.

Just past the beaver workings, a series of short switchbacks leads to rocky rubble cast down from excavation for the Grand Ditch. Views open here across the narrow valley to Mineral Point and uphill into Baker Gulch. After you walk a half mile along fractured rock slopes below the ditch, new vistas appear to the southeast, all the way to the Front Range. Chiefs Head Peak presents a very pointed aspect from this angle. From farther up the trail, Longs Peak comes into sight, looking very boxy.

You may not notice the distant peaks if your attention centers on the raspberry bushes growing among the rocks. At the right time of a good year, these bushes produce abundant and excellent fruit.

After walking for a long, hot mile over the foot-bruising rubble of ditch excavation, hikers are relieved to reenter subalpine forest. Soon the trail climbs steeply a short distance uphill to the ditch. When you cross the ditch via a substantial bridge, you enter a different world. Here no water has been diverted, and the subalpine growth is luxuriantly beautiful.

The trail becomes less distinct as it passes through three marshy meadows and enters cool, mature subalpine woods. Traveling on an easy grade, you feel real soil underfoot—dirt well laced with organic matter made available by adequate water. It is almost springy to walk on.

About a half mile from the ditch, you enter a subalpine meadow and cross the stream flowing down Baker Gulch, from the right (north). Past the stream crossing, there is a trail junction; the Baker Gulch Trail cuts right to head uphill toward Baker Pass, on the Continental Divide (see page 177). The **Parika Lake Trail** continues straight ahead and soon crosses the stream flowing from Parika Lake. It climbs directly uphill and away from the stream. There are a few switchbacks to help, but this stretch seems very steep in comparison with that below.

After a final switchback to the left, the path opens into a marsh, where you see a brook tumbling down a ravine from Farview Mountain. It is a nice setting, with little waterfalls and a pond surrounded by meadow.

The final quarter mile to Parika Lake is very steep, but rest stops offer views of the wall of the Never Summer Range, especially Baker Mountain and Mounts Stratus and Nimbus. Longs Peak still is visible far to the southeast, down Baker Gulch. After a trail runs off to the right toward Baker Pass (see page 177, it is just a few hundred yards farther to **Parika Lake.**

The lake lies in open tundra, with an unnamed 12,253-foot bump to the north, Parika Peak directly west, and Farview Mountain to the southwest. In the vicinity of the lake's outlet, a few stunted trees have been vandalized by an active ax directed by a small mind. Other unfortunate evidences of ignorant or malicious visitation appear here and there amid the krummholz, but the lakeshore itself remains relatively unspoiled.

From the outlet, a trail climbs southwest across shelves overlooking the lake before angling north uphill to a broad saddle on the Continental Divide situated between Farview Mountain and **Parika Peak.** The trail runs to the left along the divide toward Farview. From the saddle it is a fairly easy climb to the right to the double-humped top of Parika. The summit cairn is located on the northwestern part of the peak, but deciding which point really is highest is tough.

Views from the divide are similar to those from Parika Lake, except that Jack Creek drainage is visible to the north, North Park to the west, and Bowen Gulch and Bowen Mountain to the southwest. You can follow the divide down the eastern slope of Parika Peak, to a saddle between Parika and its unnamed neighbor. There you meet a trail that ascends south from the Jack Creek drainage and continues vaguely through marshy terrain downhill to the northern shore of Parika Lake.

Back at the junction a few hundred yards short of Parika Lake, the trail branching to the north goes to the vicinity of **Baker Pass.** This route runs directly uphill to the pass without losing any elevation; you would have to lose elevation from here if you wish to reach Baker Pass via the Baker Gulch Trail.

Back at the earlier junction just after the stream crossing, the **Baker Gulch Trail** heads north and away from the Parika Lake Trail, climbing gradually through a maze of elk trails and marsh. When the trail passes into forest, Engelmann spruce and subalpine fir are large, and subalpine flowers—monkshood, larkspur, tall chiming bells—are abundant. Eventually, the route becomes considerably less distinct and crosses a stream to climb to another track on the side of **Baker Mountain.** If you wish, you can keep on climbing very steeply to the east to the summit of Baker.

From the Parika Lake Trail, it is a little more than 2 miles of exploration on the Baker Gulch Trail to Baker Pass. The overall grade is not difficult and the terrain is lovely, especially above the trees. A beautiful chartreuse tundra extends from tree line to what appears to be the pass. Actually, the top of the pass is on the Continental Divide and cannot be seen from tree line.

The trail crosses the divide into the Michigan River drainage. To the east, the Never Summer Range is a high wall of broad tundra slopes, except for the black cone of Mount Richthofen and the sharp ridge of Lead Mountain at the northern end of the wall. The gentle tundra slopes of Mount Cindy are to the northwest.

To descend from the pass to Parika Lake, you may have to hunt around a bit for a trail that materializes downhill and south of the pass. Head southwest below the ridge of the Continental Divide, past mine tailings and an old cabin. Stay above tree line, and watch for a distinct path that descends into the trees. It ends about 1.5 miles later at the junction with the Parika Lake Trail, a few hundred yards east of the lake.

Onahu Creek–Green Mountain Circle

The Onahu Creek and Green Mountain Trails form a very convenient circle hike. The two trailheads are near enough to each other that car shuffling is unnecessary, and the 6.5 miles of trail are interesting, pleasant, and pretty.

Begin by dropping packs and a guard at **Onahu Creek Trailhead**, 3.3 miles north of the Grand Lake Entrance to the park and 17 miles southwest of Fall River Pass. The driver then takes the car down the road (south) for slightly more than a half mile to the parking lot at Green Mountain Trailhead. It is a very easy walk back to Onahu along a trail bordering the east (right) side of the road. In August this procedure gives the person guarding the packs just enough time to pick a handful of wild strawberries.

Starting out through willows that show signs of heavy elk browsing in winter, the Onahu Creek Trail maintains a nearly level grade through marshy meadow to forest of lodgepole pines and quaking aspens. As the grade steepens, aspens begin to be crowded out. Young Engelmann spruce and subalpine fir growing in indicate that absence of forest fire in this area is allowing plant succession to proceed toward a climax spruce-fir forest. Spruce and fir have already achieved dominance along the watercourses, where extra moisture speeds their growth.

Nevertheless, as the trail steepens considerably, lodgepole pines continue to prevail. There are enough brooks to create pleasant variety in what otherwise would be a monotonous lodgepole forest. Chickarees (red squirrels) seem to be the dominant animals here, angrily cursing every hiker who dares to trespass into their domain. The familiar buzzing calls of mountain chickadees are friendlier greetings. Wild strawberries and blueberries offer a special treat to hikers in late summer.

After only one moderately steep section, the trail levels along the main drainage of Onahu Creek. Passing from forest into meadow and back into shade along the broad valley floor, the path recrosses the creek for the last time at a distance of 3 miles from the road. Past the bridge, Long Meadows Trail runs in vaguely from the left. (Long Meadows Trail is obscure in some sections and nonexistent in others. See Timber Lake Trail page 170.)

From the creek, the well-constructed trail slants up a northern slope, where the surrounding forest is classic mature spruce and fir. But on the sunnier ridge top, lodgepole pines take over again. The trail, now running south, winds on a level grade overlooking a swampy depression and is crossed by several faint elk trails before descending fairly steeply to a junction with Tonahutu Creek Trail at **Big Meadows.**

From the junction, follow Tonahutu Creek Trail south along the side of Big Meadows for slightly more than a half mile. Take time to examine a couple of log ruins at the edge of the forest. These are the remains of a century-old haying operation run by Sam Stone. One structure was a barn, the other a human habitation. Stone plowed part of the meadows, but little came of his attempt at development. He eventually fell under the influence of a woman spirtualist, who divined that there was gold to be found in Paradise Park, on what is now the national park's southern boundary. Together she and Stone went off to look for a rich lode. Fortunately, the crystal ball was wrong; Paradise Park remained unmined, unspoiled, and true to its name.

Today, little remains of Sam Stone's ranch in Big Meadows. His buildings are slow to decay because of the chilly, dry climate, but they are at least in an advanced state of disrepair. Elephant heads have replaced his livestock in the meadows.

The Tonahutu Creek–Green Mountain Trail junction is broad and obvious. **Green Mountain Trail** once was a wagon road along which Sam Stone's hay was hauled from Big Meadows to Green Mountain Ranch. The way still is wide, singularly free of rocks, not very steep, and easy to travel. Relatively plentiful water on this northern slope makes possible a greater variety of vegetation than on the rest of the circle hike. You will reach Trail Ridge Road 1.8 miles along Green Mountain Trail from Big Meadows.

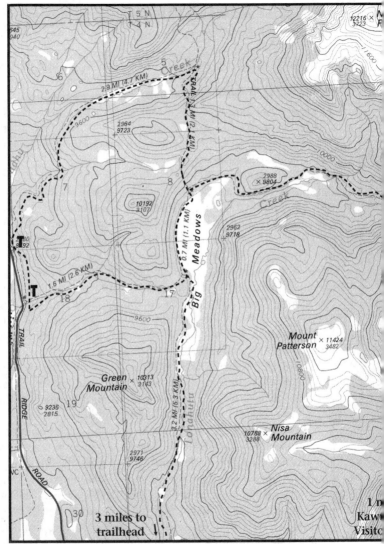

12216 ×
3723

2.9 MI (4.7 KM)

Creek

TRAIL 1.3 MI (2.1 KM)

3600

2964
9723

10000

8

7

2988
× 9804

Creek

10192
3107

0.7 MI (1.1 KM)

Big Meadows

2962
9718

50
9192

1.6 MI (2.6 KM)

T

18   17

9600

Mount
Patterson × 11424
3482

10800

TRAIL

Green × 10313
Mountain   3143

3.2 MI (5.3 KM)

Tonahutu

RIDGE

◊ 9235
2815   19

10788 ×
3288

Nisa
Mountain

ROAD

2971
9746

NC +

30

3 miles to
trailhead

1 m
Kaw
Visito

North Inlet and Tonahutu Creek Trail Systems and
Onahu Creek–Green Mountain Circle

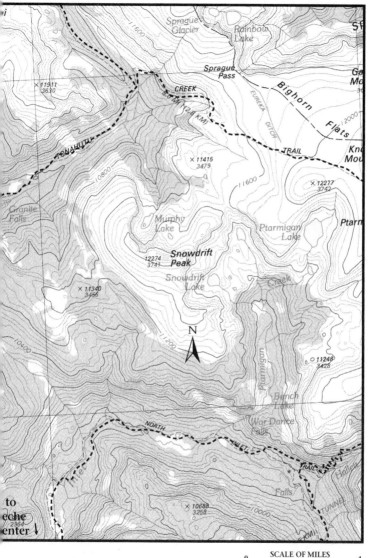

Sprague
Glacier

Rainbow
Lake

11600

Sprague
Pass

Bighorn

CREEK

Ga
Mo

Flats

12000

EUREKA

DITCH

TONAHUTU

11911
3630

TRAIL

Kn
Mo

10800

× 11415
3479

11600

× 12277
3742

Granite
Falls

Murphy
Lake

Ptarmigan
Lake

Ptarm

Snowdrift
Peak

12274
3741

Snowdrift
Lake

Creek

× 11340
3456

11200

N

Ptarmigan

× 11248
3428

10400

Bench
Lake

NORTH

War Dance
Falls

INLET

Inlet

TRAIL

Half

to
eche
enter ↓

2964

Falls

TUNNEL

× 10688
3258

10000

Colorado River Trails

The guest ranch that formerly stood at the trailhead for most routes into the Never Summer Range was called Phantom Valley Ranch. Perhaps it was named for the ghosts of trappers, miners, and irrigation ditch diggers who all figured prominently in the history of this stretch of the Colorado River.

In 1984 and 1985, the Park Service obliterated the old Phantom Valley Trailhead and the road leading to it, which was deemed a traffic hazard. The new Colorado River Trailhead was substituted on the other side of Trail Ridge Road from Timber Lake Trailhead, 9.6 miles north of the Grand Lake Entrance to the national park and 10.7 miles southwest of Fall River Pass. From the new trailhead, a trail follows the Colorado River for 0.6 mile to a split: Red Mountain Trail on the left and the Colorado River Trail to Lulu City and La Poudre Pass on the right.

Red Mountain Trail System

Shortly after the split, the Red Mountain Trail bridges the Colorado River and continues across a meadow. The grade steepens somewhat after entering lodgepole pine woods, then steepens considerably just before crossing Opposition Creek. Past the creek, a climb to the south up an open rocky slope reveals views downhill to the meadows and marshes of Kawuneeche Valley. Raspberry bushes growing among the rocks produce delicious fruit in August.

When you reenter the woods, the grade becomes less steep. A switchback turns you in the opposite direction (north) along a level walk through subalpine forest. Blueberries take over the wild edibles role along this section of trail, where there is little other ground cover. A few openings among the trees reveal occasional views to the east, and a large rocky gap in the forest gives another perspective of Kawuneeche Valley.

The way heads slightly downhill to cross Opposition and Mosquito Creeks, then climbs up to the service road that follows the Grand Ditch. The ditch is a water diversion project that

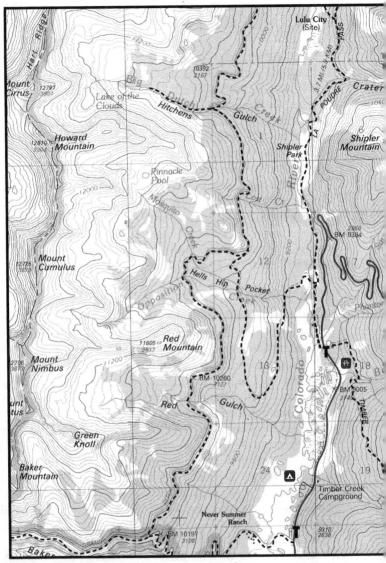

Trail Ridge Road and Red Mountain Trail

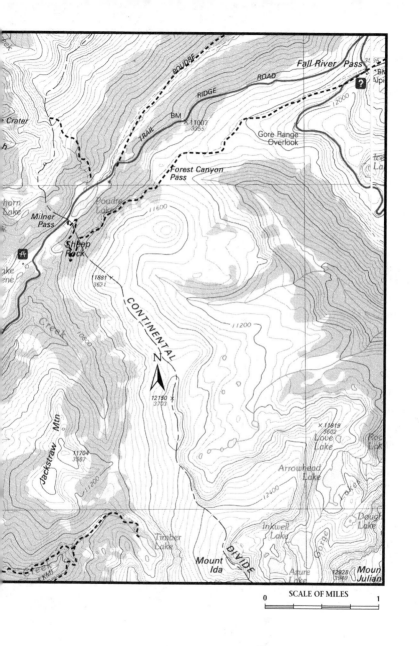

SCALE OF MILES

0   1

brings water from the damp west slope to the populous but dry plains east of the Rockies. The road, 3.4 miles from the trailhead, is closed to public vehicles and provides hiking access to many destinations in the Never Summer Range. The most popular may be **Lake of the Clouds.**

To reach the lake, take the very easy walk to the north (right) along the ditch. Red Mountain rises behind you and Mount Cumulus to the left. Directly ahead are the massive ridges of Howard and Lead Mountains. Hitchens Gulch, which leads to Lake of the Clouds, is out of sight behind Howard. Clumps of subalpine flowers—Parry primrose, tall chiming bells, senecio, brook cress—grow nicely in some spots along the ditch.

The flowers are especially fine 1.7 miles along the road at **Hitchens Gulch,** where Big Dutch Creek flows east toward the Colorado River. Cross the ditch on a bridge, and follow the Lake of the Clouds Trail uphill through switchbacks in Hitchens Gulch. The trail ascends steeply into beautiful subalpine forest where Engelmann spruce and subalpine fir grow to huge sizes, well watered by runoff from melting snowbanks. The runoff flows down to the Grand Ditch.

At a small clearing, which is the site of long-ago mining activity, the grade becomes less steep. Hikers in June may find the trail hidden by snow in some places. The forest opens a bit, and the trail crosses wet meadows here and there. Continuing west toward Hart Ridge, between Mount Cirrus and Lead Mountain, you reach a meadow with a small, marshy pond at its southern end. Keeping just inside the woods, skirt the southern shore and continue west to a short, steep slope 6.3 miles from the trailhead.

The path ends at the top of the slope by the edge of a rock glacier. Lubricated by permanent ice beneath, the whole boulder field is creeping downhill below Lake of the Clouds. This debris is an obstacle course of large, shaky, angular rocks, among which lives a healthy population of large black spiders. Looking south (left), you can see a waterfall, which drops from the cirque containing Lake of the Clouds, below Mount Cirrus.

To reach the lake, pick the most likely looking route across the rocks to a ridge to the right of the waterfall and the Lake of the Clouds cirque. Ascend this ridge to a point somewhat below the level of the lake. Then cut left, dodging snowbanks and using the most convenient rocks and ledges to make your way into the basin containing Lake of the Clouds, 6.9 miles from the trailhead.

After the grade levels in the basin, walk over the tundra and bedrock to the shore of the lake. This is the only really solid rock around Lake of the Clouds; the other shores are bounded by steep, loose rock and ice fields.

Photos taken from the solid rock are not particularly impressive, but good shots can be had from the eastern or western shore. Be careful of the snowfield on the northwest; an uncontrolled slide there would land you in water where ice still floats in July.

You might try for photos of the marmots and pikas that live around the lake. If they are feeling unfriendly, attach close-up equipment to your camera and photograph the excellent examples of tundra cushion plants among the rocks.

To ascend **Lead Mountain,** bear right from the Lake of the Clouds Trail at the spidery rock glacier. Crossing the boulders, climb to tundra slopes below the saddle situated between Lead and an unnamed summit to the east (right). Continue uphill to the saddle, staying west (left) of snowfields wherever possible. From the saddle make your way over tundra, rock, and sometimes snow to the knife ridge that leads to Lead's summit.

This is the part of the climb that sticks most firmly in everyone's memory, for the ridge top is about 3 feet wide. The footing on top, however, is reasonably solid, whereas loose rock makes for awful going below the ridge on the south side. The north side is a precipice. We recommend walking steadily along the ridgeline to the summit.

A variation on the return route is to go back down the knife ridge as far as the saddle and then descend to the north. A snowfield on the north side of Lead can be an easy way down for those equipped for and experienced in climbing on snow and ice. But after approximately mid-July, the lower and less steep part of the snowfield melts and exposes rocks. These could bring an unpleasantly sudden and painful stop to an uncontrolled slide from the steeper upper part of the snowfield, which takes longer to melt. Therefore, you may wish to descend later in the season via rocks along the edge of the snowfield, traversing carefully from time to time to reach easier rock. Failure to be careful on the snow could add another grisly incident to the history of **Skeleton Gulch,** which is situated below the snowfield. Descend into the gulch and catch a trail back to the Grand Ditch service road.

You can cross a bridge over the ditch and walk down a trail on the other side to the Thunder Pass Trail, Lulu City, and finally the Colorado River Trailhead. From the Skeleton Gulch Trail–Grand Ditch road junction to the trailhead, it is 5.3 miles via Lulu City and 7 miles via the Red Mountain Trail.

To climb **Mount Howard** from the Red Mountain Trail–Grand Ditch junction, walk south along the ditch service road 0.2 mile to Mosquito Creek. Cross the ditch on a bridge, and continue up the Mosquito Creek drainage on faint animal trails for about a mile to **Pinnacle Pool.**

Ascend the drainage of the inlet of Pinnacle Pool, cutting left of the trees below the pinnacles on the ridge leading east from Mount Howard. About a half-mile up the valley, you can turn right and begin climbing a tundra slope toward the top of Howard's east ridge. Too soon tundra is replaced by loose rock. Scramble up this stuff carefully, and avoid kicking it down on those below you. Turn left at the ridgeline, skirt a bump on the ridge, and proceed to the summit, about 5.5 miles from the trailhead. Snow cornices can make the ridge to Howard's summit a sweaty-palms adventure, with exposure to falls in early summer.

If time and weather permit, you can continue for an additional half mile to **Mount Cirrus.** Follow the Continental Divide northwest and downhill to a bump on the ridgeline between Howard and Cirrus. Skirt the bump on the left (west), and continue downhill to the saddle between the two peaks, above Lake of the Clouds. Then climb a tundra slope to the top of Cirrus, dodging to the left around rock-filled gullies near the summit.

Descend from Cirrus via the ridge extending east from the summit, overlooking Lake of the Clouds. Loose rock covering the ridge and some exposure to falls while making your way over and around obstacles require care while you descend. On the lower end of the ridge, bear left (north) to avoid cliffs above Lake of the Clouds. Follow the route from Lake of the Clouds down Hitchens Gulch to the Grand Ditch, back to the Red Mountain Trail, and then to the trailhead. Howard, Cirrus, and Lake of the Clouds are about 13.2 miles, round trip.

Mount Cumulus and **Mount Nimbus** are the peaks immediately south of Howard. They are usually climbed together and are easier to surmount than their neighbors. From the Red Mountain Trail–Grand Ditch junction, turn left and hike 0.4 mile along the ditch road to Opposition Creek. Cross the ditch on a bridge and continue west, upstream. Above tree line, the trail you have been following, which has been growing gradually less distinct, disappears altogether. Continue climbing up tundra and rocks to the saddle on the Continental Divide between Nimbus, on the left, and Cumulus, on the right. At the saddle, turn left and follow the ridgeline to the top of Nimbus, about 5.7 miles from the trailhead.

Cumulus is located about a mile from Nimbus. To reach it, go back to the saddle and climb north along the divide. Circumventing loose rock along the ridgeline requires dropping down a bit in places. Round-trip for both peaks is about 14 miles.

The peak for which the Red Mountain Trail is named sits east of Mount Nimbus. To climb **Red Mountain**, turn left at the trail's junction with the Grand Ditch, walk 1.2 miles along the ditch service road to Red Gulch, and cross the ditch on a bridge. The shortest and least difficult way up Red Mountain is to go right (north) on the west side of the ditch to whatever point seems best for climbing the peak's southeast side.

Although the mountain is not very high, its peak is strategically located for viewing high mountains to the west and the Colorado

River drainage. Early summer hikers may wish to slide down a handy snowfield to ease their descent from the summit.

Green Knoll is the next projection south of Red Mountain. There is, however, a closer approach to Green Knoll than from the Red Mountain Trail—the approach from the Never Summer Ranch (see the Trail Ridge Road chapter).

Lulu City Trail System

The trail to Lulu City is an easy 3.7-mile walk to the site of an old mining community. Many hikers may expect to find a ghost town, but all they see when they reach the site is a meadow with a few barely distinguishable remains of log cabins. To adventurers seeking mineral wealth in 1879, Lulu City was a disappointment. It is also a disappointment to modern hikers seeking tangible historic relics. But if the pay dirt you seek is wilderness beauty, the trail to the site of Lulu City and beyond is a sure path to success.

The trail to Lulu City and La Poudre Pass (**Colorado River Trail**) splits from the Red Mountain Trail 0.6 mile from the Colorado River Trailhead. The grade continues level, following the floodplain of the Colorado River almost due north. Willows and other water-loving flora line the trail, and beaver workings are obvious. The workings of humans also are evident in an 1880 mining site to the right of the trail beyond the split.

From the trailhead, the trail follows the east bank of the Colorado, sometimes closely, sometimes at a distance, over an easy grade for 2 miles to some tailings below **Shipler Mine.** The mine, an unsuccessful effort of the 1880s, is uphill to the right. (Entering the mine area is unsafe.) Two log cabins associated with the mine are situated 0.4 mile farther along the trail. The cabin on the left was built in 1876.

Continuing on the level past the cabins, the trail follows a stage road that used to run through Lulu City and then northwest over Thunder Pass to Walden, Colorado. When you at last begin to climb above the valley floor, the shade of subalpine forest through which you walk is especially welcome. The trail forks at a junction 3.5 miles from the trailhead. The right-hand fork goes to Little Yellowstone Canyon and La Poudre Pass (see page 196). The left-hand fork heads back downhill through switchbacks to the site of Lulu City, about 0.2 mile farther. The **Stage Road Trail** to Thunder Pass continues through the meadow of Lulu City and past a connecting trail that leads steeply uphill to La Poudre Pass Trail.

Heading left toward Thunder Pass, you soon cross the Colorado River amid water-loving shrubs and rocks. On the other side of the river there is another fork. The right-hand fork is yet another trail to La Poudre Pass.

To continue on the Stage Road Trail, take the left-hand fork for one very steep mile through subalpine forest. Then your way broadens and levels, bearing right through lovely meadowland to the Grand Ditch. At the ditch, turn left and continue 0.1 mile to a bridge.

Cross the ditch and walk through subalpine woods and along the edge of marshland. At the mouth of **Box Canyon** you will reach a pleasant meadow through which Lulu Creek flows, 0.6 mile uphill from the ditch. Past the meadow, the trail climbs at a very steep grade. Only a few moderating switchbacks remind you that stagecoaches once were pulled up this remarkable slope. Below Thunder Pass, subalpine flowers often put on a spectacular display. A final short, steep climb takes you to **Thunder Pass** and the national park boundary, 6.9 miles from the trailhead.

On the other side of the pass, the valley of Michigan Lakes to the west is very lovely, with Static Peak and Nokhu Crags towering dramatically on the left. The highest and largest of Michigan Lakes, Snow Lake, is hidden in the basin below the crags.

From Thunder Pass, you can climb the three tundra-covered, rounded slopes of Lulu and Thunder Mountains and Mount Neota. All these peaks provide good views of the Colorado River drainage and Never Summer Range. Turn right from the pass, and climb uphill steadily past the upper limit of krummholz for a half mile to **Lulu Mountain.**

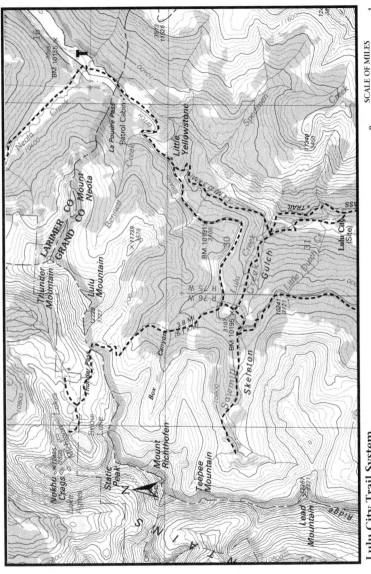

Lulu City Trail System

0   1
SCALE OF MILES

On top of Lulu, the hardest part lies behind you. It is relatively easy to pick your way along rocks and tundra on the Continental Divide and park boundary for three-quarters of a mile to **Thunder Mountain** and another three-quarters of a mile to **Mount Neota.**

Descend west from Neota until you are below the steep summit slopes. Then work your way east, via wildlife trails, through fairly open subalpine woods on the south flank of the Continental Divide ridge down to a dry crossing of the Grand Ditch at La Poudre Pass. Once on the ditch road, exit south 7.4 miles via the Colorado River Trail to Trail Ridge Road (see page 190). Or you may have arranged for transportation to the northeast at Long Draw Reservoir, a quarter mile north. (For driving instructions to Long Draw, see Mummy Pass Trail in the Mummy Range chapter.)

From Thunder Pass, you can climb **Static Peak** and **Mount Richthofen** too. Turn left (west) from the pass, and head along the north side of the divide in Routt National Forest. Your immediate goal is a saddle between Static and an unnamed lower peak east of it that rises above Thunder Pass. Once around this peak, cross the saddle and contour below the cliffs on Static Peak to a shelf extending between Static and Mount Richthofen. You can reach this point without going all the way to Thunder Pass by leaving the Thunder Pass Trail about a mile before the pass and walking up Box Canyon. This more direct route necessitates climbing onto the shelf via the north (right-hand) canyon wall.

From the shelf, pick the least cliffy route, again to the north, over loose rock to the saddle between Static and Richthofen. From there the way is relatively simple to either summit. Beyond Static, the ridge to **Nokhu Crags** is a much more challenging climb, crossing jagged and potentially dangerous terrain.

Mount Richthofen can be climbed also from the south, via the Skeleton Gulch Trail (see page 188) or a ridge extending east from Richthofen. But by far the shortest approach is from the west, via Lake Agnes. This route, which begins in Colorado State Forest, is about 2 miles long; the route from Colorado River Trailhead is 7.6 miles long.

To reach the starting point of the Lake Agnes route, take Colorado Highway 14 from Walden or Fort Collins to a point about 3 miles southwest of Cameron Pass. Turn south there on an unpaved road passable by normal passenger cars, and follow it 2 miles to the end, at a parking lot and trailhead. The parking lot holds about fifteen cars. More than fifteen would put enough hikers into the Lake Agnes area to seriously disturb the area's bighorn sheep and reduce their already uncertain chances for survival.

It is very important that hikers who are fortunate enough to see bighorn sheep do not bother them by trying to stalk them closely. Nearly 100 percent of the photos attempted by hikers pursuing sheep across the mountains result in dismal failure, and the stress that the animals undergo as a result of being chased from their feeding grounds gravely affects their health.

On one of our climbs up Mount Richthofen, we encountered a herd of ewes and lambs near Skeleton Gulch. Not wishing to disturb them, we immediately sat down and rested quietly so the sheep could go on their way. To our surprise, the ewe leading the herd brought them over to look at us! We took excellent photos while seated in comfort, and the sheep placidly grazed and went about their usual business.

Admittedly, this event is unlikely to be repeated. But you will get no bighorn photos worth looking at in any other way. It is vital not to pressure the sheep. Too much pressure from hikers will drastically reduce their numbers.

From the Colorado State Forest parking area, a trail extends for a little more than a half-mile to **Lake Agnes.** Once at the lake, continue around its western shore to the stream flowing into it from the slopes of Richthofen. Follow this stream to the south, ascending over boulders toward a saddle situated between Richthofen and an unnamed peak to the west. You must fight small loose rocks to get to the saddle. After scrambling carefully over this stuff, pick your way from the saddle up the ridgeline to Richthofen's summit. The angular rocks are fairly solid compared

Mountain chickadee on lodgepole pine

with those just climbed, but care must be taken to avoid kicking anything down on other climbers along this popular route.

From the west ridge of Richthofen, you can climb along a very rough knife ridge for a half mile to the much lower **Tepee Mountain.** The rock is loose, and there is exposure to long drops when climbing around barriers on the ridgeline. Be very careful.

Back at the trail junction 3.5 miles from the Colorado River Trailhead, **La Poudre Pass Trail** heads to the right, while the trail to Lulu City drops to the left. Soon La Poudre Pass Trail begins a gradual descent. At one point the trees open to reveal the meadow where Lulu City once stood. After 0.6 mile, you reach a trail that drops to the Colorado River on the northern edge of the same meadow.

Beyond this junction are semi-parallel trails to Poudre Pass. Signs will likely be in place to keep you from getting too confused or lost. The trail to the left drops at once to the Colorado River, following the Stage Road Trail up Lulu Creek and across the Grand Ditch to the historic route over Thunder Pass. The trail to the right loops across the Colorado River to strike north toward Poudre Pass. The trail to Poudre Pass branches right to cross Lulu Creek and rejoins the other connector to the pass. From this point the grade becomes less steep, and the dense lodgepole forest opens a bit, allowing blueberries to flourish as ground cover.

The rim of **Little Yellowstone Canyon** is about a mile past the point where the Stage Road Trail branches up to the Grand Ditch and Thunder Pass. From the top of rock pillars overlooking the river, you can see the canyon's resemblance, on a diminutive scale, to the Grand Canyon of the Yellowstone River in the world's first national park. This viewpoint is an excellent platform from which to photograph the eroded volcanic rock that gave the canyon its name.

Uphill past the viewpoint, La Poudre Pass Trail crosses a brook and climbs up switchbacks through open areas before shooting straight up to the service road paralleling the Grand Ditch. A level

1.1 miles in the sunshine along the ditch road takes you to **La Poudre Pass,** a broad, low, and wide-open point on the Continental Divide, 7.4 miles from the Colorado River Trailhead. From the pass, you have several options for your return route: back along the ditch 4.2 miles to the Stage Road Trail; back the way you came, with detours to Lulu City; or ahead a quarter mile to prearranged transportation at Long Draw Reservoir.

Grand Lake

Grand Lake is the largest natural lake in Colorado yet it is considerably smaller than the adjacent man-made reservoir, Shadow Mountain Lake, or nearby Lake Granby. In other words, there is a lot of water sloshing around this part of the Rockies. Precipitation is relatively heavy here. Streams are spectacular during most of the summer; trails are blocked by snow long into the hiking season. The forests are denser and seem more primeval than in the eastern part of the national park. Coincidentally, most approaches to various hiking goals are longer in the Grand Lake area than elsewhere.

North Inlet Trail

The North Inlet Trail and the Tonahutu Creek Trail start in almost the same place north of Grand Lake. By different routes they run east and climb to the summit of Flattop Mountain, where they come together and descend to Bear Lake. Most of the length of these trails is described in the Bear Lake Trailhead chapter. Some goals, however, are more appropriately reached from Grand Lake, so they are described here.

To reach the North Inlet Trailhead, drive east from US 34 toward Grand Lake on Colorado Highway 278 (Tunnel Road). One-third mile from US 34, CO 278 forks. Take the left-hand fork, which bypasses the village of Grand Lake and leads eventually to the West Portal of the Adams Tunnel of the Big Thompson Irrigation Project.

Leave CO 278 at 0.8 mile from the fork, turning left on a narrow unpaved road. A short distance along the unpaved road there is a parking lot on the left, which is the best place to park for the Tonahutu Creek Trail. Continue past the parking lot, go over a hill, turn right, and cross Tonahutu Creek on a bridge uncomfortably narrow for most cars. There is a parking lot just beyond the bridge.

From the parking lot, walk east along a mostly level road with a few minor ups and downs for 1.2 miles to **Summerland Park.** This road provides access to private land within the national park and is closed to driving by the public. Beyond Summerland Park, the route is an easily walked trail, passing through lodgepole pines for a few miles while running upstream along the North Inlet, the creek that flows into Grand Lake from the northeast.

Below **Cascade Falls,** the trail forks; the two branches come together above the falls. To avoid conflicts with parties on horseback, take the right-hand (lower) fork now and the upper fork on your return. Cascade Falls is located a few yards to the right of the lower fork, 3.5 miles from the trailhead. The best viewpoint for photographers is reached by climbing steeply downstream over boulders. Be careful; some of the rocks are wet and slick. Smashing your camera, not to mention your body, in a fall could cast a pall over your entire hike.

The trail remains mostly easy and well shaded for more than 6.5 miles from the trailhead. Finally, a short set of switchbacks marks the beginning of a gradually steepening grade. You reach a junction with the **Lake Nanita Trail** 7.5 miles from the trailhead. The North Inlet Trail continues on the left-hand fork to Flattop Mountain (see the Bear Lake Trailhead chapter). The right-hand fork climbs at an easy grade for 0.1 mile to a bridge over the small gorge that is the site of **North Inlet Falls.**

Past the falls, the right-hand fork climbs steeply away from North Inlet. Heavy subalpine forest opens at the ends of switchbacks to reveal views of marshes and of Lake Solitude, on the North Inlet valley floor. Overhead, Chiefs Head Peak presents an oddly pointed aspect. After four long sets of switchbacks, you climb across bedrock uphill from fine subalpine gardens where the outlet stream of **Lake Nokoni** flows.

At 9.9 miles from the trailhead, you reach Lake Nokoni itself, a classic tarn lying in a basin carved from solid rock by a glacier. Little soil and few trees mask the stone bowl shoreline. On the south, the promontories of Ptarmigan Mountain are sheer but rather blocky. A long broad slope blanketed with loose rock tends to spoil photographic composition. All in all, Nokoni is not as photogenic as might be desired. Or perhaps it suffers by comparison with Lake Nanita, a larger tarn over the ridge.

Lake Nanita is one of the most photogenic lakes in Rocky Mountain National Park. Admittedly, its attraction may be enhanced because you must work to get here. Past Lake Nokoni, the trail rises steeply before leveling in heavy subalpine forest on the ridge top. You get a few glimpses of Nanita as you descend to a marshy meadow. The lake is forgotten briefly as incredibly ragged and dramatic spires on the south face of Ptarmigan Mountain saw across the skyline. Then you pass through trees to ledges overlooking Nanita, 11 miles from the trailhead. Andrews Peak rises on the opposite side of the lake; it is every first grader's impression of exactly what a mountain should look like.

Scrambling down the rocky slope, you may be lucky enough to photograph Andrews reflected in Nanita. Afternoon or evening light is best for this shot. Should you arrive in the morning, Ptarmigan Mountain makes an even more dramatic subject from the other side of the lake.

A third tarn in the heavily glaciated vicinity of Ptarmigan Mountain is **Pettingell Lake,** an off-trail hike three-quarters of a mile from Lake Nokoni. Walk to the right from the bedrock lip of Nokoni's basin, and climb steeply uphill to a low point on the ridge north of Nokoni. From the ridge, drop down a gradually steepening slope to the basin of Pettingell.

If you are in the vicinity of Nokoni and want to climb **Ptarmigan Mountain** and **Andrews Peak,** you can start from the ridge separating Nokoni and Pettingell. Follow the ridgeline steeply uphill and climb along the edge of the Nokoni cirque to the summit of Ptarmigan, about 1.5 walking miles from Nokoni. Andrews Peak is 1.5 miles farther across tundra slopes. With unbeatable views of glacial lakes in North and East Inlet Valleys and the 13,000-foot peaks to the east, Ptarmigan and Andrews certainly are worth the climb. They are reached more easily, however, from the East Inlet Trail (see page 203) than via the long North Inlet Trail approach to Lake Nokoni.

Ptarmigan Creek, contrary to what you might expect, flows south down the north wall of North Inlet valley *opposite* Ptarmigan Mountain. It drains a magnificent basin where there are three named tarns—Bench, Snowdrift, and Ptarmigan Lakes —and many unnamed ones. Ptarmigan Creek crosses the North Inlet Trail at a point 6.7 miles from Grand Lake. From the trail you can follow the stream very steeply uphill through thick sub-alpine forest to **War Dance Falls.**

Bench Lake is located in a hanging valley about a half mile and 760 feet above the North Inlet Trail. As is typical for a glaciated landscape, the hanging valley has a broad marshy floor and steep walls. Both are barriers to hikers wishing to explore the large tarns hanging in their cirques more than a thousand feet above the hanging valley containing Bench Lake and Ptarmigan Creek.

Tonahutu Creek Trail

One approach to the Tonahutu Creek Trail is the same as the approach to the North Inlet Trail. Many folks park their cars beside Colorado Highway 278, at 0.8 mile from the Grand Lake fork, and walk along the unpaved road to the trailhead. But there is a parking lot at the trailhead, on the left of the road. From the parking lot, the Tonahutu Creek Trail follows moderate grades to the north through lodgepole pines. After 0.9 mile it reaches a junction with a half-mile spur that originates at the Kawuneeche Visitor Center. (Parking at the visitor center eliminates 0.4 mile of hiking through lodgepole pine.) The path steepens somewhat past the junction but remains moderate as it parallels Tonahutu Creek uphill to the beginning of **Big Meadows,** more than 2 miles from the trailhead. The trail skirts the edge of Big Meadows, keeping in the shade and out of marshy grassland, which is more easily trampled than is the forest. The shade is welcome, for the 4.4 miles of trail between the trailhead and a junction with the Green Mountain Trail are often hot. We recommend skipping the first part of the Tonahutu Creek Trail and hiking to the junction via the more interesting, more comfortable, and 2.6-miles-shorter Green Mountain Trail (see Onahu Creek–Green Mountain Circle in the Trail Ridge Road chapter).

Big Meadows seem to go on and on, even if you reach them at the midpoint, at the Green Mountain–Tonahutu Creek junction. From the junction, hike north on an excellent trail and pass log cabin ruins. More than a half mile north of the junction, the trail divides. The left-hand fork continues running north to Onahu Creek. The right-hand fork, the Tonahutu Creek Trail, bends to the east around the upper end of Big Meadows. Cutting between a forested hill and the northern bank of Tonahutu Creek, the trail follows an easy grade upstream most of the way to **Granite Falls,** 7.8 miles from the Tonahutu Creek Trailhead and 5.2 miles from the Green Mountain Trailhead.

More than 1.5 miles past Granite Falls, the trail crosses a stream flowing south from **Haynach Lakes** just below a pretty cascade. A little farther, a trail branches left up a drainage to the beautiful lakes, as well as numerous marshy ponds and one large tarn at the base of **Nakai Peak** (see Flattop Mountain Trail System in the Bear Lake Trailhead chapter for further description of Haynach Lakes). The lakes are an excellent 7.5-mile hike from the Green Mountain Trailhead.

Nakai Peak can be reached in an uncomplicated ascent from Haynach Lakes. Walk uphill along the drainage flowing into the largest lake to a saddle on the ridge between Nakai and the Continental Divide. Turn left at the saddle and, skirting right (west) around a bump on the ridge, follow the ridgeline to Nakai's summit. The summit is about 9 miles from the Green Mountain Trailhead.

East Inlet Trail

The East Inlet Trail runs uphill in the valley of the creek that flows into Grand Lake from the east. Its trailhead is located at the West Portal of Adams Tunnel, a point of some confusion.

To reach the trailhead from US 34, head east on Colorado Highway 278 (Tunnel Road) toward the village of Grand Lake. After one-third of a mile, the road divides; take the left-hand fork, which bypasses the town of Grand Lake and heads directly toward Adams Tunnel, a link in the Big Thompson Irrigation Project. Follow more than 2 miles of paved road to the West Portal and continue driving, bearing left on an unpaved road to the trailhead parking lot.

The parking area is large because the easy 0.3 mile to **Adams Falls** attracts many walkers. The falls are attractive; a rainbow shines from the spray in the morning. The surrounding rocks are smooth, steep, and wet. Parents should take care that children do not slip into the water and get washed over the brink.

Past Adams Falls, the trail runs on the level through lodgepole pines to a marshy meadow much loved by mosquitoes. With urging from the bugs, you tend to make excellent speed along the meadow's edge. Then there is more flat walking through lodgepole pines to a much larger meadow filled with obvious beaver workings. Bugs are not shy in this meadow, either, but there is some compensation ahead of you in the nice views of Mount Craig.

After crossing two streams in quick succession, the trail rises and falls through more lodgepoles, but each downhill pitch is a little shorter than the previous uphill pitch. You gradually gain altitude in this fashion until emerging on a rock shelf perched on the side of Mount Cairns. Switchbacks over the rocks reveal fine views to the east of the craggy walls of Mount Craig.

The trail resumes its up-and-down progress, occasionally approaching East Inlet. Along the stream, Parry primrose, globe-flower, marsh marigold, and chiming bells are common. From switchbacks through thick subalpine forests, you can catch glimpses of Mount Craig, on the opposite side of the valley, and of the tundra slopes of Andrews Peak, straight ahead.

Eventually, the trail circles a forested hill and climbs switchbacks to **Lone Pine Lake,** 5.5 miles from the trailhead. The lake is named for a single lodgepole pine that once took root in a crack

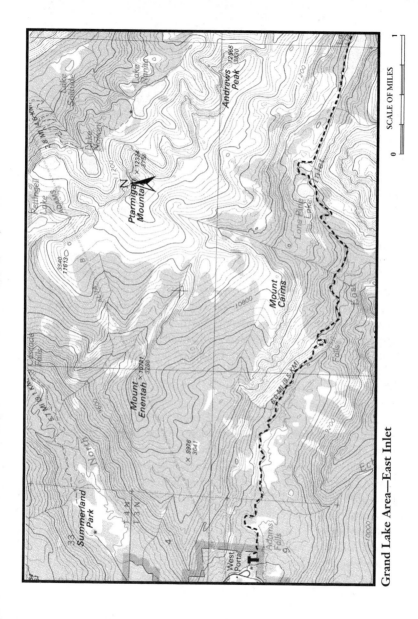

Grand Lake Area—East Inlet

SCALE OF MILES

0   1

in a rock island in the lake. Since the naming, that pioneer has succumbed to the extreme rigors of the trying environment. The tree has been replaced, however, by several young pines and by an Engelmann spruce, all growing on the same island. The mountain vistas surrounding Lone Pine Lake are unspectacular to the jaded eye so easily acquired in Rocky Mountain National Park, where remarkable views are normal.

East Inlet Trail curves to the right and follows the southeastern shore of Lone Pine Lake to a slope of large boulders. Traversing the slope, it reenters woods and winds uphill to several interesting crossings of streams cascading down Andrews Peak. Braided courses of brooks weave among trees and rocks, while the trail stays dry atop long bridges—a unique and very lovely area.

Past these streams the path turns right and traverses the upper end of the rocky slope crossed previously, just before reaching the streams. Having bypassed more boulders, the trail angles to the left above the gorge of East Inlet. The generally rocky character of the terrain is relieved occasionally by ponds and small meadows decorated with glacier lilies. More than a mile from Lone Pine Lake, at a pond just below Lake Verna, climbers heading for Andrews Peak and Ptarmigan Mountain may wish to cut left over boulders and pick their way to the top of Andrews, more than 2,300 feet higher.

The East Inlet Trail reenters subalpine forest, then leaves it on an interesting rocky ridge overlooking **Lake Verna,** 6.9 miles from the trailhead. Here may be the best view of the lake, portraying its mysterious, fjordlike quality. The trail (unmaintained beyond Verna) continues along the north shore. Cut right to the lakeshore occasionally to take in the view. Avoid crossing trampled areas that the National Park Service is trying to restore.

Spirit Lake is located more than a mile from the west (outlet) end of Lake Verna. Three-quarters of the sometimes soggy trail follows Verna's shore. Past Spirit, the trail is even less maintained for the three-quarters of a mile to **Fourth Lake.** Past Fourth, the track becomes very sketchy up to **Fifth Lake,** about 9.5 miles from the trailhead.

From Fourth Lake, it is possible to climb steeply to Boulder–Grand Pass for an outstanding view of Fourth, Spirit, and Verna lakes strung out along East Inlet (see Ouzel Falls Trail System in the Wild Basin chapter). The East Inlet chain is an excellent example of paternoster lakes. *Pater noster* is Latin for "Our Father," the first words of The Lord's Prayer; the rosary, a string of beads used as an aid while repeating the prayer, came to be known as a paternoster. When seen from above, a series of lakes in a glaciated valley resembles a string of beads, hence the name paternoster lakes. They might be located either in glacially scoured basins in bedrock or behind rock "dams"—terminal moraines—laid down by a glacier as it melted.

Paradise Park is an aptly named valley south of East Inlet. Designated a research natural area, it is given special protection so that its ecosystem will be preserved unaltered by human activity. As part of that protection, camping and horse riding are prohibited within Paradise Park and **Ten Lakes Park,** a hanging valley that overlooks it. Folks spending the day hiking in Paradise Park should exercise more than their usual care to leave no evidence of their passing. Sketchy tracks penetrate Paradise Park, starting in the vicinity of the bridge that crosses East Inlet 4.4 miles from the trailhead.

Shadow Mountain and East Shore or Outlet Trails

Shadow Mountain is not notably high or impressive looking, but an old fire lookout near the summit has a romantic, fortresslike quality and is listed on the National Register of Historic Places. The steps on the outside of the tower give hikers access to a view above the trees. You get to the Shadow Mountain Trail via the East Shore or Outlet Trail.

To reach the East Shore Trailhead, watch for Sombrero Stables as you drive into the town of Grand Lake. Bear right on the road that runs behind the stables, then take the first street to the right, which leads to the bridge crossing the canal that connects Grand and Shadow Mountain Lakes. After crossing the bridge, keep heading south for several hundred yards until you run out of paved road. What appears to be an old gravel pit serves for parking. The East Shore Trail begins on the right and probably will be marked with a sign.

Follow it along the shore of **Shadow Mountain Lake** for 0.7 mile to the park boundary and then to the Shadow Mountain Trail junction, 1.5 miles from your starting point. The first section of the trail is flat and easy to walk. Most of the way it passes through lodgepole pines, although there are a few sunny stretches where brush predominates.

The East Shore Trail continues to the right along the lake (see page 209). To climb **Shadow Mountain,** take the trail to the left, which soon begins to climb at a steady grade up the side of a lateral moraine amid lodgepoles that predominate through most of the hike. Approximately a half mile from the junction, the Shadow Mountain Trail makes a switchback, and you climb a bit more steeply in the opposite direction along the narrow ridgeline of the moraine.

After nearly a mile, the moraine merges with the bulk of Shadow Mountain, and the path bends to the right around the end of the gully between ridge and mountain. Circling a lower summit on Shadow Mountain, the path enters a level area above another gully, then bends to the right along the mountain's flank below the fire lookout. A moderate climb takes you to Ranger Creek, where a narrow wooden trough concentrates water in a tempting trickle. *Do not drink it.* You should carry your own water on this and all other hikes. Untreated water should not be assumed safe. The trough was part of the tower's water system decades ago.

Leaving Ranger Creek, the trail switchbacks steeply uphill for about a half mile to a saddle east of the lookout. A right turn away from the trail then leads to the true summit of Shadow Mountain, another half mile away and 10,155 feet above sea level. The summit is surrounded by trees, which block the view from there.

On the other hand, following the trail to the left from the saddle leads you quickly to the lookout tower. Built in 1932, it stands on a 9,923-foot promontory directly above Grand Lake. Steps around the outside of the tower climb three stories, above the surrounding pine and fir, to an excellent view. Grand Lake lies to the west, and the valley of East Inlet leads away to the east, with Mount Craig on its south wall and the higher tundra-covered slopes of Ptarmigan Mountain and Andrews Peak on the north.

To the southwest, below the even ranks of lodgepole pine tops, Shadow Mountain Lake dominates the scene. Large islands at the southern end are high points on a terminal moraine marking the end of a glacier that once extended 20 miles from cirques easily visible in the Never Summer Range to the north. South of Shadow Mountain Lake, huge Lake Granby defines the route of the **East Shore Trail.**

Past the point where the Shadow Mountain Trail leaves the shore of Shadow Mountain Lake, the way splits again almost at once. Both branches end up at the same place. The wide path to the left is usually used by horses, the path to the right by hikers. The right-hand path continues along the lakeshore, a bit wet in places, for 1.3 miles to **Shadow Mountain Dam.**

You can begin hiking the East Shore Trail by driving to the dam just east of the USDA Forest Service's Green Ridge Campground in Arapaho National Recreation Area. To drive to this campground, turn east from US 34 at the southern end of Shadow Mountain Lake by the sign that reads GREEN RIDGE COMPLEX.

From the dam, the East Shore Trail cuts inland up a draw and across a bog to join its other branch, the horse trail. The inland horse trail and the shoreline foot trail both measure about 2.4 miles, junction to junction.

From the convergence of the trails, turn right to follow the trail down to the Colorado River, which becomes Columbine Bay, an arm of Lake Granby. After 1.4 miles the **Columbine Creek Trail** begins on the left and runs to the east up Columbine Creek. The trail was built in the 1930s to provide access for forest fire control.

It was unneeded then and is little used today because it has no particular destination. The Park Service does not maintain this trail.

After a short level stretch, the Columbine Creek Trail climbs steeply above the sometimes marshy valley floor of Columbine Creek. Eventually, it crosses over a ridge to descend again, recross the main creek, and fade away about 3 miles from Columbine Bay.

Past Columbine Creek, the East Shore Trail continues for 1.5 miles to cross the boundary between Rocky Mountain National Park and Arapaho National Recreation Area, administered by the USDA Forest Service. To hikers on this trail, the difference between Forest Service and Park Service land probably will not be significant. On Park Service land, there are to be no pets, hunting, wood gathering, or camping. Beyond a Forest Service cabin at Grand Bay, the trail climbs Knight Ridge for views of **Lake Granby,** then descends to the lake. The southern trailhead of the East Shore Trail is located at Arapaho Bay Ranger Station, 12.7 miles from the northern trailhead at Grand Lake. An easier long trail is difficult to imagine. Mile after mile of lodgepoles and lakeshore, however, might get a bit monotonous after a while.

The ideal way to walk the trail is from one end to the other, having arranged for a car to be left at the end where the hike will conclude. For driving instruction to Arapaho Bay Ranger Station, see the West of the Divide chapter.

INDIAN PEAKS WILDERNESS

National Park and National Forest— Two Administrative Styles

Congress established Indian Peaks Wilderness Area in 1978 within Roosevelt and Arapaho National Forests to preserve the natural, recreational, and scenic value of this rugged rampart of mountains. Adjacent to the south boundary of Rocky Mountain National Park, Indian Peaks Wilderness derives its name from the many dramatic peaks it contains that are named for Indian tribes.

Although the trail systems of Indian Peaks and the national park interconnect very slightly, the two areas are virtually identical with regard to their recreational wilderness resources. Both are unexcelled in their mountain grandeur, and both are very accessible to hikers.

The main difference between Indian Peaks and the national park is administrative. The U.S. Department of Agriculture Forest Service manages Indian Peaks, and the U.S. Department of the Interior National Park Service manages Rocky Mountain National Park.

Although the USDA Forest Service has a generally broader duty in its care of the national forests than the Park Service's mission in caring for national parks, the differences between the two agencies may seem somewhat obscure. Public confusion about who runs Indian Peaks and who runs Rocky Mountain National Park is not remarkable because the two managing agencies happen to manage these adjacent pieces of glorious landscape for nearly identical goals. There are some notable differences, however.

The National Park Service has a more elaborate system for handling visitors to Rocky Mountain National Park than the Forest Service system for Indian Peaks. Rocky Mountain National Park uses nine centers for educating visitors, sponsors lectures in five locations every summer evening, and hires a division of employees whose main responsibility is to conduct programs about the park for visitors. The USDA Forest Service cooperates with the Park Service to some extent in these efforts. Moreover, many if not most visitors to Indian Peaks also visit Rocky Mountain National Park, and benefit from the Park Service's educational efforts.

Another difference is that Congress established Rocky Mountain National Park sixty-three years before it established Indian Peaks Wilderness. In those intervening years between 1915 and 1978, some worn spots developed in Indian Peaks at points of visitor concentration (Isabelle Lake, for instance), and they did not receive the kind of remedial attention overused spots ordinarily receive in a national park.

Since 1978, however, Forest Service management of Indian Peaks has narrowed to focus primarily on the area's recreational wilderness resources. Vigorous preservation of these resources has reduced trampling in particular spots, despite steadily increasing use of Indian Peaks. To hikers familiar with Indian Peaks before wilderness designation, Forest Service efforts are already obvious. In this austere climate where healing is slow, signs of previous wear and tear remain detectable. However, the trend toward restoration clearly is in the right direction and is evidence of good Forest Service stewardship.

To reduce wear and tear, backcountry camping regulations in both the national park and Indian Peaks require backpackers to obtain wilderness camping permits. Differences exist between the Forest Service and Park Service permit systems. Permit applications and rules for camping in specific zones in Indian Peaks are available from USDA Forest Service offices at 2140 Yarmouth Avenue, Boulder, CO 80301; (north side of town along US 36) 9 Ten Mile Drive, P.O. Box 10, Granby, CO 80446; 1311 South College, Fort Collins, CO 80524; and 161 Second Street, Estes Park, CO 80517. Permits are also available at Indian Peaks Ace Hardware at Nederland Shopping Center in Nederland, Colorado. Backcountry campers in Indian Peaks do not need permits in winter. For more information, call (303) 541–2519.

For hikers, perhaps the main difference between the administration of Indian Peaks Wilderness and Rocky Mountain National Park trails is that leashed dogs can accompany hikers on Indian Peaks trails but not on the national park trails. This is not an inherent difference between the two agencies; leashed dogs may hike on trails in some other areas administered by the National Park Service. Administrators of Rocky Mountain National Park, however, came to feel that problems caused by unsupervised dogs on trails were too great and they banned them from the trails. Leashed dogs may still visit developed outdoor areas within the national park, such as campgrounds and along roads.

This administrative decision came about primarily because a significant number of irresponsible hikers with dogs failed to obey park regulations to keep dogs leashed. Letting dogs run loose conflicted with park wildlife management goals and annoyed or intimidated some park visitors who came to the national park for relief from annoyance.

Those people who hiked with unleashed dogs did not understand that they were jeopardizing canine companionship on park trails and decreasing the wilderness value of the national park. Even hikers who kept their dogs on leashes probably failed to understand that the future of dogs on trails in the national park was grim.

Since they lost the right to hike with their dogs on national park trails, dog owners were eager for dogs to be allowed on the trails of Indian Peaks. In public hearings preceding Congressional

213

establishment of Indian Peaks Wilderness, various witnesses proclaimed the virtues of hiking with dogs. Unfortunately, leash regulations were often violated. Proposals to ban dogs from Indian Peaks have met with heavy public opposition, however, as the community of dog owners has learned to define the value of dogs in the wilds and to suggest effective management alternatives to a complete ban. These include self-registration of hikers with dogs at trailheads, backcountry-use permits, limited access of dogs to certain trails, and special-use permits. Present Indian Peaks regulations, however, merely require that all dogs be leashed; violators are subject to fine.

The Forest Service deems peer pressure to be more effective than fines in enforcing the leash regulation. To help with this cause, the American Dog Owners Association printed pocket-sized cards entitled "A Few Good Reasons to Leash Your Dog," which the Forest Service hands out to dog owners. The Forest Service encourages dog owners to take several copies of these cards (available from the Forest Service office in Boulder) to hand out to other dog owners encountered on the trails of Indian Peaks.

Forest Service managers strive to accommodate hikers' desires to hike with dogs because dogs contribute to the purposes of wilderness preservation in at least nine ways.

1. Pack dogs provide historic association with previous wilderness travelers dating back as far as 11,000 years. (Although leather does not survive like a stone projectile point, we can assume that the leash is one of the oldest of human inventions.)
2. Dogs share their senses of smell and hearing with humans, pointing out natural occurrences that we otherwise would miss and frustrating the rare mountain lion that might consider humans its prey.
3. Pack dogs expand human appreciation of scenic values by making room in human packs for binoculars, cameras, and guidebooks.

4. Even on relatively short hikes, pack dogs can be important for families who need to carry extra things for small children or hikers who are a bit infirm due to chronic skeletal problems brought on by years of toting heavy packs.

5. Dogs are the easiest pack animals to transport to trailheads, requiring less room for parked vehicles.

6. Dogs have less impact on the wilderness than any other pack animal; they do not pose grazing competition for wild animals, reduce trailside flowers, or erode trails.

7. Dogs, with a couple of paws still in the world of wild canines, help hikers step outside a strictly human viewpoint. Dogs thereby become what John Muir described as windows through which he looked with greater sympathy into all other living things.

8. Traveling wilderness trails is supposed to be fun, and many people have more fun when accompanied by dogs they regard as family members. This is especially true of the increasing number of childless people.

9. Canine companionship allows a hiker to enjoy the wilds alone, without the inherent discomfort that solitude instills in many humans, just as human companionship relieves the discomfort a dog feels when separated from a pack.

To gain most of these benefits, hikers need to leash their dogs. Dogs also benefit from leashes. Leashing a dog is the only way to prevent it from drinking from streams and lakes, a practice certain eventually to infect the dog with giardia, native parasites that cause the same gastric discomfort and diarrhea in dogs as in humans. (Dogs, like humans, should drink only purified water, excellent contents for dog packs.) Leashes also protect dogs from becoming lost, which happens far too often, and leashes protect dogs from unfamiliar hazards, such as porcupines, predators, and precipices.

Clark's nutcracker on subalpine fir

East of the Divide (Roosevelt National Forest)

Because trailheads are situated relatively high on Indian Peaks east of the Continental Divide, many destinations are close to roads. The combination of short easy trails to spectacular spots and proximity to a large urban area guarantees crowds at Indian Peaks.

There are two ways to avoid the crowds. First, start hiking at dawn. This practice is less painful than it seems and yields benefits far too numerous to list. Second, get together with hiking friends and use two vehicles, leaving them at opposite trailheads. Thus, one group can start at each trailhead, rendezvous on the trail and exchange car keys. Alternatively, you can set up a complicated shuttle and have everyone begin at the same trailhead. Starting in one spot and ending in another is a logistical bother, however, so relatively few people do it. Somewhere between the two trailheads, the crowds begin to thin out. Of course, you also experience more terrain this way.

Pawnee Pass Trail

To reach trailheads in the **Brainard Lake** area, drive to the old mining town of Ward on Colorado Highway 72. Just north of Ward, turn west at a sign that indicates the paved access road to Brainard Lake.

Early in the season (June), this road may be closed at a temporary trailhead a few miles from the highway. A 0.3-mile hike past this road closure takes you to **Red Rocks Lake,** which has a good view of striking peaks to the west. After 1.7 miles more you reach Brainard Lake, a highly developed but very scenic campground area. A paved road circling the lake runs one-way to the right, crossing a bridge at the outlet. The road is the shortest route on foot to the Long Lake and Mitchell Lake Trailheads.

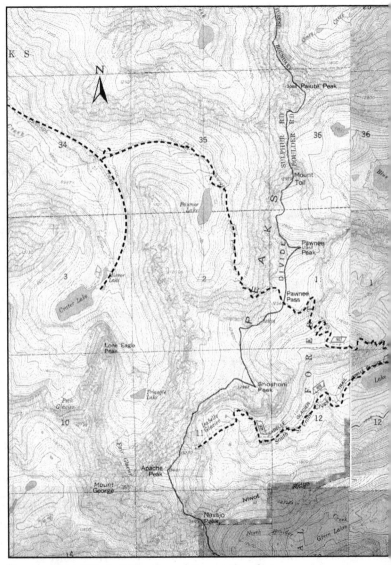

Pawnee Pass, Mitchell Creek, and Beaver Creek to Mount Audubon Trails

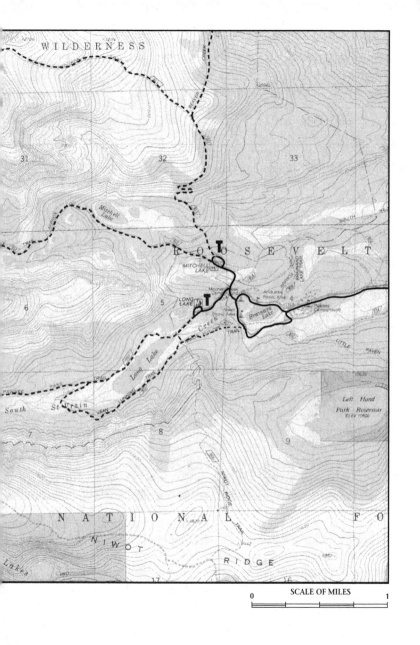

31

32

33

R O O S E V E L T

Mitchell
Lake

MITCHELL
LAKE

5

Mitchell Lake

Arikaree Picnic Area

4

Brainard Lake

Pawnee Campground

LONG
LAKE

6

Long Creek

Long Lake

South St Vrain

7

8

9

Left Hand
Park Reservoir
ELEV 10600

RAVEN

LITTLE

N A T I O N A L

F O

N I W O T

R I D G E

Lakes

17

16

Once the access road is free of melting snow, the soggy sub-alpine soil presumably has dried enough to withstand the tramping of thousands of booted feet. Hoping that everybody will stay on trail, the Forest Service then opens the access road all the way to Brainard Lake and the two trailheads. At a fork in the road on the west side of Brainard, 5.7 miles from CO 72, you can turn right to reach the trailheads. About 200 yards up this road, you reach another fork. To the right are the Mitchell Lake Trailhead and Beaver Creek Trailhead; to the left is the Long Lake Trailhead. The Pawnee Pass Trail, which connects Long Lake with Lake Isabelle, begins at the Long Lake Trailhead.

Forest Service practice reserves the parking areas at the Long and Mitchell Lakes trailheads for day hikers. Backpackers who wish to leave a car overnight should drop their gear at the trailhead (with a friend to stand guard) and park the car at designated areas about a half mile back down the road toward Brainard Lake. This practice makes for more efficient use of parking space and cuts down on the demand for land to be bulldozed and paved.

Nature Walk to Lake Isabelle (Subalpine Zone)

The forest around the Pawnee Pass Trail is a good example of the subalpine zone of vegetation. Many hikers feel that a path in this zone provides the most pleasant walking found anywhere. The first stretch of the trail is particularly nice because it is flat.

The dominant growth along the way is Engelmann spruce and subalpine fir. Both are short-needled conifers whose needles grow individually from the twigs. Close examination reveals obvious differences between the two trees. The easiest test is to grab a branch. If it hurts, the tree is a spruce. Spruce needles are four-sided, stiff, and sharp. Fir needles are flat, soft, and blunt.

There are other differences as well. Engelmann spruce cones are brown, have parchmentlike scales, and hang down from the branches. You probably can see some of these small (less than 2 inches long) cones that have fallen to the ground. Fir cones, on the other hand, are dark purple to black and grow erect in the top of the tree. When fir cones are ready to spread their seeds, the scales do not open as do those of spruce and pine. Rather, the scales merely fall off, leaving the cores of the cones standing bare and upright.

The trunk of a subalpine fir is generally smooth and gray in color; after it grows to a foot or so in diameter, it becomes furrowed near the base. Blisters containing pitch are scattered over the smooth bark. The bark of an Engelmann spruce begins to flake off while the tree is still young. With age the trunk becomes red-brown and develops a scaly texture.

The plant life along this section of trail is relatively lush because the subalpine zone, extending from 9,000 feet to about 11,500 feet above sea level, gets more moisture than any other zone in Colorado. More than 22 inches of annual precipitation is normal here, almost double the amount expected down on the plains. Snow blown from the mountaintops accumulates in this zone, providing moisture vital to luxuriant growth.

Protected by the trees from wind and hot rays of the sun, snow remains here far into the summer. Melting slowly, snowbanks serve as reservoirs, constantly watering the trees during their short growing season. Thanks to the steady water supply, the forest grows taller and denser, providing more shade to protect more snow to nourish more growth, and so on in a circle of cooperation. There is a fascination in this system's efficiency that only water-starved westerners can appreciate fully.

The forest shade is not the only reason for a supply of water. The forest floor is rich with years' accumulation of rotting needles and other plant material. Their decay adds humus to the bits of minerals produced by disintegrating rock. The combination of organic and inorganic material creates fine-grained dark soil that retains water.

In drier areas in the mountains, where plant growth is much slower, little organic material is contributed to the soil. There the soil is light in color and consists of larger particles. It has no humus to hold it together, and water percolates quickly away. In the case of water so essential to plant survival, it is surely true that "them that has, gets."

Forming a continuous ground cover over much of the damp forest floor is grouseberry, or broom huckleberry. This type of blueberry has small leaves that turn bright red in fall, and tiny urn-shaped flowers, which mature to small red berries. The berries are fairly tasty, although less so than some other members of the blueberry family. They are a favorite food of many species of wildlife, including the blue grouse.

Flowers common in shady areas along the trail include Jacob's ladder, with sky blue blossoms and ladderlike leaves whose leaflets grow opposite each other on a central stalk, and arnicas, which are totally yellow composites. Growing in sunny areas is the brilliant, dark pink fireweed, named not for its color but for a tendency to invade areas that have been opened up by forest fires or other disturbances, such as avalanches.

Less conspicuous plants are the lichens, the gray-green splotches that you see on rocks next to the path. Lichens represent a relationship in nature called mutualism, or symbiosis—a partnership between algae and fungi. The algae, which contain chlorophyll, produce food for the fungi. The fungi, in turn, absorb and store water for the algae. They cooperate so well that lichens thrive where no other plants can survive. On bare rocks in hot deserts and in the frigid Arctic, lichens of many varieties display the advantages of partners working together for their common good.

These crusty plants actually contribute to the disintegration of rocks and the building of soil. Lichens adhere very strongly to the rock surface. When they are wet, their colors (which can be far more varied than they are here) are brilliant, but when they dry out and their colors fade, they shrink or curl up. This small movement tends to loosen the bits of rock to which the lichens are attached, causing some particles to fall away as sand.

Lichens further break down rock by secreting small amounts of organic acids, which, mixed with water, gradually dissolve the bonding material that holds the rock together. Such acids are comparatively weak, of course, and the wearing away of a rock is not noticeable in several human generations.

Soon after leaving the trailhead, you see the woods to your left opening up along the banks of South St. Vrain Creek. The name of St. Vrain is scattered all over the Indian Peaks and Wild Basin areas, and it has a colorful history. The brothers Ceran and Marcellin St. Vrain were nineteenth-century traders who swapped goods with Native Americans in exchange for furs and hides.

The profit was vanishing from the beaver trade in 1837, when the St. Vrain brothers built Fort St. Vrain on the South Platte River, yet they and their partners, the Bents, managed to do well. Experienced traders, they exploited the expertise of mountain men like Kit Carson, who knew the trapping business well but had been reduced to picking the bones of a dying trade. Such men still operated efficiently in the Colorado Rockies, which had not yet been trapped out like the mountains farther north in Wyoming.

The site of the St. Vrain trading post was well chosen, being easily accessible to Native Americans. The Bents and St. Vrains were the fairest traders in a generally unscrupulous business. Soon their honorable dealings had gained them the entire business of the Southern Cheyenne and most of the Arapaho. By their unheard-of honesty, they were able to maintain a nearly permanent truce among their constantly warring customers in the vicinity of the post.

But mainly the St. Vrains were just smart businessmen: They diversified. Their economic base consisted not only of the very shaky beaver trade but of trade with Santa Fe and a general retail business. Eventually, after gold was discovered, there was a St. Vrain trading post in the new town of Denver.

South St. Vrain Creek, which you see from the Pawnee Pass Trail, flows into a creek that in turn flows into the South Platte just upstream from the St. Vrain brothers' 1837 trading post. The peaks that surround you were named for the St. Vrains' Native American customers.

Big-rooted spring beauty

A quarter mile from the trailhead, **Long Lake** is reached. Here, just inside the wilderness boundary, the trail divides. The left-hand branch crosses the bridge and divides again: A turn to the left on the Niwot cutoff trail takes you back down to Brainard Lake at the Niwot picnic area. A turn to the right takes you on a loop trail (Jean Lunning Trail) that circles Long Lake, providing fine views of the jagged peaks rising overhead, and meets the Pawnee Pass Trail above the lake.

From the east end of the loop trail, the Niwot Ridge Trail heads uphill to the tundra slopes on broad **Niwot Ridge.** If you elect to go all the way to the ridge top, you will arrive at the boundary of the Boulder Watershed. The city of Boulder is very diligent about keeping people out of this area, however, and you would be better off acceding to its wishes.

It is even more important to avoid disrupting the natural history experiments being conducted on Niwot Ridge by the Institute of Arctic and Alpine Research. Years of data collecting can be ruined by one careless step or handling of markers. It also is wise to refrain from poking around inside the mountain research station building that IAAR maintains on the ridge.

Back on the Pawnee Pass Trail, at the east end of Long Lake, follow the right-hand fork along a level grade roughly parallel to the lake's northern shore. Long Lake is long indeed, extending about a third of the way to Isabelle Lake. In several places the trail is built up above bogs. These are excellent spots to observe the results of plant succession.

Pools of water are formed by glacial action or by the blocking of drainages by beavers or human beings. Tiny algal plants are the first vegetation to invade these pools. Some algae float; others find a home on wet rocks at the water's edge. Among the rocks, moisture-loving mosses and liverworts (some species resemble lobed livers; *wort* is Old English for "plant") also establish plant communities. These pioneer plants help to create soil on the margin of the pond, as do lichens on the surface of a rock. Although it is a small beginning, it is important.

The seeds of various plants land on the mud at the shoreline. Others end up in shallow water; still others come to rest in deeper water. Then they germinate and grow according to specific adaptations to specific pond environments. Some species grow submerged entirely in deep water. Others are rooted in mud in shallower water, and their leaves float on the surface. There are no floating-leaf varieties along this path, but they are obvious in Red Rocks Lake, which you passed en route to Brainard Lake.

The most common and varied seed-producing water plants are the sedges, rushes, and water grasses growing in shallow water along the pond's margin. Various willows and other deciduous shrubs spring up around the soggy shore. Farther from the water are dry land grasses and then the coniferous forest. You can easily see most of these concentric zones of vegetation in the marshes next to Long Lake.

Year after year the plants grow and die, slowly depositing layers of organic material. The process of decay builds soil composed mostly of humus. Humus and other material carried by wind and running water gradually fill in the pond, lowering the water level and drying out the margins.

Plants that require drier habitat invade the filled-in edges of the pond. The ones that need water over their roots begin to grow in a ring closer to the pond's center as the entire body of water becomes shallower. Plants requiring deep water, which no longer exists, no longer can survive in the pond.

The plant life continues to change as the pool gradually shrinks and is succeeded by marsh, which is succeeded by meadow, which is succeeded by forest. In the subalpine zone, plant succession stops with Engelmann spruce and subalpine fir, the so-called climax plants. Of course, fire can destroy a spruce-fir forest, including its humus soil. In such a situation, lodgepole pine and quaking aspen tend to succeed. Centuries later, spruce and fir again will take over and will grow until beavers or people build another pond or until fire sweeps the area once more. Change is the most universal condition in nature.

The flowers that are obvious along this section of the Pawnee Pass Trail are typical of wet subalpine areas. White marsh marigold is the first to appear after snow has melted in the sunny bogs. In midsummer, rose crown, with its fleshy leaves, is very conspicuous. The deep pink spikes of elephant head blossoms are beautiful from a distance and fascinating close-up. Each blossom looks like the flower's name. Fireweed grows in drier areas, a brightly garbed herald of the encroaching forest.

Past the marshes, the trail once more enters pure subalpine climax forest. Frequently on grand old trees you will see burls, which are flattened hemispheres bulging from the trunks. A burl generally originates at the site of an adventitious bud, a bud that grows at an abnormal place, such as the side of a tree trunk, where the plant is not putting on any length. Such buds have no vascular system to carry water or minerals to nourish growth. The buds are eventually covered by trunk tissues—burls—having very dense, contorted, wild, and disorderly grain structure. Such analogous growths on humans are termed cancer.

We hope that the medical term will not spoil burls for you. Burls are benign in that they do no harm to the tree. When trees are cut for lumber, burls themselves can be valuable. Their natural shape suggests their transformation into wooden bowls, which are much desired for their beautiful mottled grain. The grain makes burls appropriate as veneer, thin slices of wood used to overlay less attractive wood, particularly in furniture.

Furthermore, burls are beautiful growing on the tree. The way their round shapes contrast with the rough texture of the bark inspires some very fine photos. Often a tripod and a slow shutter speed are necessary for getting maximum depth of field in close-ups in less than bright forest light.

The philosopher of Ecclesiastes stated that God "has made everything beautiful in its time." That broad generalization is proven true in the forest, where even a cancerous deformity becomes a thing of beauty. Conservationist John Muir observed that all things in nature, "however mysterious and lawless at first sight they may seem, are only harmonious notes in the song of creation, varied expressions of God's love."

About three-quarters of a mile from the trailhead, and in other places along the trail, you may notice a familiar-looking plant, a clover. Its leaves and flowers are easily recognized. Although there are native clovers in the Rockies, the clovers growing alongside this section of trail are aliens. They were introduced here by horses that ate hay brought in from the plains. The hay contained clover seeds, which passed through the horses' digestive systems and were deposited along the trail, fertilized and ready to grow.

No horses have been permitted on the Pawnee Pass Trail since 1965. Therefore it seems that these alien plants have been maintaining their population for a significant length of time without the help of any new seeds. So far as is known, the alien clover does not have a serious impact on the local ecosystems, but man's accidental introduction of alien organisms into natural areas often has been catastrophic. Water hyacinth clogs waterways in the South; alien insects have caused the destruction of chestnuts, elms, and dogwoods in the East. Many more horror stories emphasize that we must be extremely careful not to introduce chaos into a delicately balanced system.

Past the western end of Long Lake, the trail divides. The left-hand fork is the loop trail around the lake. The right-hand fork begins, gradually at first, to climb toward Lake Isabelle and Pawnee Pass.

Soon the way levels out, and you will notice more marshland on the left. This is a classic example of plant succession, showing almost all the stages. There still remains a central pool, but it has been taken over almost completely by marsh.

This pool was considerably larger following the retreat of the last glacier 8,000 years ago. The moving masses of ice carried rocky rubble to this point and dropped it when the ice melted. The ridge or moraine thus formed was piled up next to an older landform, and the depression between them filled with water.

Plant succession began very slowly at first because there was little time for plant development in the short growing season and little or no soil for plant habitat. But succession picks up momentum, progressing at ever increasing speed as more and more plants throw themselves into the task of creating soil. In terms of land formation, succession at the marsh is racing along at this time. Some change might be observable within one human generation.

As you walk past the marsh, high jagged peaks that have been hidden from sight for the last mile come into view to the west, supplying new drama and awesomeness. The sculpting power of snowflakes becomes immediately impressive.

About 27,000 years ago, the climate in this area cooled to the extent that snow at the top of the mountains failed to melt in summer. Snow began to accumulate in the low places between the peaks, where wind from the west dumped extra amounts and where it was protected to some extent from the sun. As more and more snow piled up, the bottom layers were crushed by the weight of the upper layers. The compacting pressure squeezed out all the air spaces, creating a solid mass of ice under perhaps 100 feet of snow. Eventually, the weight of snow and ice became so great that it forced the ice at the bottom to flow downhill, like molten plastic.

As a glacier flows, it carves the surrounding mountains in several ways. At the headwall, where the glacier first forms, summer meltwater seeps into cracks in the rocks, only to refreeze at night or when winter returns. As it freezes, water expands, forcing the cracks to widen and eventually wedging off chunks of rock. The chunks are frozen into the glacier's mass and carried away in its flow.

Through the centuries this quarrying action forms steep cliffs, many of them shaped like bowls. The cliff-sided basin at a glacier's headwall is called a cirque. A part of a cirque is visible on the left side of Shoshoni Peak, the main double-pointed summit that dominates the view from the trail. The cirque's distinctive shape is not obvious from here though. You will be able to pick out two classic cirques from Lake Isabelle.

As a glacier moves downhill, it quarries the rock beneath it too. In this way it widens the floor and steepens the walls of the valley through which it flows, giving the valley a typical U-shape. Simultaneously, the ice carves away at softer areas of bedrock, forming giant ledges or stairs on the valley floor. The tons of rock carried by the ice act as the rasps on a file, enabling the glacier to scour basins on the ledges. When the ice finally melts, the basins become glacial lakes, or tarns. Lake Isabelle is a tarn sitting on such a shelf.

To reach **Lake Isabelle,** you must leave the nearly level grade where you have been walking and turn onto switchbacks that climb through the forest. It may seem easier to bypass the switchbacks and head straight uphill. This course might be quicker, but presumably you are having a good time and are in no big hurry to finish your walk.

More importantly, shortcutting switchbacks does great harm. It causes unnecessary wear to the vegetation and soil, setting up a perfect path for destructive erosion. In one area along these switchbacks, the Forest Service is trying to restore land severely damaged by shortcutting hikers.

Many folks are surprised to learn that trails are designed not so much to be easy on hikers as to be easy on the terrain. It is a happy arrangement that trails that protect the land also follow the easiest way to walk.

At the top of the switchbacks, you traverse a steep meadow with a brook tumbling down it. The meadow is lush with colorful wildflowers. Particularly eye-catching is the dark pink Parry's primrose, which grows right next to the water or on a cushion of soil atop rocks in the middle of the stream.

Ford the stream and bear left. Lake Isabelle is situated on the other side of a low ridge facing you to the west. Very likely you will have to cross a short patch of snow to get there.

Lake Isabelle has been enlarged by a small dam and converted to a reservoir. When the water is drawn down (as happens more and more frequently), the lake becomes an ugly mudflat, commemorating the corruption of what could be one of the loveliest tarns in Colorado. In any case, the mountains are always fine. As you face the lake, the long ridge rising behind you on the left is Niwot Ridge. The conical peak is Navajo; the double-humped peak to the right of Navajo is Apache. Shoshoni, on the far right, was pointed out earlier. There is a cirque with a permanent snowfield between Navajo and Apache, and a second one between Apache and Shoshoni. In this second cirque lies Isabelle Glacier, the source of South St. Vrain Creek.

Isabelle Glacier is the most easily accessible glacier described in this book. Like all the other glaciers in the area, it was born just 3,000 years ago during a slight cooling following a period when the climate was warmer than today. It is not a very active glacier; it is barely holding its own against the sun.

To reach Isabelle Glacier, follow a path along Lake Isabelle's northern shore. At the western end of the lake, follow South St. Vrain Creek upstream from the inlet until krummholz forces you to the right. Ascend over rocks and through small gullies, surmounting a series of glacial ledges toward the eastern end of the glacier, roughly 2 miles from the eastern end of Lake Isabelle.

An irresistible urge to climb up the glacier and slide down comes over some hikers at this point. That is unfortunate, because the rocks at the bottom of the glacier have no trouble resisting sliders who splat down against them at high speed. The glacier is especially steep on the Apache Peak side. There have been serious injuries and at least two fatalities here. Be careful.

No marked path exists up **Apache Peak,** but the least difficult route is obvious from the glacial shelves above Lake Isabelle. Bearing southwest of the South St. Vrain Creek drainage, pick your way over the boulders and head for the saddle on top of Apache between the left (lower) and right summits. Note a very steep slope covered with large loose rocks, called talus, to the right of the permanent snowfield between Navajo and Apache.

This talus slope is the least difficult way past the cliffs that guard Apache's east face. Please do not kick the loose rocks down on the heads of the climbers below you.

The most popular route for climbing **Navajo Peak** begins in the same way as the route up Apache, on the glacial shelves above Lake Isabelle. On the level, bouldery floor of the cirque below Navajo's permanent snowfield, turn left to head up "airplane gully." Of the two obvious ravines on Navajo's flank, it's the one on the left, marked by the wreckage of a late 1940s plane crash scattered throughout its entire length and at its base.

Airplane gully is full of small loose rocks, called scree. This stuff is extremely difficult to walk on (wade through) because it keeps slipping underfoot and carrying you back downhill. Even worse, it presents the real threat of accidentally bombarding climbers below with dangerous rocks.

A group's best method of overcoming this gully is to climb very close together so as to catch bounding rocks before they can pick up momentum. Stay alert to what is happening above. No stolid concentration on your feet here; you'd miss a lot of scenery that way, anyhow. Short gaiters are nice for keeping rocks out of your boots.

At the top of the gully, turn right onto a tundra saddle. Continue west straight up the southeastern shoulder of Navajo toward the cliff-bound summit tower. At the base of the southeastern section of the tower, look for a vertical gully, or chimney, that provides an interesting but easy climb to the summit.

Back in the meadow at the northeast end of Lake Isabelle, the trail to **Pawnee Pass** turns to the right. It climbs for a short way, then veers left (west), following a contour above the lake. About three-quarters of the way along the northern shore, it runs through a series of switchbacks that climb to a bench situated about 1,000 feet above Lake Isabelle. There is a good overlook of the lake and excellent views of Navajo Peak as the trail winds up this bench toward Pawnee Pass. At a final series of switchbacks, you leave the tundra of the bench and climb through boulders to more tundra at the pass.

West of Pawnee Pass, the trail goes downhill to **Pawnee Lake.** The slope is very steep and rocky, and the path is the most masterful example of sinuous, switchbacking trail construction in the entire area covered by this book. (For a description of Pawnee Pass Trail beyond Pawnee Lake, see Cascade Trail to Pawnee Pass in the West of the Divide chapter). The spire-decked western cliffs of Pawnee Peak are certainly worth a photo themselves, and they make a dramatic frame for a picture of Pawnee Lake. Photos of the spires need a hiker in the distant foreground to provide size perspective.

Turning right from the trail at Pawnee Pass, you can follow the Continental Divide over easy terrain, given the nearly 13,000-foot altitude, to the top of **Pawnee Peak.** Continuing north along the divide from Pawnee Peak is considered by many to be the easiest way up Mount Toll (see Mitchell Creek Trail).

To climb **Shoshoni Peak,** strike left (south) from the Pawnee Pass Trail just before the final set of switchbacks east of the pass. Traverse the steep, rocky slope to the saddle between Shoshoni and an unnamed rise south of Pawnee Pass. Once on the saddle, you face a gentle tundra walk almost to the summit. The last 10 or 20 feet up the summit knob requires an easy rock scramble that might make acrophobic folks nervous.

Mitchell Creek Trail

To reach the Mitchell Creek Trailhead, drive to the road junction beyond Brainard Lake, 5.7 miles from Colorado Highway 72 (see Pawnee Pass Trail). A right turn at the fork in the trailhead access road about 200 yards from the Brainard Lake road takes you to the trailhead parking area, which is reserved for day use only. Backpackers should leave their cars at the designated parking places close to Brainard Lake.

The Mitchell Creek Trail begins on the left-hand (southwest) side of the parking lot. (The Mount Audubon Trail System begins on the north side.) Mitchell Creek is less than a half mile away; the path runs fairly level through fine subalpine woods. After crossing the creek, the trail bears to the left, winds uphill to the level of **Mitchell Lake** and meanders through more open woods to the lake itself. You may want to compose a photo of Mount Audubon rising from behind the trees on the opposite shore. At the outlet end of Mitchell Lake you can take a picture of Mount Toll, prominent behind a relatively low ridge at the side of Audubon.

The trail climbs the Mitchell Creek drainage for about a mile beyond the lake to a large snowbank near tree line. Far into the summer the stream's channel-cutting underneath the snow and tumbling over rocks make an interesting photo, with Toll rising over a ridge in the background. The trail passes to the right of this snowbank (over it, earlier in the season) and continues over rock slabs and around outcrops to reach **Blue Lake** at tree line, 2.4 miles from the trailhead.

Mount Toll soars more than 1,600 feet right out of the water. The lake is frozen well into summer, thawing first at the spot where Mitchell Creek cascades over a waterfall into the northwestern end. The stream tumbles from a shelf 500 feet above Blue Lake, on which is located a fairly good-sized tarn unofficially called **Little Blue Lake,** the source of Mitchell Creek.

To reach this tarn, follow a faint path around Blue Lake's northern shore as far as the waterfall. Be careful there. It is farther—straight down—to the lake than you would imagine. The frigid water will instantly paralyze anyone who falls in. Boots and cameras are heavy, and the lake is 100 feet deep. From the falls, follow Mitchell Creek very steeply upstream to Little Blue Lake.

To climb **Mount Toll** from Blue Lake, circle to the waterfall via the track on the northern shore, then climb to a glacial shelf above the lake and traverse south along the base of Toll. Below the saddle between Toll and Pawnee Peak, the mountain to the left, head straight uphill by whatever route looks least steep to reach the saddle. From there it is an uncomplicated boulder hop to the summit. This route is less popular as an ascent than as a descent for climbers who have reached the saddle by traversing the top of Pawnee Peak from Pawnee Pass (see page 232). Similarly, you can climb **Paiute Peak,** located north of Mount Toll, from Little Blue Lake.

Ascend an extremely steep energy-sapping gully filled with loose rock to the low point in the ridge between Paiute and Mount Audubon, to the northeast. The preferred route, however, is to climb Mount Audubon first, follow the ridge to Paiute, and then use the steep gully for the descent.

Mount Audubon Trail System

The Beaver Creek Trail to Mount Audubon begins at the north (right-hand) side of the Mitchell Creek Trailhead parking lot. The path climbs steadily to the northwest through typical subalpine forest for more than a half mile to a long set of switchbacks. From the western end of the second switchback, you get a fine view of Mount Toll rising behind a steep rocky slope of Mount Audubon. As the trail zigzags, the trees change to limber pines, then back to scrubby spruce and fir as you near tree line.

A short distance above tree line, the trail divides. The Beaver Creek Trail continues straight ahead and eventually leads to Coney Flats Trailhead. There the trail heads due west, eventually connecting to the Coney Creek Trail and the Buchanan Pass Trail (see Routes from Beaver Reservoir).

At the trail division a short way above tree line, the **Mount Audubon Trail** goes to the left and bends up a gradual tundra slope. In July and August, displays of alpine wildflowers are excellent in this area. Watch for alpine pedicularis, whose deep pink blossoms are uncommon on the tundra.

The trail winds across tundra toward a large snowbank, then zigzags up some distance to the right of it. The terrain is very rocky in the switchbacks; it is an excellent place to see cushion plants such as moss campion. Once above the switchbacks, the trail levels on tundra. Follow the tundra uphill into the saddle immediately north of the main bulk of Audubon. Turn sharply to the left and climb steeply, following cairns and snatches of trail to the summit. Watch for big-rooted spring beauty; it has white blossoms tinged with pink blooming around a large rosette of fleshy leaves, which turn brilliant red in autumn. This plant seems to be much more common on Audubon and the rest of Indian Peaks than on the mountains farther north in the national park.

You can descend from Audubon by the same route you ascended, or you can descend the southwestern ridge to climb **Paiute Peak**. From the saddle between Audubon and Paiute, the easier route tends toward the northern side of the ridge and up to Paiute's summit. Glaciers cut high cliffs that drop steeply on all sides. Be careful.

Descend Paiute from the low point in the ridge between Audubon and Paiute, via a very steep gully to the Mitchell Creek drainage. There is much loose rock in this narrow couloir; be careful not to kick it down and batter the body of a fellow climber. When you finally reach Blue Lake, an easy tramp of 2.5 miles lies ahead to the Mitchell Creek Trailhead parking lot, where you began hiking. This is an excellent and exciting circle trip, one of the very few with no worries about shuffling cars.

Beyond its junction above tree line with the Mount Audubon Trail, the **Beaver Creek Trail** ascends straight ahead on the right. After a few yards, it descends by relatively easy grades and a few wide switchbacks toward Coney Flats, a broad open area along Coney Creek. Soon after it begins its descent, the path reaches tree line, a mixed limber pine, Engelmann spruce, and subalpine fir woodlands.

This path is a pleasant walk that crosses branches of Beaver Creek and passes the junction of the so-called Stapp Lakes Trail. Actually, the Stapp Lakes Trail goes nowhere near Stapp Lakes, which are on private property visible from above tree line on Mount Audubon. The Stapp Lakes Trail comes out on a four-wheel-drive road connecting Coney Flats with Beaver Reservoir.

From where the Beaver Creek Trail reaches Coney Flats, it is a 3.5-mile hike through lodgepole pines down a four-wheel-drive road to Beaver Reservoir and a road passable by normal passenger cars.

Routes from Beaver Reservoir

To reach Beaver Reservoir, drive 7.4 miles on Colorado Highway 72 south of its junction with Colorado Highway 7, or 5.8 miles north of the town of Ward. Turn west on an unpaved road and drive 2.5 miles to a roadside parking spot on the northern shore of Beaver Reservoir.

This is the beginning of a 3.5-mile four-wheel-drive road to **Coney Flats,** a wide, open area made marshy by beaver activity around Coney Creek. This road definitely should not be attempted in a normal passenger car. There is room to park a few cars at the spot where the four-wheel-drive road leaves **Beaver Reservoir.** Additional parking is available on Forest Service land bordering the road immediately before you reach the reservoir.

Walking up the four-wheel-drive road takes you through easy grades in lodgepole pine forest past an occasional beaver-made marsh. This road has large, loose, rounded rocks that vehicles constantly dislodge. The rocks are hard on your feet. After 2 miles this road splits; hikers go right and vehicles, left. The hiking route originally was also for vehicles and still contains large rocks that are no easier on the feet than the road surface. The split at least separates backcountry pedestrians from automobiles.

Hikers for a while follow the top of the south wall of Middle St. Vrain Valley. The valley is barely visible through the trees, but you still get the feeling of being on the edge.

After more than a mile of segregation, hikers arrive at a short reintegration of their route with the four-wheel-drive road and a branch of Coney Creek, which they cross on a bridge. Here the **Beaver Creek Trail** arrives from the south. Follow this trail to a nearby second bridge that takes you across Coney Creek at the Indian Peaks Wilderness Boundary. This is the end of the four-wheel-drive road at the Coney Flats Trailhead.

From the trailhead, the broad trail runs toward **Buchanan Pass,** the low saddle (11,837 feet) with a permanent snowfield below it and to the left, 3.5 miles west of Coney Flats. The trail is in good condition, running first through quaking aspens and limber pines, then through Engelmann spruce and subalpine fir. Ultimately, trees give way to tundra and tundra to rocks as the trail snakes steeply through switchbacks to the pass. A left turn at Buchanan Pass leads across a half mile of tundra, gaining 467 feet of elevation to **Sawtooth Mountain,** the easternmost point on the Continental Divide.

About 0.2 mile from the Coney Flats Trailhead, the Coney Lakes Trail branches left (southwest) from the main trail and follows the Coney Creek drainage to **Coney Lake** and **Upper Coney Lake** (about 2 and 3 miles, respectively). Beyond the lower lake, the route becomes less distinct and more rugged. Upper Coney Lake has a very dramatic setting in the cirque between Paiute Peak and Mount Audubon.

Especially around Upper Coney Lake, the steep slopes covered with loose rocks are ideal habitat for the pika, or cony (also spelled coney). This little round-eared cousin of the rabbit has caused a certain amount of confusion about locations. Nearby to the north in Rocky Mountain National Park's Wild Basin is Cony Lake, source of Cony Creek. The two spelling variations of the animal's name are no help in alleviating the confusion.

After 1.4 miles from where the Coney Lakes Trail branches left, another trail branches right (north) to **Red Deer Lake.** (On maps, this trail to Red Deer Lake is called the Buchanan Pass Trail because it heads to the pass from the Middle St. Vrain Valley. The easiest way to the pass, however, is from Beaver Reservoir, as described earlier.) The first part of the trail to Red Deer Lake is fairly easy, ascending over snowfields in early summer that later melt to boost wildflower displays. However, as you pass over the top of the ridge and begin to descend more steeply, interior alarms begin to ring that perhaps you missed the lake somehow. Fear not. Before descending all the way into the Middle St. Vrain Valley, the trail switchbacks to climb again toward the lake.

Eight-tenths of a mile from the previous trail junction, you can turn left to ascend rather steeply toward Red Deer Lake. The right branch descends gently to an old sawmill site and the St. Vrain Glacier Trail along Middle St. Vrain Creek. The Red Deer Lake Trail climbs steadily for about a half mile to the open, rocky glacial debris of the Red Deer Lake basin and the lakeshore.

Red Deer Lake, about 6.5 miles from Beaver Reservoir, is a rock- and krummholz-rimmed tarn enlarged by a small dam. Red deer is the European name for the animal that Americans call elk. From the place where the trail reaches the lakeshore, you can see a mountain called Elk Tooth peeking over the top of a ridge on the opposite side of the lake. In the entire area covered by this book, these two features are the only ones named for the most spectacular animal you are likely to see along the trails.

Another four-wheel-drive road, a little less than a mile long, connects Coney Flats with the Middle St. Vrain road. The Middle St. Vrain road is a trail, but the connecting track to Coney Flats is for folks who enjoy repairing their vehicles. It has deteriorated to the point that only hikers can get much pleasure out of the thick spruce-fir forest through which it passes.

Middle St. Vrain Trail System

To reach the Middle St. Vrain Trail System, turn west from Colorado Highway 72 at Peaceful Valley onto an unpaved road. Peaceful Valley is situated 4 miles south of the junction of Colorado Highways 7 and 72, or 9.2 miles north of the town of Ward. Follow the unpaved road for a mile to the second campground, Camp Dick.

The 5-mile road beyond Camp Dick is a severe trial even for high-clearance four-wheel-drive vehicles, so hikers riding in a normal passenger car must begin to walk. For a very pleasant 4 miles, the Buchanan Pass Trail follows Middle St. Vrain Creek from Camp Dick to the wilderness boundary. Although it is called the Buchanan Pass Trail, the trail along Middle St. Vrain

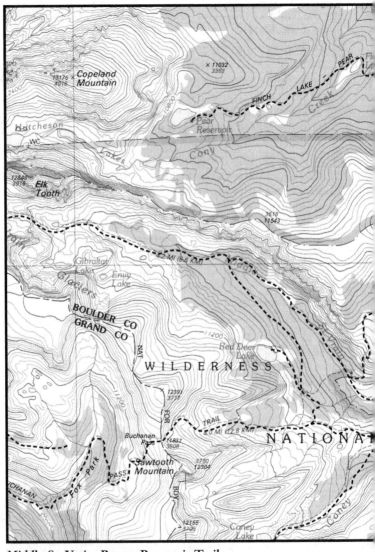

**Middle St. Vrain, Beaver Reservoir Trails,
and East End Buchanan Pass Trail**

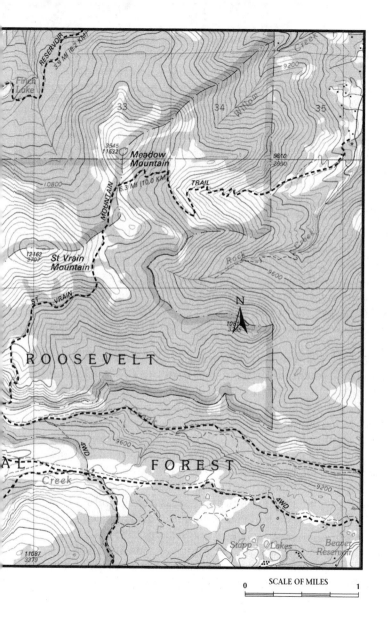

RESERVOIR

3.9 MI (6.2 KM)

Finch Lake

9200

33   34   35

Wild Creek

3545
11632

Meadow Mountain

9810
2990

6.3 MI (10.0 KM)   TRAIL

10800

MOUNTAIN

12162
3707

St Vrain Mountain

Roc   Creek

9600

ST   VRAIN

N

109
33/6

R O O S E V E L T

9600

4WD

A L   F O R E S T

9200

Creek

4WD

11087
3379

Stapp   Lakes   Beaver Reservoir

SCALE OF MILES

0   1

Creek is not the easiest route to the pass (see Routes from Beaver Reservoir). Just inside the wilderness boundary, the St. Vrain Mountain Trail (see page 243) climbs very steeply to the right.

The Buchanan Pass Trail continues west from the wilderness boundary along an old logging road now closed to bicycles and motorized vehicles. About 1.3 miles west of the St. Vrain Mountain Trail intersection, you reach a fork in the trail. The Buchanan Pass Trail bears left to cross the creek on a log bridge, beginning a long switchback east that leads eventually to the pass. About 1.1 miles along the way is the trail that branches up to Red Deer Lake (see Routes from Beaver Reservoir).

Veering right at the fork takes you up the Middle St. Vrain Valley on the St. Vrain Glacier Trail. Eventually, a bend to the left climbs 0.5 mile into a cirque containing **Lake Gibraltar,** source of Middle St. Vrain Creek. The outlet from Lake Gibraltar flows at once into a smaller lake unofficially called **Little Lake Gibraltar.** Over a low ridge to the east of the trail at Lake Gibraltar there is another cirque, which contains **Lake Envy.** Towering above all these lakes are spectacular cliffs on which hang **St. Vrain Glaciers.**

For those who can drive to the road closure, the Middle St. Vrain Trail System offers alternative routes to two Wild Basin destinations. To reach **Hutcheson Lakes,** leave the trail about 3.5 miles beyond the road closure. Climb over loose rock up the very steep north wall of the Middle St. Vrain Valley wherever it looks least difficult. From the top of the ridge between Middle St. Vrain and Cony Creek drainages, descend with care over more loose rock to Hutcheson Lakes.

A shorter approach to **Ogalalla Peak** leads to a much more difficult final climb than do the approaches from Ouzel Peak or Cony Pass. When the trail bends south to Lake Gibraltar, keep going west, uphill, to a small tarn unofficially called **Pika Lake.** Continue on to the head of the Middle St. Vrain Valley, and climb into the cirque containing the largest and northernmost of the St. Vrain Glaciers. Ogalalla lies straight north of this body of ice. Between the cliff above the glacier and the peak there is a very steep slope covered with loose rock. Climb this talus slope to the lowest point on the skyline southwest of Ogalalla. This spot is on the Continental Divide. Once there, you have a short walk east over relatively level tundra to the summit of Ogalalla.

St. Vrain Mountain Trail

The trail to Meadow and St. Vrain Mountains begins near the town of Allenspark, which is on Colorado Highway 7, about 17 miles south of Estes Park. To reach the trailhead, turn right off CO 7 onto Business Route 7 (across the road from the fire department), which winds through Allenspark. After 0.6 mile turn right onto an unpaved road. The road is named Ski Road, but the sign might be missing. (There is another Ski Road off of Business 7 a short distance from CO 7, so be sure you drive 0.6 mile before turning on the second—possibly unsigned—Ski Road.)

After 0.5 mile, Ski Road comes to a T-junction; turn left. Follow this road another 0.9 mile to Roosevelt National Forest. At 0.3 mile inside the forest boundary you will reach a fork (1.2 miles from the T-junction). The left-hand fork goes downhill to Rock Creek and miscellaneous four-wheel-drive logging roads. The right-hand fork goes uphill about a half mile to the St. Vrain Mountain Trailhead.

To reach **Meadow Mountain,** follow the trail as it zigzags through a wide and long slope cleared by forest fire for more than 2 miles up to krummholz. Once above tree line, strike off for the rounded hump of Meadow to the north whenever it looks convenient. The final scramble up Meadow is very rocky but, logically enough, the top is covered by alpine meadow, thick with tundra flowers in July and August. The summit marks the Rocky Mountain National Park boundary.

The St. Vrain Mountain Trail levels below Meadow Mountain and heads south through mixed tundra and krummholz. Another rounded hump, which rises ahead to the southwest, is **St. Vrain Mountain.** From the trail in the saddle east of the mountain, you gaze over boulders and patches of tundra to the summit, 700 feet above. The summit of St. Vrain, also on the park border, is about 4 miles from the trailhead. From there you get good views north to Longs Peak, Mount Meeker, and the eastern end of Wild Basin. To the southwest are many fine but nameless peaks overlooking Middle St. Vrain Creek.

For about 0.5 mile along the ridge between Meadow and St. Vrain Mountains, the trail runs just inside the boundary of Rocky Mountain National Park. This passing from one jurisdiction to another occurs because of a boundary adjustment made to conform with natural topographic divisions. Park Service managers wisely treat this bit of trail as though it were in the national forest.

From St. Vrain's summit you may see hikers laboring up the St. Vrain Mountain Trail from Middle St. Vrain Creek. St. Vrain Mountain is harder to climb from the south. From the summit, the trail appears to drop into the Middle St. Vrain Valley—and it does.

Some maps indicate a trail heading from the St. Vrain Mountain Trail, a short distance south of the saddle below the summit, downhill into the valley of **Rock Creek.** This route soon wanders through a maze of elk paths in marshes and krummholz at the creek's source. Below tree line, it enters another maze, this one of logging roads cutting through the forest. These roads can be driven only with four-wheel-drive vehicles, but they are easily walked. Follow your feet downhill; they will naturally take you on the logical road near Rock Creek, away from St. Vrain Mountain. This route is used mostly by people out for a walk from lovely unimproved campsites they have discovered beside Rock Creek.

Arapaho Glacier Trail (Glacier Rim Trail)

The Arapaho Glacier Trailhead is located in Rainbow Lakes Campground. To reach the campground, drive on Colorado Highway 72 for 5 miles south of Ward or 8 miles north of Nederland. Turn west on an unpaved county road identified as the road to the University of Colorado Mountain Research Station. The road forks after 0.8 mile; take the left-hand fork for a bumpy 4-mile drive uphill to the campground. Drive all the way through the campground and park at its west end.

A trail to **Rainbow Lakes** begins at the very end of the road. It is a short, easy walk up to these ponds, which are connected by a web of fishermen's trails. From the highest lake you can look up past subalpine forest to a small cirque and the long tundra ridge of Caribou, a 12,310-foot projection unspecified except by the name of a deer.

A few dozen yards from the beginning of the trail to the lakes, the Arapaho Glacier Trail leaves the northwestern side of the campground. A sign marks it as the Glacier Rim Trail.

The trail begins by climbing steeply through the forest, then moderates its grade along the fence marking the border of the Boulder Watershed. Numerous signs will inform you as to which side of the fence you should travel. More than a mile from the trailhead, the path turns left away from the fence and zigzags nearly to tree line.

From the crest of a ridge above the trees, you can look down on the beautiful valley of the south fork of North Boulder Creek. Again the edge of the Boulder Watershed is marked; occasional signs may name the reservoirs below. At the head of the valley, to the west, a line of grand but unnamed 12,000-foot peaks follows the Continental Divide. The "thirteeners," North Arapaho and Arikaree, are high points on the left and right of your view. Mount Albion stands out massively across the gorge.

Be sure to photograph the valley and the peaks before you follow the trail in a sharp left turn up the ridge. As you climb higher past the switchback, the lake-filled valley will drop below your view. The peaks still will be magnificent but will rise out of a tundra slope somewhat less dramatically than from the depths of the valley.

The tundra where you walk is well carpeted with flowers; alpine sunflowers may be the most prominent. Through wide switchbacks the trail winds up the slope north of Caribou, then flattens on top of the ridge. Peak baggers may wish to walk a few

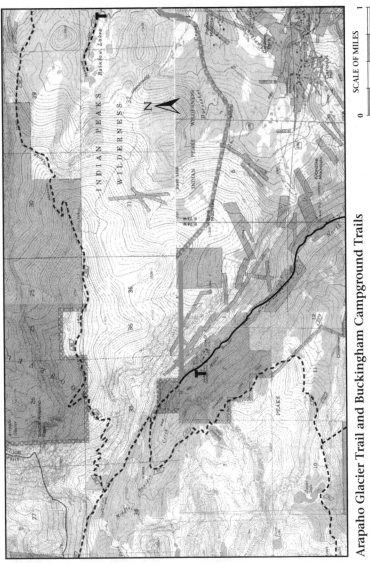

Arapaho Glacier Trail and Buckingham Campground Trails

dozen yards to the left (east) of the trail to the cairn marking the top of Caribou. Because several bumps on the same ridge are hundreds of feet higher than this point, we speculate that it was singled out to be named because it was visible from some point below. Try to step on rocks, and avoid trampling the rosettes of fleshy leaves that belong to the big-rooted spring beauty.

Past Caribou the trail crosses to a south-facing slope and switchbacks up the ridge. Above 12,600 feet the path undulates gradually across the tundra for a few miles. The view of colorful alpine flowers at your feet competes with the view of rugged peaks and hanging lakes across the valley to the south. Six miles from Rainbow Lakes Campground, the trail joins another coming up from the valley of North Fork Middle Boulder Creek. (Yes, the watercourses around here have confusing names.)

From the junction, walk uphill a few yards to the **viewpoint for Arapaho Glacier,** the southernmost glacier in the Rockies. The dramatic conical mountain rising directly above you is **South Arapaho Peak.** The route to the top is easy to follow over boulders on the south slope, to the left of the east-facing cliffs. A bronze peak finder is cemented into the summit to elaborate on the fine view, especially to the south and west as far away as Mount of the Holy Cross.

The climb over to **North Arapaho Peak** is somewhat more challenging. It is a half-mile trip—farther than it appears. The route involves boulder scrambling and a little easy climbing. Before you have gone far on the southwestern side of the ridge extending between the two Arapahos, splashes of red paint appear on the rocks, marking the route. (These are camouflaged in autumn, however, when the abundant rosettes of the big-rooted spring beauty turn bright red.)

It seems to us—and we are not avid rock climbers—that the route to North Arapaho is interesting without being scary or exposed to dangerous falls. Yet we have met enough wide-eyed folks returning from the peak and exclaiming that they had stared death in the face to suggest that our assessment is wrong.

Or perhaps some of the climbers bothered by exposure to long falls got off-route too far to the right and too close to the east-facing precipice above the glacier.

Anyone who has had enough climbing experience to use a rope effectively will probably be experienced enough not to need one on North Arapaho. But a rope in the leader's hands, belaying a nervous member of the party, may be a useful psychological protection. At any rate, all climbers should be extremely careful.

There is a huge cairn on the summit of North Arapaho—from far and wide a visible monument to the activity of the human species *Homo constructus*. You can climb the cairn to have your picture taken on the tip-top of the mountain or hold a square dance on the monument, if you like. But the best subject for a dramatic photo is a secondary promontory south of the true summit. The photographer stands on the true summit, focusing across at fellow climbers atop an absolutely sheer cliff that juts over Arapaho Glacier with South Arapaho behind them. Do not get too daring as you shoot. It is fatally far to fall.

From the Arapaho Glacier viewpoint below South Arapaho, it is only 3.5 miles down to the trailhead at Buckingham Campground. This is about half the distance of the hike back to Rainbow Lakes Campground. Moreover, the trail to Buckingham, on the banks of North Fork Middle Boulder Creek, is very pleasant. Try to work out the logistics of having transportation waiting for you at the campground.

Buckingham Campground Trails

Driving instructions to Buckingham Campground begin at the town of Nederland, west of Boulder at the junction of Colorado Highways 119 and 72. From the south side of Nederland, a half mile from the road junction, turn west toward the Lake Eldora Ski Area. At the spot where the road forks uphill (left) toward the ski area, continue on the lower (right) fork through the town of Eldora. Its pavement ends shortly. A mile past Eldora the road forks again. The left fork soon ends at Hessie (see page 249). The right fork climbs for 4 rough miles to a parking area at the upper end of the campground. Forest Service signs direct hikers to the trail to **Arapaho Pass** and **Diamond Lake.**

Almost a mile up the path, the Diamond Lake Trail drops down to cross North Fork Middle Boulder Creek. From the creek, it winds and climbs through dense subalpine woods and flowery marshes for another mile to the lake. Beyond Diamond Lake, the trail surmounts a lovely tundra ridge before descending to the Devils Thumb Trail, about 2.3 miles from Diamond Lake. A right (west) turn leads after a half mile to **Jasper Lake.**

Another 0.8 mile of trail through the woods to tree line brings you to **Devils Thumb Lake,** dominated by the rock spire that named the lake, rising above a skirt of scree and talus. The route continues past the lake to climb steep tundra and rock slopes to Devils Thumb Pass and the Corona Trail (see the West of the Divide chapter). From Jasper Lake, the broad Devils Thumb Trail descends the Jasper Creek drainage 4.4 miles to Hessie.

The Arapaho Pass Trail climbs past the Diamond Lake Trail junction for less than a mile to the century-old **Fourth of July Mine,** which yielded silver and a little gold. From a trail junction at the mine site, the right-hand path climbs to Arapaho Glacier (see page 247). The left-hand trail cuts steeply uphill for a mile across the rocky slope east of Arapaho Pass. From the pass it is an easy walk over tundra and boulders to **Lake Dorothy,** hanging below Mount Neva. Beyond Lake Dorothy follow an old wagon road to Caribou Pass, or you can descend steeply along a sinuous path from Arapaho Pass to Caribou Lake; it is a long way back up (see Caribou Pass Trail in the West of the Divide chapter).

Trails from Hessie

A quarter mile from the road to Buckingham Campground (see page 248) is the site of the 1890s mining camp of Hessie, a beginning point for trails in the drainage of South Fork Middle Boulder Creek. If beaver dam construction has thwarted the efforts of trailhead reconstruction, you might have to walk the quarter mile from roadside parking to the trailhead. Otherwise, the spur road to the trailhead should be well marked and passable. The trail into Indian Peaks Wilderness once was a four-wheel-drive road, built before the establishment of Roosevelt National Forest. USDA Forest Service signs help guide hikers through a maze of old mining and reservoir roads to popular destinations.

Less than 1 mile up the old road, the Devils Thumb bypass trail to Jasper and Devils Thumb lakes branches to the right. This trail rejoins the old road system on the reservoir service road for Jasper Lake. Heading up the trail on the north side of Jasper Creek and returning down the old road adds variety to a hike to Jasper and Devils Thumb Lakes. Photographers may wish to pay special attention to dramatic cascades on the part of South Fork Middle Boulder Creek just upstream from the old road bridge a few yards beyond the junction with the trail to Devils Thumb Lake.

About a mile up the old road, the quarter-mile Lost Lake Trail heads left to **Lost Lake,** the site of mines that supported Hessie. Just beyond the Lost Lake spur, the **King Lake Trail** heads left to follow South Fork Middle Boulder Creek for 3.5 miles, eventually climbing steeply above tree line to an indistinct splitting of the way. Where the King Lake Trail turns sharply left after reaching a milder grade atop a glacier-carved shelf below the Continental Divide, you can turn sharply right to reach **Betty** and **Bob Lakes,** 6 and 6.2 miles from Hessie. Easy-to-miss snatches of trail here and there lead through krummholz and across moraines to the lakes. Both are dammed by terminal moraines formed during successive pauses in the retreat of a glacier that originated in the cirque now occupied by Bob Lake. The view from Bob up to the divide is particularly memorable. The mosquitoes in August can also be very memorable.

Perched below Rollins Pass, King Lake is 5.2 miles from Hessie. It is an easy 6-mile walk downhill from the crumbled site of Corona, at Rollins Pass, past King Lake to Hessie. Arranging transportation at both ends of the trail can be complicated. The eastern side of the Rollins Pass Road is closed just above Yankee

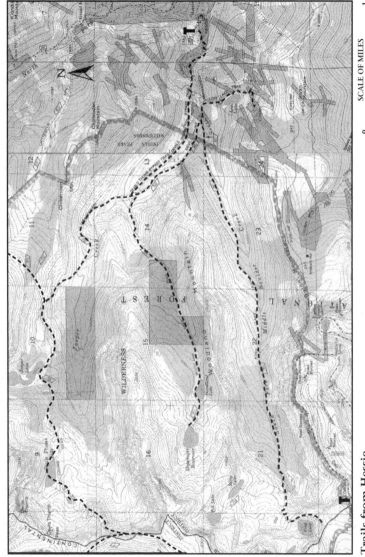

Trails from Hessie

Doodle Lake on the east side. The only way to drive to Rollins Pass is from US 40 near Winter Park (see Corona Trail in the West of the Divide chapter).

Continuing right from the King Lake Trail, the old road follows Jasper Creek to Jasper Lake (see Buckingham Campground Trails). On the way, another branch left leads to **Woodland Lake** and **Skyscraper Reservoir.** Rotting cabins appear from time to time amid raspberry bushes along the old road to Woodland Lake, 4.2 miles from the trailhead. Almost a half mile beyond is Skyscraper, nestled between two ridges jutting east from the Continental Divide. Bob and Betty Lakes are on the opposite side of the lower ridge, seen to the south (left) across Skyscraper. Surmounting this ridge will lead to an alternate route back to Hessie along the King Lake Trail.

West of the Divide (Arapaho National Forest)

I ndian Peaks Wilderness Area west of the Continental Divide has only one destination that is close to a road. Although you must walk a ways to get to most hiking goals, the effort is worth it. To exaggerate the splendor of the west side of Indian Peaks is difficult. The entire area defies hyperbole, yet most of the hiking traffic funnels into one trail system.

Four of the six Indian Peaks trail systems west of the divide are reached from Grand County Road 6 (Forest Development Road 125.1) south of Lake Granby. To reach this road, drive along US 34 to a point 11 miles south of the town of Grand Lake and 6 miles north of the town of Granby. Turn east onto the unpaved road, which winds generally east along the south shore of Lake Granby to Arapaho Bay Campground and Monarch Lake.

After about 9 miles, the unpaved road crosses a bridge over the narrow neck of the southernmost tip of Lake Granby. Past the bridge, Forest Development Road (FDR) 125.1I branches left (north) 0.8 mile to the beginning of the Roaring Fork Trail System. Past the left-hand branch to Roaring Fork, the unpaved road (FDR 125.1) from US 34 bends right (south) and dead-ends after about a mile at a parking lot a short distance from Monarch Lake (see Buchanan Pass Trail, Cascade Trail to Pawnee Pass, and Arapaho Pass Trail).

As we mentioned earlier, regulations for wilderness use in the national forest are not terribly different from regulations instituted to protect the national park backcountry. National forest regulations require backcountry camping permits. For more information, see the chapter National Park and National Forest —Two Administrative Styles.

Roaring Fork Trail System

The parking lot for the Roaring Fork Trail System is on the right (east) side of the road, near the Forest Service's Arapaho Bay Campground's Roaring Fork Loop.

The Roaring Fork Trail heads east from the trailhead and climbs immediately through steep switchbacks above Arapaho Bay to a welcome level stretch that leads to a crossing of Roaring Fork. (Roaring Fork was a fork of Arapaho Creek until Lake Granby backed up, converting Arapaho Creek into Arapaho Bay.) In easy grades the trail follows the broad Roaring Fork Valley upstream, sometimes in marsh, sometimes in lodgepole pine. In a wide, shrubby meadow about 2.5 miles from the trailhead, turn right to recross Roaring Fork.

Beyond the crossing, a trail branches left (north), zigzagging 1.5 miles up to **Watanga Lake.** From the last of three level stretches, just below the last series of switchbacks up to the lake, is a fine view of the Fraser Valley below and the Continental Divide above. Flower-filled subalpine woods become ever more delightful as you climb higher. Finally, you reach the top of a terminal moraine that dams Watanga Lake. The lake is relatively small, and the peaks above are not as spectacular as is normal in Indian Peaks. A gravel bottom around the edge supports water grasses, providing spawning habitat and good feeding areas for a rather dense trout population (mostly rainbows, some brown). This trail usually melts free of snow by mid-July.

Beyond the branch to Watanga Lake, the Roaring Fork Trail climbs steeply through deep woods and flowery meadows to the **Irving Hale Divide,** a broad saddle north of Mount Irving Hale. This section of trail has only a few switchbacks to lessen the grade. It is a real lung-popper until you reach the Irving Hale Divide. Here displays of wildflowers—tall chiming bells, yellow senecio, various colors of paintbrush—can be spectacular, especially when the trail sloshes through bogs. Paintbrush is abundant also in the drier subalpine meadows, along with some alpine flowers extending their range down from the tundra.

Mount Irving Hale is an easy climb up a tundra ridge from the Irving Hale Divide. On the double-humped top of Irving Hale are two large cairns. From a distance they look like two mountaineers standing watch over Hell Canyon. The summit is about 2 miles from the crossing of Roaring Fork.

Vistas from the top of Irving Hale are magnificent. To the west, Lake Granby stretches out in Middle Park, and the Gore Range defines the horizon. Mount Toll, Paiute Peak, and Mount Audubon tower on the southeastern skyline. Hell Canyon extends to the east, with Crawford and Long Lakes far below your feet at the base of craggy cliffs on Irving Hale.

Back down at the Irving Hale Divide, the trail descends slightly to the east past ponds and puddles. Early in the season, abundant glacier lilies testify to heavy snow accumulation. In a particularly lovely meadow with a fine view east to the Continental Divide, a tumbledown log cabin can add a romantic element to your photos.

Descending past this old sheepherder's cabin, the trail drops along a ridge into **Hell Canyon.** Another view of Crawford Lake is visible during the descent. It is possible, from a point a mile below the Irving Hale Divide, to descend cross-country to Crawford and Long Lakes. A sometimes faint path continues down Hell Canyon to the Cascade Trail, Monarch Lake, and down 2 miles of road to Arapaho Bay Campground, where you began hiking.

The trail to Stone Lake continues on, marked in faint stretches by rock cairns. **Stone Lake** lies in a stone basin that was scoured out by a glacier roughened into a rasping tool by the tons of rock it carried. Unlike many such tarns, Stone Lake is not particularly deep. Interspersed among the rounded rocks that form its shoreline are patches of subalpine meadow and trees of the forest's upper margin. A narrow track leads up the valley over meadow and rock slabs to **Upper Lake.** The trail stops at Upper Lake, but you can continue upstream over flowery tundra meadows to a pass overlooking Paradise Park. From lake to pass there is a rise of 800 feet in about a mile; the terrain makes for easy walking.

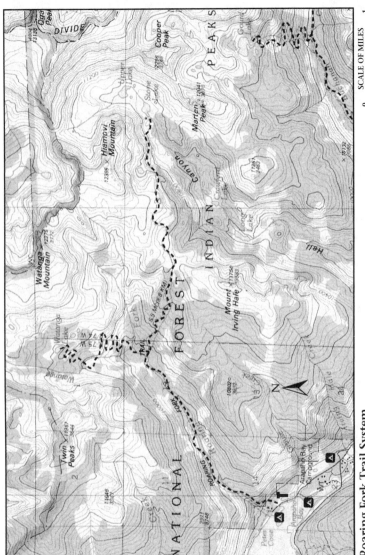

Roaring Fork Trail System

SCALE OF MILES

0   1

The pass is in a unique position between Paradise and Hell. But it is difficult to feel like Dante in a spot where both places are covered with tundra flowers and where Paradise and Hell are sublimely similar. Paradise Park lies within Rocky Mountain National Park and has been set aside as a research natural area. It is a preserve for scientific study; horses and camping are prohibited to maintain this remote mountain valley in a totally pristine condition. If you continue into Paradise Park, please be extra careful to leave no evidence of your passing.

Buchanan Pass Trail

To reach the Buchanan Pass Trail, drive to Monarch Lake. (Driving instructions are at the beginning of this chapter.) Hiking around the lake is a trip of more than 3 miles. The trail along the left (north) shore is the western end of trails traversing both Buchanan and Pawnee Passes. These trails run together for about 1.5 miles along the lakeshore and beyond to a junction where a spur trail branches right. The spur connects with the Arapaho Pass Trail (see page 265) to continue on around Monarch Lake's opposite shore.

The trail to Buchanan Pass and Pawnee Pass bears left from the junction and follows Buchanan Creek. Between a series of switchbacks and a bridge over Hell Canyon Creek, a fishermen's track to the left climbs up Hell Canyon. The path is easy to miss (watch for a charred log as a landmark); if you get to the bridge, just head up the creek or backtrack about 150 feet to the path. It is possible to follow this track up to Long and Crawford Lakes, but this steep trail is better used as a path of descent after having reached Crawford via the Roaring Fork Trail (see page 254).

The Cascade Trail continues on to **Shelter Rock.** This large boulder with overhanging ledges is an easy 4-mile walk from the trailhead at Monarch Lake. A few hundred yards beyond Shelter Rock is another trail junction. The right-hand fork leads up Cascade Creek to Pawnee Pass (see page 261).

The left-hand fork is the Buchanan Pass Trail, which climbs steeply through lodgepole to a more moderate grade at the edge of beaver-made meadows along Buchanan Creek. Continuing to climb gradually, the trail crosses outlet streams of Island Lake and Gourd Lake. About 0.2 mile past the brook flowing from Gourd Lake, you arrive at the junction with the **Gourd Lake Trail.**

The 1,280-foot difference in elevation between the trail junction and the top of the Gourd Lake Trail is gained in a long 2 miles of twisting through innumerable switchbacks. Along the way, the views of Paiute Peak are extremely dramatic. Oddly enough, the best shot can be had from near the bottom as you approach the eastern end of a switchback amid aspens. To frame Paiute with aspen leaves, continue walking a few more yards east, off trail, from where the switchback turns west. Afternoon light is best; a short telephoto lens with polarizing filter will be helpful. Farther up the trail the view expands to include double-topped Mount Toll and, across the valley, Thunderbolt Peak.

When you finally reach **Gourd Lake,** follow a faint trail around to the right (east) shore for the best photos. The surface of the lake's deeply indented bays is frequently still enough to reflect Cooper Peak.

At the base of Cooper Peak, the large tarn called **Island Lake** hangs above tree line. Patches of krummholz around its rocky shores do little to soften the austerity of the setting. The ascent from Gourd to Island Lake calls for a rise of 600 feet in about a mile. Follow the eastern shore of Gourd Lake to that part of the northern shore having the least steep slope above it. Scramble up this slope to a glacial shelf where there is a small unnamed pond. Bear northwest across this shelf and climb up the least steep route to a higher bench where there are more nameless ponds, then contour along the outlet stream past even more small tarns to Island Lake.

The Buchanan Pass Trail continues past the Gourd Lake Trail at an almost level grade until it meets the valley of Thunderbolt Creek. The same glacier that so dramatically sculpted the tower of Paiute carved deeply down the Thunderbolt Creek Valley. It cut faster than a tributary glacier flowing from farther north on the divide at the head of Buchanan Creek. Thus the valley of the

Pygmy nuthatch on Engelmann spruce

tributary glacier was left hanging 700 feet up on the mountainside, overlooking Thunderbolt Creek.

Fox Park lies on the floor of this hanging valley. To get to it, the Buchanan Pass Trail climbs, climbs, climbs through switchbacks distressingly reminiscent of those on the Gourd Lake Trail. Yet if you happen to be at Gourd Lake and want to reach Fox Park (or vice versa), you do not have to lose and regain 1,000 feet of elevation and walk 2 extra miles between these two points. What you do is follow an unimproved but marked and mostly distinct trail that extends directly down to a meadow just above Fox Park from the southeastern slope of a low forested ridge adjacent to the lake's southeastern shore. This route is not appropriate for horses. In a couple of places, the path heads straight uphill to avoid traversing steep rock. In others, it crosses obvious avalanche slopes, which can be very dangerous in early spring. Sometimes it fades away in sheltered places where snowbanks remain into autumn.

But most of the trail is a pure joy of subalpine flowers and magnificent views up Thunderbolt Creek toward Paiute and Toll. Finally, the track fades away completely in a marshy meadow with a good view that will be unavailable in Fox Park, only a short way down a tributary brook to Buchanan Creek.

Buchanan Pass rises in plain sight 1,400 feet above Fox Park. The climb for the next 2 miles promises to be tough, but it looks worse than it turns out to be. The steepest part climbs through classically beautiful subalpine forest, which gives way abruptly to alpine tundra. Farther uphill the trail steepens somewhat again on a rocky slope below Buchanan Pass.

From the pass, you can leave the trail and climb to the south over tundra slopes to the top of **Sawtooth Mountain,** the easternmost point on the Continental Divide. Sawtooth is a half mile from Buchanan Pass and 467 feet higher. To the east there are 3 downhill miles of rocky trail to a four-wheel-drive road at Coney Flats and another 3 miles along this road to a road for passenger cars at Beaver Reservoir (see Middle St. Vrain Trail System and Routes from Beaver Reservoir in the East of the Divide chapter).

Cascade Trail to Pawnee Pass

The trail along Cascade Creek is the most heavily used trail on the west side of Indian Peaks, despite relatively long distances to the most popular destinations. Although the dramatic scenery in Cascade Creek's drainage can be equaled on other trails, it cannot be surpassed. If you have a choice, make every effort to enjoy this trail at times other than obviously crowded holidays and weekends.

The Cascade Trail to Pawnee Pass branches right from the Buchanan Pass Trail at the trail junction 4 miles from Monarch Lake, just past Shelter Rock (see page 257). A short level walk takes you to Buchanan Creek, which is spanned by a substantial bridge. From there a short and rather steep stretch moderated by one switchback leads to the edge of a canyon cut by Cascade Creek. The grade moderates from the canyon edge as you continue up the valley through lodgepole pines.

About a mile from Shelter Rock, the trail bends to the right and crosses the creek on a bridge. The open marshy area here is in a middle stage of plant succession from beaver pond to forest. Located upstream from the old beaver workings is your first clear example of how Cascade Creek got its name. Falls like this, too numerous to be named individually, make the trail itself a hiking destination, rather than merely a route to the lakes at the base of the peaks.

Twisting through many tight switchbacks, the trail climbs along the cascades onto the next highest glacier-cut shelf. The views of rushing water will slow you down even more than the steepness of the climb. Various spur paths branch off to viewpoints of the cascades. If you are in a rush, keep to the right on the main trail. Near the level of the next shelf, the trail bends to the left to recross the creek over water-smoothed rock above particularly fine falls.

A bit more climbing takes you to another broad level area where Cascade Creek meanders lazily through old beaver ponds, seemingly resting before its spectacular rush down the falls. Amid

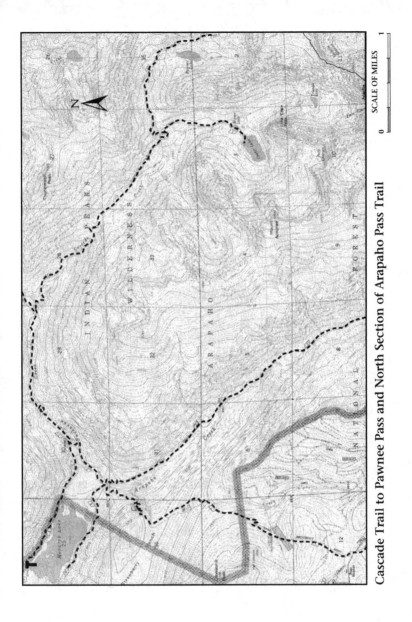

Cascade Trail to Pawnee Pass and North Section of Arapaho Pass Trail

the rock-covered slopes overhead on the left, groves of quaking aspens have pioneered a place to live among the boulders. Leaving the creek on the valley floor, the trail traverses uphill along a sunny south-facing slope. Peaks in the vicinity of Mount George, to the east, draw your attention as you climb.

The trail reenters deep spruce and fir forests before crossing Pawnee Creek. A short winding way uphill is a trail junction, about 7 miles from Monarch Lake. The right-hand fork, Crater Lake Trail, continues up Cascade Creek to Mirror and Crater Lakes.

The Pawnee Pass Trail branches left and recrosses Pawnee Creek. Switchbacks just past the crossing wind up through quaking aspens and narrow spires of Engelmann spruce. These trees are good frames for effective photos of Lone Eagle Peak flanked by Peck and Fair Glaciers (see Crater Lake Trail, page 264).

Variations on this spectacular view continue as the trail climbs east, parallel to Pawnee Creek. Lone Eagle and its glaciers are last seen from an open avalanche slope covered with large boulders. The trail continues ascending through spruce-fir forest into the cirque containing **Pawnee Lake.** The lake is a little more than a mile from the junction of the Crater Lake Trail.

Pawnee Lake is extremely grand. Spires on the slopes of Pawnee Peak, east of the lake, are picturesquely jagged. The glacier-quarried peaks on the north and west, although unnamed, are nearly as spectacular. A wide-angle lens will be very helpful in composing photos in which spruce and fir trees along the eastern shore lead your eye into this picture.

Beyond Pawnee Lake, the 2.5-mile ascent to **Pawnee Pass** is very steep. The path, however, is a remarkable example of superb trail construction. In tight switchbacks, it snakes up terrain that must approach the maximum limit of steepness and ruggedness for trail building. If you climb it, be sure to use your rest stops to photograph over the switchbacks to Pawnee Lake, using rock spires on Pawnee Peak for a frame. East of Pawnee Pass are various trail systems in the vicinity of Brainard Lake (see Pawnee Pass Trail in the East of the Divide chapter).

The **Crater Lake Trail** branches from the Pawnee Pass Trail about 7 miles from Monarch Lake. As you ascend the sometimes wet, sometimes rocky path to Crater Lake, the impossibly pointed spire of Lone Eagle Peak comes into view above the trees, echoing their sky-etching quality. The classic view of Lone Eagle is from **Mirror Lake,** a shallow, rock-rimmed tarn a few hundred yards past the third crossing of Cascade Creek. Fair Glacier is on the left of Lone Eagle, Peck Glacier on the right. A wide-angle lens is needed at Mirror Lake to include Lone Eagle and its reflection in one photo.

Less than a half mile past Mirror is **Crater Lake,** where the view of Lone Eagle is more believable. But the setting of subalpine forest, large deep lake, spires and cliffs of Mount Achonee on the right, incredibly jagged ridge on the left, and the sheer face of Lone Eagle rising straight up to a point is a scene of extravagant grandeur. The one-time occupants of a tumbledown old cabin perched atop glacially smoothed bedrock at the lake's western end had quite a view when they arose each morning.

If you can stop staring at Lone Eagle, there are several interesting hikes to take from Crater Lake. To reach **Peck Glacier,** circle Crater Lake to the right (west), and climb along the base of Lone Eagle's western flank. It is a steep mile from the lake's northern shore to the glacier.

The spire of **Lone Eagle Peak** that is seen from Crater Lake is not a true summit. Lone Eagle really is a jagged ridge extending north from Mount George. The highest point on the ridge (12,799 feet; the spire above the lake reaches 11,950 feet) can be climbed from the east. Cross the outlet stream of Crater Lake to the slopes of loose rock below Lone Eagle ridge. Scramble up this rock, following the base of the ridge.

Eventually, you will come upon snatches of faint trail and cairns that lead south and up rock slabs at a relatively moderate grade for more than a half mile. Watch carefully for cairns, and do not try to cut uphill too soon, or cliffs will block your way. After you are well south of the high point on the ridge, the route cuts back to the north and begins to climb ramps to the ridgeline at a point south of the summit. From here you must descend a few feet over slabs on the western side of the ridge, circling a small spire. This spot is exposed to a long drop and, though not difficult, can be unnerving.

Climbing back over the ridgeline toward the summit spire, you ultimately must head to the right (east) side of the ridge and then ascend to the very top from the northeast. The summit is not so sharp that it hurts to sit on it, but there is room for only a few climbers at a time. The entire climb is exciting, dramatic, and less difficult than it appears from below. On the other hand, Lone Eagle has claimed its share of lives, so be very careful. Turn back when rain threatens to make rocks slick or if you anticipate a storm.

Triangle Lake is an aptly named tarn lying in the valley below the route to Lone Eagle. To reach Triangle, cross the outlet of Crater Lake, and ascend the valley through forest and meadow. Clamber up a short steep barrier of boulders to the lake, about a mile from Crater. Triangle's water is milky, which indicates that powdered rock is being carried into the lake in meltwater from Fair Glacier. Evidently, enough ice is still flowing in the glacier to keep it actively grinding rocks.

Arapaho Pass Trail

The Arapaho Pass Trail begins by following the southwestern (right) shore of Monarch Lake. (For driving instructions to Monarch Lake, see the beginning of this chapter.) About 1.5 miles from the parking lot end of Monarch Lake, the High Lonesome Trail branches off to the right from the Arapaho Pass Trail. Eventually, the High Lonesome Trail connects with trails along the Continental Divide to Rollins Pass. The trail was named for the High Lonesome Mine. Along this section of trail are ruins of a late nineteenth-century cabin near the junction and an abandoned mine 2.8 miles from the junction. Passing through logged areas, the trail descends to the road to Junco Lake, near Meadow Creek Reservoir. (See Caribou Pass Trail.)

Bear left at the High Lonesome junction and follow the Arapaho Pass Trail across a bridge over Arapaho Creek. Just past the bridge, the trail divides. The left-hand branch continues on around Monarch Lake by connecting with the Cascade Trail. The Arapaho Pass Trail turns sharply right and, after a series of switchbacks, climbs a steep slope forested by lodgepole pines. Above the switchbacks, the trail follows a more moderate grade, paralleling Arapaho Creek. Most of the creek is out of sight behind trees and willows, but now and then side trails lead down to the water. The main trail runs south along the base of a steep ridge.

In occasional open spaces, wet-habitat-loving subalpine flowers such as tall chiming bells and monkshood grow thickly. Before long, the lodgepole pines mix with Engelmann spruce and subalpine fir. Gradually, pines become less common and spruce and fir more so until the last lodgepole is left behind in a field of boulders. Except in areas opened up by avalanches, the trail passes through a thick spruce-fir forest, which provides the shade and beauty for a pleasant walk up the long valley. Should you desire to climb **Mount Achonee,** pick one of the avalanche-cleared slopes for the best route to the tundra slopes below the summit.

Just past an avalanche slope about 3.5 miles from the last trail junction, the path climbs away from Arapaho Creek in a series of long switchbacks. It proceeds on a gentle uphill grade for less than a half mile to meet the creek again at a point where a throne-shaped rock has been frost-wedged from the cliff. You might as well rest here; you will rarely find a rock more suitable for sitting.

Past the chair rock, the trail climbs through more switchbacks in forest of increasing density. After crossing various creeks at the mouth of Wheeler Basin, it steepens somewhat, and wildflowers begin to become more abundant. Then the path meanders through the meadows of **Coyote Park.** Early in the season the ground is yellow with snow lilies. From Coyote Park, a route winds left up into Wheeler Basin. Uphill from Coyote Park, the woods are less thick, and the open spaces are multihued with flowers. Switchbacks keep the grade moderate until you reach **Caribou Lake,** at tree line.

Caribou Lake lies in a cirque walled in by cliffs between Arapaho and Caribou Passes. A walk along a narrow trail on the marshy western shore presents superb views across the lake of jagged Apache and Navajo Peaks. Patches of krummholz, willow, and alpine flowers add nice details to the lakeshore in the foreground.

Clearly visible from the lake is the continuation of the Arapaho Pass Trail; it climbs remarkably in many tight switchbacks up the very steep slope of loose rock below **Arapaho Pass.** From a distance, the rock looks like the last word in sterility. But the actual ascent reveals patches of richly blooming tundra flowers growing in loose gravel seemingly devoid of soil. Especially impressive are perfect spheroid cushions of moss campion and broad-leaved or dwarf fireweed, the latter rarely found this far south in the Rockies. The tenuous hold that these heroic plants maintain on the scree is easily destroyed by a careless step. Cutting through switchbacks is bad anywhere, but it would be especially damaging and disgusting on this delicate terrain.

From Arapaho Pass you can descend to the Arapaho Glacier Trail (see the Indian Peaks, East of the Divide chapter) or head west up gradual tundra and rock slopes to Lake Dorothy and beyond that to Caribou Pass, the easiest and most enjoyable gate to Arapaho Pass and Caribou Lake. If you can work out the car shuttle, hiking the Caribou Pass Trail to Lake Dorothy, going downhill to Caribou Lake, and exiting via Monarch Lake is by far the best way to travel the magnificent Arapaho Pass Trail.

Caribou Pass Trail

The trailhead for the Caribou Pass Trail is located on an unpaved road overlooking Meadow Creek Reservoir (on old maps the lake occupies a site called Sawmill Meadow). Begin by leaving US 40 about a half mile east of the town of Tabernash or 3.5 miles north of the town of Fraser. Turn east onto unpaved Grand County Road 84 immediately south of the spot where US 40 crosses a railroad track via an overpass. Very soon the road forks; take the left-hand fork and stay on the main road going to Meadow Creek Reservoir (Forest Development Road 129). Continue past the campground, along Meadow Creek, then follow the main road uphill through switchbacks almost to Meadow Creek Reservoir. Just before you reach the dam, bear left; the road climbs through forest past a great pile of sawdust left from lumbering operations. (*Note:* Meadow Creek Reservoir can be reached on foot via the High Lonesome Trail; see Arapaho Pass Trail, page 265.)

About 3 road miles from the dam (12 miles from the highway), above the reservoir, the road forks again. The main road (FDR 129) goes to the right through an open grassy area. The left-hand fork leads to a parking area at Junco Lake.

From Junco Lake, the High Lonesome Trail winds through meadows and woods, crossing marshes and creeks for 4 miles to Devils Thumb Park and a junction with the Corona Trail (see page 271). Where the way is confused in logged woodlands, follow blazes and red dots on trees and cairns.

To climb the Caribou Pass Trail, hike from Junco Lake up an old roadbed along Meadow Creek past two fallen-down log cabins; the footing is sloppy in places. After about 1.7 miles there is a trail junction. The Caribou Pass Trail goes to the left; the Columbine Lake Trail branches off to the right.

The **Columbine Lake Trail** follows a gradual grade for about 175 yards to the forest edge, where it becomes increasingly steep. A level meadow appears about a half mile from the trail junction, and a third smaller meadow above the second. The trail climbs steeply along Meadow Creek before bending to the left to wander amid boulders and trees, soon meeting the creek again and crossing it. A short climb past the creek crossing takes you to the level of the shelf on which lies **Columbine Lake,** at tree line. The trail mucks around in marsh, half losing itself, before reaching the lake several hundred yards past the stream crossing and 3 miles from the trailhead.

Columbine Lake has numerous slabs of granite along its shoreline that serve well for lunch and relaxation. Glacier-quarried cliffs rise overhead, but the summit of the nearest prominent peak, Mount Neva, sits back out of sight to the south.

To climb **Mount Neva** from Columbine Lake, circle a short way to the right around the western shore, and climb a surprisingly well-constructed trail to an obvious pass in the ridge south of the lake. From the pass climb steeply up the ridge to the summit. It is a long mile from the lake.

Back at the Caribou–Columbine Lake junction, the **Caribou Pass Trail** heads steeply uphill to the left. It climbs through thick subalpine forests and sunny flower-filled meadows. It crosses rivulets and passes bogs and old mine sites, all without a single switchback. But the surrounding wilderness beauty supplies ample inspiration to offset any weariness caused by the direct ascent. Soon you are above tree line and then at **Caribou Pass,** 1.5 miles from the junction.

It is a vast understatement to say that the view to the east from Caribou Pass is spectacular. Your eye will be drawn particularly to the double-humped summit of Apache Peak and the adjacent cone of Navajo Peak, on the right. Caribou Lake lies at tree line, 850 feet below your boots. Uphill from the lake stretches as perfect a terminal moraine as you will ever see. There is a tiny pond behind it, a memento of the melted glacier.

From Caribou Pass, a half mile walk north along the ridgeline takes you to the top of **Satanta Peak.** South of Caribou Pass, the Caribou Pass Trail follows a dramatic wagon route blasted long ago from a cliff face. Large mats of moss campion grow amid rock slides at the trail's edge. After a half mile of trail bordered by cliff and campion, you find **Lake Dorothy,** the highest and deepest lake in Indian Peaks, hanging in a cirque below Mount Neva. A short way down the path beyond Dorothy are **Arapaho Pass** and the trails to Caribou Lake and Arapaho Glacier (see Arapaho Pass Trail, page 265, and Arapaho Glacier Trail in the East of the Divide chapter).

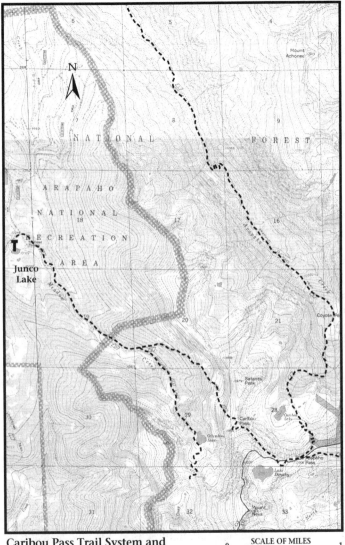

**Caribou Pass Trail System and
South Section of Arapaho Pass Trail**

SCALE OF MILES

0   1

Corona Trail

The Corona Trail runs 6 miles from Rollins (Corona) Pass to Devils Thumb Park—a grand downhill hike if you arrange transportation at both trailheads. The Rollins Pass Road follows part of the tortuous grade of a railroad between Rollinsville and Middle Park. At 11,671 feet, the now crumbled construction town of Corona was the highest railway station in the world in 1901. In 1927, Moffat Tunnel replaced the rails over the pass. East of Rollins Pass, the road is closed. From the west, the Rollins Pass Road leaves US 40 opposite Winter Park Ski Area. Ascent of the 14-mile rough road to the pass takes an hour.

To reach the Devils Thumb Park Trailhead, turn east from US 40 onto County Road 8 on the north side of Fraser. Drive 7.8 miles and turn right on a spur road. Drive 0.3 mile along the spur to park at a dam on Cabin Creek. Cross the creek above the dam, and hike a few yards through the woods before turning left on a four-wheel-drive road that reaches **Devils Thumb Park** after about a half mile.

Finding your way through the maze of beaver-made swamps in the park is interesting. Binoculars help to spot blazes on trees marking the south end of the High Lonesome Trail to the left across the park (see Caribou Pass Trail). A direct tramp to this point will be wet; wend through the woods along the meadow's edge until you strike the trail. To find the Corona Trail, wander toward a barely visible rock "thumb" on the skyline in Devils Thumb Pass (to the right as you enter the meadow from the four-wheel-drive road). Beaver ponds cause detours from the trail, which becomes clear and dry along Cabin Creek beyond Devils Thumb Park.

Traveling from the south end of the trail at Rollins Pass, hike straight uphill (north) to the wilderness boundary. The Corona Trail climbs past a steep descent to King Lake (see Trails from Hessie in the preceding chapter). Avoid a precipitous snowfield east of the pass. A slip and uncontrolled slide to the rocks below have caused at least one serious injury. Soon the Corona Trail reaches a less steep grade and meanders across lovely tundra meadows just below the Continental Divide. To view lakes perched

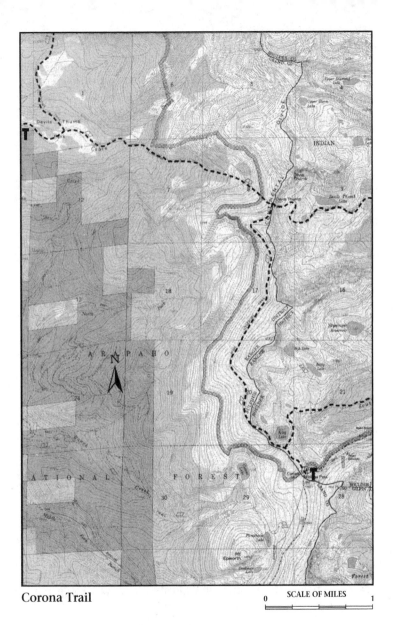

Corona Trail

SCALE OF MILES

0   1

below highly glaciated cliffs on the eastern flank of the divide, hikers have to detour up to the ridgeline. If you do this, tread gently on the tundra. The view of **Devils Thumb Lake** and Jasper Lake when the trail reaches Devils Thumb Pass (3.5 miles from Rollins Pass) is as good as any you receive by detouring.

The thumb is curiously inconspicuous from the pass because the spire blends in with cliffs to the north. The path that crosses Devils Thumb Pass is also inconspicuous but, like the thumb, becomes more obvious below the pass, either to the east (see Buckingham Campground Trails) or to the west on the Corona Trail. Subalpine gardens decorate the trail with myriad colors below willow thickets at tree line as you descend very steeply to the west. The way becomes less steep among lodgepole pine and beaver ponds at a crossing of Cabin Creek. Here the Corona Trail bends left (south) and continues for less than a mile to Devils Thumb Park. From the Cabin Creek crossing, faint paths penetrate the tangled valley to the north, where the creek flows from the flanks of Mount Neva.

Destination Tables

You will find the following abbreviations appearing among more common ones in the destination tables that follow.

CG = Campground
Ck. = Creek
CPW = Comanche Peak Wilderness
Fk. = Fork
Md. = Meadow
NRA = National Recreation Area

R. = Ranger
Res. = Reservoir
Rg. = Ridge
Sta. = Station
TH = Trailhead

Distances to destinations in Rocky Mountain National Park appearing in these tables were determined by Park Service personnel, who pulled wheeled measuring devices over the trails. We determined the distances to off-trail destinations in the national park and national forest by running a measuring device over topographic maps. This method proved to be surprisingly accurate when tested against distances measured on the ground by the Park Service.

Depths of lakes came from direct-measurement figures supplied by the National Park Service and USDA Forest Service. Many lakes have not been measured directly, and in those cases no measurements are given.

Fish species in Rocky Mountain National Park lakes were identified for the U.S. Fish and Wildlife Service by a volunteer, Alan Jones. Information on the fish in Indian Peaks lakes came from the Colorado Division of Wildlife.

Destination	Starting Point	Distance from Start. Pt. (in miles)	Elevation Gain TH to High Pt.	Altitude (in feet)	Alt. Rank National Park	Alt. Rank Indian Peaks	Size of Lake (in acres)	Depth of Lake (in feet)	Fish in Lake
Achonee, Mt.	Monarch Lake	6	4,303	12,649		17			
Acoma, Mt.	Green Ridge CG	4	2,118	10,508	101	35			
Adams Falls	East Inlet	0.3	79	8,470					
Adams Lake	East Inlet	9	2,819	11,210	41		4.6		Colorado River cutthroat
Adams, Mt.	East Inlet	5	3,730	12,121	69				
Alberta Falls	Glacier Gorge Jct.	0.6	160	9,400					
Albion, Mt.	No Access, Boulder Watershed			12,609		18			
Alice, Mt.	Wild Basin R. Sta.	9	4,810	13,310	12				
Andrews Glacier	Glacier Gorge Jct.	5	2,460	11,700					
Andrews Pass	Glacier Gorge Jct.	5.25	2,704	11,980					
Andrews Peak	East Inlet TH	7.5	4,174	12,565	42				
Andrews Tarn	Glacier Gorge Jct.	4.7	2,150	11,390	27		2.4		fishless
Apache Peak	Long Lake TH	6.5	2,861	13,441		2			
Arapaho Glacier	Rainbow Lakes CG	6	2,740	12,700					
Arapaho Glacier Overlook	Buckingham CG	3.5	2,579						
Arapaho Pass	Buckingham CG	3	1,785	11,906					
	Junco Lake	4.5	1,866						
Arapaho Peak, North	Rainbow Lakes CG	7	3,542	13,502	1				
	Buckingham CG	4.5	3,381						

Name	Access								Notes
Arapaho Peak, South	Rainbow Lakes CG	6.5	3,437	13,397		4			
	Buckingham CG	4	3,276						
Arch Rocks	Fern Lake TH	1.5	45	8,200					
Arikaree Peak	No Access, Boulder Watershed			13,150		7			
Arrowhead	Glacier Gorge Jct.	5.5	3,147	12,387	53				
Arrowhead Lake	Milner Pass	6.5	1,050	11,130	47		34.9		greenback cutthroat
Audubon, Mt.	Mitchell Ck. TH	3.75	2,743	13,223		6			
Azure Lake	Milner Pass	7.75	1,150	11,900	3		13.8		fishless
Baker Mtn.	Trail Rg. Rd.	5.5	3,533	12,397	52				
Baker Pass	Trail Rg. Rd.	5.75	2,389	11,253					
Balanced Rock	Twin Owls	3.8	910	8,240					
Bald Mtn.	Caribou (townsite)	2.5	1,340	11,340		32			
Battle Mtn.	Boulder Brook TH	5	3,194	12,044	71				
Bear Lake	On road			9,475	111		11.2	33	greenback cutthroat
Beaver Mtn.	U. Beaver Mds.	2	1,971	10,491	102				
Bench Lake	North Inlet TH	7.5	1,610	10,150	95		6.4	6	Colorado River cutthroat
Betty Lake	Hessie	6	2,451	11,460		4			
	Rollins Pass	1.6	240						
Bierstadt Lake	Bierst L. TH	1.4	566	9,416	112		7.4		fishless
	Bear Lake	1.6	255						

Destination	Starting Point	Distance from Start. Pt. (in miles)	Elevation Gain TH to High Pt.	Altitude (in feet)	Alt. Rank National Park	Alt. Rank Indian Peaks	Size of Lake (in acres)	Depth of Lake (in feet)	Fish in Lake
Bighorn Lake	Milner Pass	0.5	180	10,930	58		0.9	6	fishless
Bighorn Mtn.	Lawn Lake TH	4	2,923	11,463	86				
Big Meadows	Green Mtn. TH	1.8	606	9,400					
Black Lake	Glacier Gorge Jct.	4.7	1,390	10,620	72		9.2		brook
Blue Lake (Indian Peaks)	Mitchell Ck. TH	2.5	840	11,320		7	25.7	100	cutthroat, rainbow
Blue Lake (RMNP)	Glacier Gorge Jct.	5.5	1,900	11,140	45		2.8		fishless
Blue Lake, Little	Mitchell Ck. TH	3.5	1,353	11,833		2			
Bluebird Lake	Wild Basin R. Sta.	6	2,478	10,978	57		22		fishless
Bob Lake	Hessie	6.2	2,591	11,600		3			
	Rollins Pass	1.8	360						
Boulder Field	Longs Peak R. Sta.	5.9	3,360	12,760					
Boulder-Grand Pass	Wild Basin R. Sta.	8	3,561	12,061					
Box Lake	Wild Basin R. Sta.	6.5	2,240	10,740	69		6.4		brook
Brainard Lake	On road			10,360		33	15.6		rainbow, brook, brown, suckers
Bridal Veil Falls	Cow Creek TH	3	1,060	8,900					
Bryant, Mt.	East Shore TH	6.5	2,644	11,034	93				
Buchanan Pass	Beaver Reservoir	6	2,676	11,837					
	Monarch Lake	9.75	3,491						

					CPW				
Cairns, Mt.	East Inlet TH	4.5	2,489	10,880	95				
Calypso Cascades	Wild Basin R. Sta.	1.8	700	9,200					
Caribou	Rainbow L. CG	3.5	2,350	12,310		21			
	Buckingham CG	5.5	2,189						
Caribou Lake	Buckingham CG	3.75	1,785	11,147	12	7	8		cutthroat
	Junco Lake	5.75	1,866						
	Monarch Lake	9.5	2,801						
Caribou Pass	Buckingham CG	4	1,940	11,851					
	Junco Lake	3.5	1,811						
Cascade Falls	North Inlet TH	3.5	300	8,840					
Castle Lake	Wild Basin R. Sta.	6.75	2,650	11,150	44		1.8	15	fishless
Chapin, Mt.	Chapin Cr. TH	1.5	1,814	12,454	50				
Chasm Lake	Longs P. R. Sta.	4.2	2,360	11,760	7		19.3	100	fishless
Chickadee Pond	Wild Basin R. Sta.	4.75	1,510	10,010	98		0.9	4	fishless
Chickaree Lake	Onahu Crk. TH	1.75	525	9,290	113		4.6		fishless
Chief Cheley Peak	Milner Pass	5	2,130	12,804	28				
	Timber Lake	6.5	3,880	13,579					
Chiefs Head Peak	Copeland Lake	7	5,267		3				
Chipmunk Lake	Lawn Lake TH	4.1	2,180	10,660	71		0.1		fishless
Chiquita Lake	Lawn Lake TH	5.5	2,810	11,350	30		3.7	35	fishless
Chiquita, Mt.	Chapin Cr. TH	2.4	2,429	13,069	20				
Chittenden, Mt.	Buckingham CG	3	739	10,860		34			
Cirque Lake	Pingree Park	5.25	1,970	11,000			2.3	13	fishless

Destination	Starting Point	Distance from Start. Pt. (in miles)	Elevation Gain TH to High Pt.	Altitude (in feet)	Alt. Rank National Park	Alt. Rank Indian Peaks	Size of Lake (in acres)	Depth of Lake (in feet)	Fish in Lake
Cirrus, Mt.	Colo. Riv. TH	6.4	3,807	12,797	29				
Clouds, Lake of the	Colo. Riv. TH	6.9	2,440	11,430	23		11.2		fishless
Columbine Falls	Longs Pk. R. Sta.	4	2,160	11,440		15			
Columbine Lake	Junco Lake	3	1,000	11,040					
Comanche Peak	Corral Ck. TH	6.75	2,702	12,702	37				
Coney Lake	Beaver Res.	5	1,439	10,600		29	9	21	cutthroat
Coney Lake, Upper	Beaver Res.	6	1,779	10,940		18	16	31	cutthroat
Cony Lake	Finch L. TH	9	3,042	11,512	19		16.5		fishless
Cony Pass	Wild Basin R. Sta.	7.25	3,860	12,360					
Cooper Peak	Roaring Fork TH	7.75	4,015	12,296		23			
Copeland Falls	Wild Basin R. Sta.	0.3	15	8,515					
Copeland Lake	On road		117	8,312					
Copeland Mtn.	Wild Basin R. Sta.	6.75	4,676	13,176	16				
Cracktop	Milner Pass	5.5	2,010	12,760	30				
Craig, Mt.	East Inlet TH	7.5	3,616	12,007	73				
Crater, The	Milner Pass	1	730	11,480					
Crater Lake	Monarch Lake	8.25	1,934	10,280		34	20	78	brook, cutthroat
Crawford Lake	Roaring Fk. TH	7.25	1,789	10,070		37	2	3	cutthroat, rainbow

Crystal Lake	Lawn Lake TH	7.7	2,980	11,520	18		24.8	125	greenback cutthroat
Crystal Lake, Little	Lawn Lake TH	7.5	2,972	11,512	19		3.7	20	fishless
Cub Lake	Cub Lake TH	2.3	540	8,620	115		10.1	3	fishless
Cumulus, Mt.	Colo. Riv. TH	5.6	3,735	12,725	31				
Dark Mtn.	McGraw Ranch	4	3,019	10,859	96				
Deer Mtn.	Deer Rg. Jct.	3	1,083	10,013	108				
Deserted Village	North Fork TH	3	200	8,160					
Desolation Peaks	Chapin Ck. TH	5.5	2,309	12,949	21				
Devils Thumb Lake	Hessie	5.2	2,131	11,140		13			
	Rollins Pass	4.4	253						
	Buckingham CG	6.5	1,019						
Devils Thumb Pass	Rollins Pass	3.5	253	11,747					
Diamond Lake	Buckingham CG	2	1,191	10,920		19			
Dickinson, Mt.	North Fork TH	14	3,871	11,831	77				
Dorothy, Lake	Buckingham CG	3.5	1,940	12,061		1	16	100	cutthroat
	Junco Lake	3.5	2,021						
Doughnut Lake	Milner Pass	7.25	1,050	11,250	37		7.4		fishless
Dream Lake	Bear Lake	1.1	425	9,900	103		5.5	14	greenback cutthroat
Dunraven, Lake	North Fork TH	10.75	3,300	11,260	35		11.2		fishless
Dunraven, Mt.	North Fork TH	11.75	4,611	12,571	41				

Destination	Starting Point	Distance from Start. Pt. (in miles)	Elevation Gain TH to High Pt.	Altitude (in feet)	Alt. Rank National Park	Alt. Rank Indian Peaks	Size of Lake (in acres)	Depth of Lake (in feet)	Fish in Lake
Eagle Cliff	Moraine Park	0.5	786	8,906	112				
Eagle Lake	Wild Basin R. Sta.	6.75	2,310	10,810	64		11.9		fishless
Eagles Beak	Wild Basin R. Sta.	7.25	3,700	12,200	74				
Elk Tooth	Middle St. Vrain	9	4,210	12,848	26	15			
Embryo Lake	Glacier Gorge Jct.	3.5	1,120	10,360	83		0.1	3	fishless
Emerald Lake	Bear Lake	1.8	605	10,080	96		6.3		fishless
Emerald Mtn.	Glacier Basin CG	0.5	637	9,237	111				
Emmaline Lake	Pingree Park	5.5	1,930	10,960	CPW		5.7	23	cutthroat
Enentah, Mt.	East Inlet TH	3	2,390	10,781	97				
Envy, Lake	Middle St. Vrain	8	2,382	11,020		16	2	18	cutthroat
Estes Cone	Lily Lake TH	3.7	2,369	11,006	94				
	Longs Peak R. Sta.	3.3	1,606		94				
Eugenia Mine	Longs Peak R. Sta.	1.4	508	9,908					
Fairchild Mtn.	Lawn Lake TH	8.75	4,962	13,502	6				
Fair Glacier	Monarch Lake	9.75	3,814	12,160					
Falcon Lake	Wild Basin R. Sta.	7.5	2,560	11,060	53		4.6		fishless
Fall Mtn.	Corral Ck. TH	7.5	2,258	12,258	62				
Fay Lakes	Lawn Lake TH	6	2,210-2,660	10,750-11,200	42		4.6 (Middle)	26	fishless
Fern Falls	Fern Lake TH	2.7	645	8,800					

Lake	Access	Distance	Elev. Gain	Elevation	Acres		Depth	Max	Fish
Fern Lake	Fern Lake TH	3.8	1,375	9,530	110		9.2	31	greenback cutthroat
	Bear Lake	4.7	1,215						
Fifth Lake	East Inlet TH	9.25	2,459	10,850	62		7.4	15	Colorado River cutthroat
Finch Lake	Finch Lake TH	4.5	1,442	9,912	102		7.4	15	fishless
	Allens Park TH	3.8	1,392						
Flatiron Mtn.	Corral Creek TH	5	2,335	12,335	56				
Flattop Mtn.	Bear Lake	4.4	2,849	12,324	58				
Forest Canyon Pass	Milner Pass	2	530	11,280					
Forest Lake	Rock Cut	2	-2,258	10,298	87		7.4	8	
Fourth Lake	East Inlet TH	8.25	1,989	10,380	82		7.4	20	brook
Fourth of July Mine	Buckingham CG	2	1,119	11,240					
Fox Creek Falls	McGraw Ranch	3	660	8,400					
Frigid Lake	Wild Basin R. Sta.	7.75	3,315	11,815	6		11.9		fishless
Frozen Lake	Glacier Gorge Jct.	5.75	2,340	11,580	14		7.4		fishless
Gabletop Mtn.	Bear Lake	7	2,849	11,939	76				
Gem Lake	Twin Owls	1.8	910	8,830	114		0.2	5	fishless
	Gem Lake TH	2	1,090						
George, Mt.	Monarch Lake	10.25	4,530	12,876		14			
Gilbraltar Lake	Middle St. Vrain	7.75	2,562	11,200		9	5.7	44	cutthroat
Gilbraltar L., Little	Middle St. Vrain	8	2,562	11,200		9	2.0	18	fishless

Destination	Starting Point	Distance from Start. Pt. (in miles)	Elevation Gain TH to High Pt.	Altitude (in feet)	Alt. Rank National Park	Alt. Rank Indian Peaks	Size of Lake (in acres)	Depth of Lake (in feet)	Fish in Lake
Glacier Knobs	Glacier Gorge Jct.	1.75	985	10,225					
Glass, Lake of	Glacier Gorge Jct.	4.2	1,580	10,820	63		4.6		brook, greenback, cutthroat
Gourd Lake	Monarch Lake	8	2,454	10,800		24	2.0	50	cutthroat
Grace Falls	Bear Lake	3.25	1,215	10,280					
Granby, Lake	On road			8,280	Arapaho NRA				rainbow, brown, kokanee
Grand Lake	On road			8,367	116				rainbow, brown, kokanee
Granite Falls	Green Mtn. TH	5.2	1,046	9,840					
Granite Pass	Longs Pk. R. Sta.	4.2	2,680	12,080					
	Glacier Gorge Jct.	6.8	2,840						
Green Knoll	Nvr Sum Ranch	5	3,396	12,280	60				
Green Lake	Glacier Gorge Jct.	5.75	2,310	11,550	15		3.7		fishless
Green Mtn.	Green Mtn. TH	2	1,519	10,313	106				
Hagues Peak	Lawn Lake TH	9	5,020	13,560	4				
	North Fork TH	13	5,600						
Haiyaha, Lake	Bear Lake	2.1	745	10,220	90		15.6	29	cutthroat
	Glacier Gorge Jct.	3	980						
Half Mtn.	Glacier Gorge Jct.	2.5	2,242	11,482	85				

Hallett Peak	Bear Lake	5	3,238	12,713	34				fishless
Hayden Lake	Bear Lake	10	2,849	11,140	45		7.4		
Hayden Spire	Bear Lake	9.75	3,005	12,480	48				
Haynach Lakes	Green Mtn. TH	8.25	2,286	11,080	50		6.4		Colorado River cutthroat
Hazeline Lake	Corral Ck. TH	4.5	11,110	11,110	48		7.4	3	fishless
Helene, Lake	Bear Lake	2.9	1,215	10,580	77		2.8	3	fishless
Hiamovi Mtn.	Roaring Fork TH	6.5	4,114	12,395		19			
Highest Lake	Milner Pass	8.25	1,675	12,425	2		7.4		fishless
Homestead Meadows	US 36	1.75	1,040	8,040					
Horsetooth Peak	Meeker Park	2	1,572	10,344	105				
Hourglass Lake	Fern Lake TH	6.5	3,065	11,220	38		9.2		fishless
Howard Mtn.	Red. Mtn. TH	5.25	3,770	12,810	27				
Husted, Lake	North Fork TH	10.25	3,120	11,080	50		10.1	21	greenback cutthroat
Hutcheson Lakes	Finch Lake TH	8.5	2,382	10,852	61		7.4		greenback cutthroat
Icefield Pass	North Fork TH	11.75	3,880	11,840					
Ida, Mt.	Milner Pass	4.5	2,130	12,880	25				
	Timber Lake	6	3,880						
Inkwell Lake	Milner Pass	7.5	1,050	11,460	21		30.3		fishless
Irene Lake	Milner Pass	0.5	-150	10,598	74		1.8	12	fishless
Irene Lake	Fern L. TH	7.25	3,705	11,860	4		1.8		fishless
Irving Hale, Mt.	Roaring Fork TH	5.75	3,473	11,754		30			fishless

Destination	Starting Point	Distance from Start. Pt. (in miles)	Elevation Gain TH to High Pt.	Altitude (in feet)	Alt. Rank National Park	Alt. Rank Indian Peaks	Size of Lake (in acres)	Depth of Lake (in feet)	Fish in Lake
Isabelle Glacier	Long Lake TH	3.75	1,440	11,920					
Isabelle, Lake	Long Lake TH	2	388	10,868		21	30	37	rainbow
Island Lake	Monarch Lake	9	3,054	11,400		6	19	39	cutthroat
Isolation Peak	Wild Basin R. Sta.	8	4,618	13,118	19				
Italy Lake	Glacier Gorge Jct.	6	2,380	11,620	12				
Jackstraw Mtn.	Timber L. TH	4.5	2,704	11,704	80				
Jade, Pool of	Bear Lake	2.75	1,885	11,360	28				fishless
Jasper Lake	Hessie	4.4	1,805	10,814		23			
	Buckingham CG	5.75	693						
Jewell Lake	Glacier Gorge Jct.	3	710	9,950	100		4.6		rainbow
Jims Grove	Longs Pk. R. Sta.	2.9	1,600	11,000					
Joe Mills Mtn.	Bear Lake	3.5	1,603	11,078	92				
Julian Lake	Timber L. TH	5.75	2,800	11,100	49		5.5	30	fishless
Julian, Mt.	Milner Pass	6	2,178	12,928	23				
Junco Lake	Wild Basin R. Sta.	6.75	3,130	11,630	11		9.2	45	fishless
Keplinger Lake	Copeland Lake	6.25	3,374	11,686	10		9.2		fishless
Keyhole, The	Longs Pk. R. Sta.	6.25	3,750	13,150					
King Lake	Hessie	5.2	2,422	11,431		5			
	Rollins Pass	0.8	80	11,431		5			
Kiowa Peak	No Access, Boulder Watershed			13,276		5			
Knobtop Mtn.	Bear Lake	6	2,856	12,331	57				

Feature	Access	Distance	Elev. Gain	Elevation					Fish
Lady Washington, Mt.	Longs Pk. R. Sta.	5.5	3,881	13,281	13				
La Poudre Pass	Colo. Riv. TH	7.4	1,165	10,175					
Lark Pond	Wild Basin R. Sta.	6.5	2,840	11,340	32		4.6		fishless
Lawn Lake	Lawn L. TH	6.2	2,249	10,789	65		20		greenback cutthroat
Lead Mtn.	Colo. Riv. TH	7.4	3,547	12,537	44				
Lily Mtn.	Lily Mtn. TH	1.5	1,006	9,786		Roosevelt NF			
Lion Lake No. 1	Wild Basin R. Sta.	7	2,565	11,065	52		7.4		fishless
Lion Lake No. 2	Wild Basin R. Sta.	7.5	2,900	11,400	26		3.7		fishless
Little Matterhorn	Bear Lake	5.5	2,111	11,586	83				
Loch, The	Glacier Gorge Jct.	2.7	940	10,180	94		14.6		brook, greenback cutthroat
Lone Eagle Peak	Monarch Lake	9.5	3,574	11,920		29			
Lone Pine Lake	East Inlet TH	5.5	1,494	9,885	104		12.9		brook
Lonesome Lake	Bear Lake	9.5	3,085	11,700	9		7.4		fishless
Long Lake	Long Lake TH	0.25	41	10,521		30	39.5	18	rainbow, brook
Long Lake	Roaring Fork TH	7.75	1,639	9,920		38	5	8	cutthroat, rainbow
Longs Peak	Longs Pk. R. Sta.	8	4,855	14,255	1				
	Glacier Gorge Jct.	10.6	5,015						
Lookout Mtn.	Meeker Park	2.5	1,943	10,715	100				

Destination	Starting Point	Distance from Start. Pt. (in miles)	Elevation Gain TH to High Pt.	Altitude (in feet)	Alt. Rank National Park	Alt. Rank Indian Peaks	Size of Lake (in acres)	Depth of Lake (in feet)	Fish in Lake
Loomis Lake	Fern L. TH	5.2	2,065	10,220	90		2.8	15	greenback cutthroat
Lost Falls	North Fork TH	7.4	1,840	9,800					
Lost Lake	North Fork TH	9.7	2,750	10,710	70		9.2	21	greenback cutthroat
Lost Lake (Indian Peaks)	Hessie	1.25	777	9,786		39			
Louise, Lake	North Fork TH	10.75	3,070	11,030	55		6.4		greenback cutthroat
Love Lake	Milner Pass	6.25	1,050	11,260	35		1.8	10	fishless
Lulu City	Colo. Riv. TH	3.7	350	9,360	63				
Lulu Mtn.	Colo. Riv. TH	7.5	3,218	12,228	103				
MacGregor Mtn.	Fall R. Ent. Sta.	1.25	2,206	10,486	103				
McHenrys Peak	Glacier Gorge Jct.	6.75	4,087	13,327	10				
Mahana Peak	Wild Basin R. Sta.	7.75	4,132	12,632	39				
Many Winds, Lake of	Wild Basin R. Sta.	7.75	3,110	11,610	13		0.9	6	fishless
Marguerite Falls	Fern L. TH	3.75	1,285	9,440					
Marigold Lake	Bear Lake	3.5	1,215	10,220	90		0.2	2	fishless
Marigold Pond	Bear Lake	2.2	1,215	10,580	77		0.1	6	fishless
Marmot Point	Fall River Pass	0.5	113	11,909					
Marten Peak	Roaring Fork TH	7.5	3,760	12,041		25			
Meadow Mtn.	St. Vrain Mt. TH	3	2,832	11,632	81	31			

Meeker, Mt.	Longs Pk. R. Sta.	5.5	4,511	13,911	2			
	Copeland Lake	6	5,599					
Mertensia Falls	Wild Basin R. Sta.	6	1,860	10,360				
Mill Ck. Basin	Hollowell Park	1.6	600	9,000				
Mills Lake	Glacier Gorge Jct.	2.5	700	9,940	101	15.6		rainbow
Mirror Lake	Corral Ck. TH	6.1	1,020	11,020	56	21	84	brook, brown
Mirror Lake (Indian Peaks)	Monarch Lake	8	2,034	10,380	31			fishless
Mitchell Lake	Mitchell Ck. TH	1.25	240	10,720	27	13.8	8	brook, cutthroat
Monarch Lake	On road			8,340	40			
Mummy Mtn.	Lawn L. TH	8.25	4,885	13,425	8			
	North Fork TH	12.5	5,465					
Mummy Pass	Corral Ck. TH	6.3	1,120	11,120				
	Pingree Park	6.5	2,090					
Murphy Lake	Green Mt. TH	7.75	2,426	11,220	38	7.4		fishless
Nakai Peak	Green Mt. TH	9	3,422	12,216	64			
Nanita, Lake	North Inlet TH	11	2,240	10,780	66	34.0		Colorado River cutthroat
Navajo Peak	Long Lake TH	6.25	2,929	13,409	3			
Neota Mtn.	Colo. Riv. TH	8.4	2,724	11,734	78			
Neva, Mt.	Junco Lake	4.25	2,774	12,814	16			
Nimbus, Mt.	Colo. Riv. TH	5.9	3,716	12,706	36			
Nisa, Mt.	Tonahutu Ck. TH	3.5	2,233	10,778	98			

Destination	Starting Point	Distance from Start. Pt. (in miles)	Elevation Gain TH to High Pt.	Altitude (in feet)	Alt. Rank National Park	Alt. Rank Indian Peaks	Size of Lake (in acres)	Depth of Lake (in feet)	Fish in Lake
Niwot Ridge	Long Lake TH	4	2,543	13,023		10			
Nokhu Crags	Lake Agnes TH	3	2,640	12,485	Colorado SF				
Nokoni, Lake	North Inlet TH	9.9	2,240	10,780	66		24.9	50	fishless
North Inlet Falls	North Inlet TH	7.6	1,000	9,540					
Notchtop Mtn.	Bear Lake	5.75	2,849	12,129	68				
Nymph Lake	Bear Lake	0.5	225	9,700	108		0.9		fishless
Odessa Lake	Bear Lake	4.1	1,215	10,020	97		8.4	22	greenback cutthroat
	Fern L. TH	4.4	1,865						
Ogalalla Peak	Middle St. Vrain	9	4,500	13,138	18	8			
	Wild Basin R. Sta.	9.75	4,638						
Orton, Mt.	Copeland Lake	5.25	3,412	11,724	79				
Otis Peak	Bear Lake	6	3,011	12,486	47				
Ouzel Falls	Wild Basin R. Sta.	2.7	950	9,450					
Ouzel Lake	Wild Basin R. Sta.	4.9	1,510	10,010	98		6.4		greenback cutthroat
Ouzel Peak	Wild Basin R. Sta.	8.5	4,216	12,716	33				
Pagoda Mtn.	Glacier Gorge Jct.	6.5	4,257	13,497	7				
Paiute Peak	Mitchell Ck. TH	4.5	2,608	13,088		9			
Parika Lake	Trail Rdg. Rd.	5	2,496	11,360	Never Summer Wilderness				
Parika Peak	Trail Rdg. Rd.	6	3,530	12,394	Never Summer Wilderness				
Patterson, Mt.	Green Mt. TH	3.25	2,630	11,424	88				

Pawnee Lake	Monarch Lake	8.25	2,494	10,840		22	11	22	cutthroat
	Long Lake TH	6	2,061						
Pawnee Pass	Long Lake TH	4	2,061	12,541					
	Monarch Lake	9.75	4,195						
Pawnee Peak	Long Lake	4.5	2,463	12,943					
Peacock Pool	Longs Pk. R. Sta.	4	1,885	11,285	34	13	4.6		brook
Pear Lake	Finch Lake TH	6.5	2,112	10,582	76		16.5		greenback cutthroat
	Allens Park TH	5.8	2,062						
Peck Glacier	Monarch Lake	8.75	3,174	11,520					
Petingell Lake	North Inlet TH	10.75	1,970	10,510	81			10	cutthroat
Pika Lake	Middle St. Vrain	7.5	2,282	10,920		19	2.0	10	cutthroat
Pilot Mtn.	Wild Basin R. Sta.	8	3,700	12,200	65				
Pinnacle Pool	Colo. Riv. TH	4.9	2,310	11,300	33		3.6		fishless
Pipit Lake	Wild Basin R. Sta.	6.75	2,915	11,415	25		12.9	50	fishless
Pool, The	Fern L. TH	1.7	245	8,400					
Potts Puddle	Lawn L. TH	5.75	2,360	10,900	59		3.7	3	fishless
Poudre Lake	On road			10,750	68		13.8		brook
Powell, Lake	North Inlet TH	12.5	3,010	11,550	15		12.9		fishless
Powell Peak	Glacier Gorge Jct.	7.25	3,968	13,208	14				
Ptarmigan Lake	Bear Lake	6	2,849	11,460	21		21.1		fishless
Ptarmigan Mtn.	East Inlet TH	9.25	3,933	12,324	58				
Ptarmigan Pass	Bear Lake	5	2,705	12,180					
Ptarmigan Point	Bear Lake	5.25	2,888	12,363	56				

Destination	Starting Point	Distance from Start. Pt. (in miles)	Elevation Gain TH to High Pt.	Altitude (in feet)	Alt. Rank National Park	Alt. Rank Indian Peaks	Size of Lake (in acres)	Depth of Lake (in feet)	Fish in Lake
Rainbow Lake	Fern L. TH	7	3,585	11,740	8		12.9		fishless
Rainbow Lakes (#3)	Rainbow L. CG	0.5	240	10,200		35	4	14	brook
Ramsey Peak	Pingree Park	7	2,552	11,582	84				
Red Deer Lake	Middle St. Vrain	7.25	1,734	10,372		32	16	58	brook, suckers
Red Mtn.	Red Mt. TH	5.5	2,565	11,605	82				
Red Rocks Lake	On road			10,160		36	6.5	4.5	rainbow
Ribbon Falls	Glacier Gorge Jct.	4.5	1,330	10,570					
Richthofen, Mt.	Colo. Riv. TH	7.2	3,910	12,940	22				
	Lake Agnes TH	2	2,640						
Rock Lake	Milner Pass	7	1,050	10,320	84		5.5	10	greenback cutthroat
Rock Lake, Little	Milner Pass	7.25	1,050	10,320	84		0.7	20	greenback cutthroat
Round Lake	Roaring Fork TH	6.25	2,879	11,160		11			
Round Pond	Bear Lake	2.5	845	10,320	84		0.2	1.5	fishless
Rowe Glacier	Lawn L. TH	9	4,660	13,200	84				
Rowe Glacier Lake	Lawn L. TH	9	4,560	13,100+	1		7.4		fishless
	North Fork TH	13	5,140						
Rowe Mtn.	North Fork TH	14	5,224		15				
	Lawn L. TH	10	4,644	13,184					

Rowe Peak	North Fork TH	13.5	5,440						
Saddle, The	Lawn L. TH	9.5	4,860	13,400	9				
	Lawn L. TH	8.25	3,858	12,398					
St. Vrain Glaciers	Middle St. Vrain	8	2,562	11,200					
St. Vrain Mtn.	St. Vrain Mt. TH	4	3,362	12,162	66	24			
Sandbeach Lake	Copeland Lake	4.2	1,971	10,283	89		16.5	40	greenback cutthroat
Satanta Peak	Junco Lake	4	1,939	11,979		26			
	Buckingham CG	4.5	1,858						
Sawtooth Mtn.	Beaver Res.	6.5	3,143	12,304		22			
Shadow Mtn.	East Shore TH	5	1,765	10,155	107				
Shadow Mtn. Lake	On road		8,367	Arapaho NRA					rainbow, brown, kokanee
Shadow Mtn. Lookout	East or Outlet TH	4.8	1,533	9,923					
Sharkstooth, The	Glacier Gorge Jct.	4.75	3,390	12,630	40				
Sheep Mountain	McGraw Ranch	2	1,838	9,678	109				
Shelf Lake	Glacier Gorge Jct.	4.25	1,980	11,220	38		3.7		fishless
Shipler Mtn.	Milner Pass	2.2	567	11,317	89				
Shipler Park	Colo. Riv. TH	2.3	110	9,120					
Shoshoni Peak	Long Lake TH	4.25	2,487	12,967		12			
Signal Mtn.	North Fork TH	6	3,302	11,262	CPW				
Signal Mtn., South	North Fork TH	5.5	3,316	11,276	90				

Destination	Starting Point	Distance from Start. Pt. (in miles)	Elevation Gain TH to High Pt.	Altitude (in feet)	Alt. Rank National Park	Alt. Rank Indian Peaks	Size of Lake (in acres)	Depth of Lake (in feet)	Fish in Lake
Skull Point	Pingree Park	7.5	2,996	12,026					
Sky Pond	Glacier Gorge Jct.	4.6	1,660	10,900	59		11.2		brook
Skyscraper Res.	Hessie	4.6	2,212	11,221		8			
Snowbank Lake	Wild Basin R. Sta.	8	3,021	11,521	17		7.4		fishless
Snowdrift Lake	North Inlet TH	8.75	2,620	11,160	43		9.2		fishless
Snowdrift Peak	Bear Lake	8	2,799	12,274	61				
Solitude Lake	Glacier Gorge Jct.	4.5	2,180	11,420	24		7.4		fishless
Solitude, Lake	North Inlet TH	8.5	1,180	9,720	107		7.4	4	Colorado River cutthroat
Specimen Mtn.	Milner Pass	2.2	1,739	12,489	46				
Spectacle Lake, Lower	Lawn L. TH	5	2,810	11,350	30		7.4	80	fishless
Spectacle Lake, Upper	Lawn L. TH	5.25	2,820	11,360	28		11.2	60	fishless
Spirit Lake	East Inlet TH	7.75	1,899	10,290	88		18.4	20	brook
Sprague Glacier	Fern L. TH	7.75	3,705	11,860					
Sprague Glacier Lake	Fern L. TH	7.75	3,705	11,860	4		5.5		fishless
Sprague Lake	On road			8,710	115		12.9	9	brook
Sprague Mtn.	Bear Lake	9	3,238	12,713	3				
Spruce Lake	Fern L. TH	4.6	1,515	9,670	109		3.7	8	greenback cutthroat

Static Peak	Lake Agnes TH	2.5	2,640	12,560	43				
Steep Mtn.	Cub Lake TH	4.25	1,458	9,538	110				
Stone Lake	Roaring Fork TH	6.75	2,879	10,643		28	6.0	8	rainbow, cutthroat
Stone Man Pass	Glacier Gorge Jct.	6.25	3,240	12,480					
Stones Peak	Bear Lake	10	3,447	12,922	24				
Storm Pass	Lily Lake	3	1,323	10,250					
	Longs Pk. R. Sta.	2.6	850						
	Boulder Brook TH	3.75	1,400						
Storm Peak	Longs Pk. R. Sta.	6.25	3,926	13,326	11				
Stormy Peaks	Pingree Park	5.25	3,118	12,148	67				
Stormy Peaks Pass	Pingree Park	5	2,570	11,600					
Stratus, Mt.	Nvr Sum Ranch	5	3,636	12,520	45				
Sugarloaf Mtn.	Pingree Park	6.25	3,090	12,120	70				
Sundance Mtn.	Trail Ridge Road	0.5	446	12,466	49				
Tanima Peak	Wild Basin R. Sta.	8.5	3,920	12,420	51				
Taylor Glacier	Glacier Gorge Jct.	5.25	3,913	11,800					
Taylor Peak	Glacier Gorge Jct.	6.25	3,678	13,153	17				
Tepee Mtn.	Lake Agnes TH	2.5	2,060	12,360	55				
Terra Tomah Mtn.	Milner Pass	6.75	2,010	12,718	34				
Thatchtop	Glacier Gorge Jct.	5	3,428	12,668	32				
Thunder Falls	Wild Basin R. Sta.	7.25	2,420	10,920					
Thunder Lake	Wild Basin R. Sta.	6.8	2,074	10,574	79	16.5			brook, greenback cutthroat

Destination	Starting Point	Distance from Start. Pt. (in miles)	Elevation Gain TH to High Pt.	Altitude (in feet)	Alt. Rank National Park	Alt. Rank Indian Peaks	Size of Lake (in acres)	Depth of Lake (in feet)	Fish in Lake
Thunder Mtn.	Colo. Riv. TH	7.85	3,030	12,040	72				
Thunder Pass	Colo. Riv. TH	6.9	2,321	11,331					
Thunderbolt Peak	Monarch Lake	6.25	3,592	11,938		28			
Tileston, Mt.	Lawn L. TH	4.5	2,714	11,254	91				
Timber Lake	Timber Lake TH	4.8	2,060	11,060	53		10.1		Colorado River cutthroat
Timberline Falls	Glacier Gorge Jct.	4	1,210	10,450					
Timberline Pass	Trail Ridge Road	1.75	566	11,484					
Toll, Mt.	Mitchell Ck. TH	5.25	2,499	12,979		11			
Toll Memorial	Rock Cut	0.5	260	12,310					
Tourmaline Lake	Bear Lake	4.5	1,115	10,590	75		1.8	12	fishless
	Fern L. TH	4.8	2,435						
Triangle Lake	Monarch Lake	9.25	2,774	11,120		14			
Trio Falls	Wild Basin R. Sta.	7.25	2,800	11,300					
Twin Lakes, Lower (Radcliff Pond)	Wild Basin R. Sta.	3.5	1,270	9,770	106		4.6	15	fishless
Twin Lakes, Upper	Wild Basin R. Sta.	3.5	1,270	9,790	105		1.8		fishless
Twin Owls	Twin Owls TH	0.5	869	8,789					
Twin Peaks	Roaring Fork TH	4	3,776	11,957	75	27			

Twin Sisters Peaks	Lily Lake	3.9	2,338	11,428	87				
Two Rivers Lake	Bear Lake	2.5	1,125	10,600	73	4.6		5	fishless
Tyndall Glacier	Bear Lake	4.75	2,725	12,200					
Upper Lake	Roaring Fork TH	7.25	2,879	10,730		7	26	6	cutthroat
Verna, Lake	East Inlet TH	6.9	1,809	10,200	93	33.1			brook
War Dance Falls	North Inlet TH	7	1,260	9,800					
Watanga Lake	Roaring Fork TH	4.25	2,509	10,790			25		rainbow, brown
Watanga Mtn.	Roaring Fork TH	5.5	4,094	12,375	54		20		
Wescott, Mt,	East Inlet TH	5.5	2,030	10,421	104				
West Creek Falls	McGraw Ranch	2	600	8,160					
Windy Gulch Cascades	Upper Beaver Meadows	2	680	9,200					
Woodland Lake	Hessie	4.2	1,963	10,972			17		
Woodland Mtn.	Hessie	5	2,211	11,220			33		
Wuh, Mt.	Bear Lake	2.5	1,286	10,761	99				
Yellowstone Canyon, Little	Colo. Riv. TH	4.6	990	10,000					
Ypsilon Lake	Lawn L. TH	4.5	2,180	10,540	80	7.4		55	Colorado River cutthroat
Ypsilon Mtn.	Chapin Ck. TH	3.5	2,874	13,514	5				

Destinations Index

A

Abandoned Road, 164
Achonee, Mount, 266
Adams Falls, 204
Agnes, Lake, 194
Alberta Falls, 78
Alice, Mount, 135
Allen's Park Trail, 142
Andrews Glacier, 96
Andrews Peak, 201
Andrews Tarn, 80
Apache Peak, 231
Arapaho Glacier Overlook, 247
Arapaho Glacier Trail, 244–48
Arapaho Pass, 249, 265–67, 269
Arch Rocks, 65
Arrowhead, 86
Arrowhead Lake, 169
Audubon, Mount, 235–37
Azure Lake, 169

B

Baker Gulch
  Trail System, 173–77
Baker Mountain, 173, 177
Baker Pass, 177
Balanced Rock, 37
Battle Mountain, 89
Bear Lake Road, 71–90
Bear Lake Trailhead, 91–101
Beaver Creek Trail, 236, 237
Beaver Mountain Trail, 149

Beaver Reservoir, 237
Bench Lake, 202
Betty Lake, 250
Bierstadt Lake, 74, 94
Bierstadt Lake Trail, 76
Bighorn Flats, 97
Bighorn Mountain, 56
Big Meadows, 179, 202
Black Canyon Trail, 57
Black Lake, 84
Blue Lake (Glacier Gorge), 85
Blue Lake (Indian Peaks), 234
Bluebird Lake Trail, 130
Bob Lake, 250
Boulder Brook Trail, 75
Boulder Field, 90
Boulder–Grand Pass, 134
Box Canyon, 191
Box Lake, 136
Brainard Lake, 217
Bridal Veil Falls, 58
Buchanan Pass, 238
Buchanan Pass Trail, 257–60

C

Calypso Cascades, 128
Caribou, 245
Caribou Lake, 267
Caribou Pass, 269
Caribou Pass Trail, 267–68, 269
Cascade Creek, 261
Cascade Falls, 200

Cascade Trail, 261–65
Chapin, Mount, 59
Chapin Creek Trail, 59
Chapin Pass Routes, 58–62
Chasm Lake, 109
Chickadee Pond, 131
Chief Cheley Peak, 168
Chiefs Head Peak, 137
Chipmunk Lake, 53
Chiquita Lake, 54
Chiquita, Mount, 59
Cirque Lake, 47
Cirrus, Mount, 188
Clouds, Lake of the, 186
Colorado River Trail, 190
Columbine Creek Trail, 209–10
Columbine Falls, 109
Columbine Lake, 268
Columbine Lake Trail, 268
Comanche Peak, 47
Coney Flats, 237
Coney Lake, 238
Cony Lake, 142
Cony Pass, 132
Copeland Falls, 125–28
Copeland Lake, 125
Copeland Mountain, 130
Corona Trail, 271
Corral Creek Trailhead, 47–50
Cow Creek Trailhead, 58
Coyote Park, 266
Cracktop, 168
Crater, The, 166
Crater Lake, 264
Crawford Lake, 255

Crystal Lake, 57
Cub Lake Trail, 67–69
Cumulus, Mount, 189

D

Deer Mountain Trail, 162–64
Deserted Village, 39
Desolation Peaks, 61
Devils Thumb Lake, 249, 273
Devils Thumb Park, 271
Diamond Lake, 249
Dickinson, Mount, 42
Dorothy, Lake, 249, 269
Doughnut Lake, 169
Dream Lake, 92
Dream Lake Trail System, 91–94
Dunraven, Lake, 42
Dunraven, Mount, 42
Dunraven Trail, 38

E

Eagle Lake, 132, 136
Eagles Beak, 136
East Edge, 113–17
East Inlet Trail, 203–7
East Shore Trail, 209
Elk Tooth, 239
Emerald Lake, 92–93
Emmaline Lake, 47
Envy, Lake, 242
Estes Cone, 117–19
Eugenia Mine, 111–12
Eureka Ditch, 97

F

Fairchild Mountain, 56, 61
Fair Glacier, 265
Falcon Lake, 134
Fall Mountain, 47
Fay Lakes, 54
Fern Falls, 66
Fern Lake, 66
Fern Lake Trail System, 63–67,
Fifth Lake, 206
Finch Lake, 141
Finch Lake Trail System, 140–42
Flatiron Mountain, 61
Flattop Mountain, 95
Flattop Mountain Trail System,
   94–100
Forest Canyon Pass, 146
Fourth Lake, 206
Fourth of July Mine, 249
Fox Creek Falls, 43–44
Fox Creek Trail, 44
Fox Park, 260
Frigid Lake, 132, 136
Frozen Lake, 85

G

Gabletop Mountain, 97
Gem Lake, 27–37
Gibraltar, Lake, 242
Glacier Gorge Trail, 78–90
Glacier Knobs, 79
Glass, Lake of, 81
Goblins Forest, 103
Gorge Lakes, 169
Gourd Lake, 258

Gourd Lake Trail, 258
Grace Falls, 106
Granby, Lake, 210
Grand Lake, 199–210
Granite Falls, 203
Granite Pass, 90
Green Knoll, 172
Green Lake, 85
Green Mountain Trail, 179

H

Hagues Peak, 42, 56
Haiyaha, Lake, 79, 93
Half Mountain, 89
Hallett Peak, 95
Hayden Spire, 67
Haynach Lakes, 98, 203
Helene, Lake, 100
Hell Canyon, 255
Highest Lake, 168
Hitchens Gulch, 186
Hollowell Park, 74
Homer Rouse Trail, 121
Homestead Meadows, 123–24
Homestretch, 106
Horsetooth Peak, 144
Hourglass Lake, 67
Howard, Mount, 188
Husted, Lake, 43
Hutcheson Lakes, 142, 242

I

Icefield Pass, 43
Ida, Mount, 167, 171
Inkwell Lake, 169

Irving Hale, Mount, 255
Isabelle Glacier, 231
Isabelle, Lake, 220, 230
Island Lake, 258
Isolation Peak, 132
Italy Lake, 85

J

Jackstraw Mountain, 171
Jasper Lake, 249
Jewel Lake, 84
Julian Lake, 171
Julian, Mount, 168
Junco Lake, 132, 268

K

Keplinger Lake, 140
Keyhole, 104
King Lake Trail, 250
Knobtop Mountain, 97

L

Lady Washington, Mount, 108–9
La Poudre Pass, 197
La Poudre Pass Trail, 196
Lark Pond, 131
Lawn Lake, 43, 51
Lawn Lake Trail, 54–55
Lead Mountain, 187
Lily Lake Trail, 119
Lily Mountain, 122–23
Lion Gulch Trail, 123
Lion Lake No. 1, 134
Lion Lake No. 2, 135

Lion Lakes Trail, 134
Little Blue Lake, 234
Little Crystal Lake, 57
Little Lake Gibraltar, 242
Little Matterhorn, 100
Little Rock Lake, 169
Little Yellowstone Canyon, 196
Loch, The, 80
Loch Vale Trail, 79–80
Loft, 111
Lone Eagle Peak, 64
Lone Pine Lake, 204–6
Long Lake (Indian Peaks, East), 225
Long Lake (Indian Peaks, West), 255
Long Meadows, 170
Longs Peak, 103–112, 140
Longs Peak Trail, 103
Lookout Mountain, 144
Loomis Lake, 67
Lost Lake (Indian Peaks), 250
Lost Lake (Mummy Range), 42
Lost Lake Trail, 39–42
Louise, Lake, 43
Love Lake, 169
Lulu City Trail System, 190–97
Lulu Mountain, 191

M

McHenrys Peak, 86–87
Mahana Peak, 136
Many Winds, Lake of, 134
Meadow Mountain, 243
Meeker, Mount, 111, 139

Middle St. Vrain Trail System, 239–43
Mill Creek Basin, 74, 94
Mills Lake, 84
Mills Moraine, 104
Mirror Lake (Indian Peaks), 264
Mirror Lake (Mummy Range), 47
Mirror Lake Trail, 50
Mitchell Creek Trail, 233–35
Mitchell Lake, 234
Monarch Lake, 267
Moraine Park, 63–90
Mummy Mountain, 57
Mummy Pass, 47
Mummy Pass Trail, 46–51

N

Nakai Peak, 203
Nanita, Lake, 200, 201
Narrows, 106
Navajo Peak, 232
Neota, Mount, 193
Neva, Mount, 269
Nimbus, Mount, 173, 189
Niwot Ridge, 225
Nokhu Crags, 193
Nokoni, Lake, 200
North Arapaho Peak, 247
North Boundary Trail, 43, 58
North Fork Trail, 37–46
North Inlet Falls, 200
North Inlet Trail, 99, 199
North Longs Peak Trail, 88
Notchtop Mountain, 97
Nymph Lake, 91

O

Odessa Gorge, 100
Odessa Lake, 100
Odessa Lake Trail, 100–101
Ogalalla Peak, 132, 242
Old Ute Trail, 146–50
Onahu Creek Trail, 178–81
Orton, Mount, 137
Otis Peak, 96
Ouzel Falls, 128
Ouzel Falls Trail System, 125–37
Ouzel Lake, 130
Ouzel Peak, 132

P

Pagoda Mountain, 85, 139
Paiute Peak, 235–36
Paradise Park, 207
Parika Lake, 176
Parika Lake Trail, 175–76
Parika Peak, 176
Paul Bunyans Boot, 35
Pawnee Lake, 233, 263
Pawnee Pass, 232, 263
Pawnee Pass Trail, 217–20
Pawnee Peak, 233
Peacock Pool, 109
Pear Lake, 141–42
Peck Glacier, 264
Pettingell Lake, 201
Pierson Park, 124
Pika Lake, 242
Pinnacle Pool, 188
Pipit Lake, 131
Pool, The, 63

Pool of Jade, 93
Potts Puddle, 57
Poudre Lake, 165
Poudre River Trail, 166
Powell Peak, 96
Ptarmigan Lake, 97, 202
Ptarmigan Mountain, 201
Ptarmigan Point, 97

R

Rainbow Lake, 67
Rainbow Lakes, 245
Red Deer Lake, 238
Red Mountain, 189
Red Mountain Trail System,
  183–90
Red Rocks Lake, 217
Ribbon Falls, 84
Richthofen, Mount, 193
Roaring Fork Trail System,
  254–57
Rock Creek, 244
Rock Lake, 169
Rowe Glacier, 43
Rowe Mountain, 43

S

Saddle, The, 57
St. Vrain Glaciers, 242
St. Vrain Mountain, 243
Sandbeach Lake, 137
Sandbeach Lake Trail System,
  137–40
Satanta Peak, 269

Sawmill Loop, 124
Sawtooth Mountain, 238, 260
Shadow Mountain, 207–10
Shadow Mountain Lake, 208
Sharkstooth, 80
Shelf Lake, 87
Shelter Rock, 257
Shipler Mine, 190
Shipler Mountain, 167
Shoshoni Peak, 233
Signal Mountain Trail, 45–46
Skeleton Gulch, 188
Skull Point, 44
Sky Pond, 81–83
Skyscraper Reservoir, 252
Snowbank Lake, 135
Snowdrift Lake, 202
Solitude, Lake, 200
Solitude Lake, 87
South Arapaho Peak, 247
Spearhead, 85
Specimen Mountain, 166
Spectacle Lakes, 53
Spirit Lake, 206
Sprague Glacier, 97
Sprague Mountain, 97
Spruce Canyon, 67
Spruce Lake, 66
Spruce Lake Trail, 66
Squally Pass, 144
Stage Road Trail, 191
Static Peak, 193
Steep Mountain, 74
Stone Lake, 255

Stone Man Pass, 86
Stones Peak, 67, 97
Storm Pass, 118
Storm Pass Trail, 75, 117–19
Storm Peak, 108
Stormy Peaks Trail, 44–45
Stormy Peaks Pass, 44
Stratus, Mount, 172
Sugarloaf Mountain, 44
Summerland Park, 200

T

Tanima Peak, 134
Taylor Glacier, 81
Taylor Peak, 96
Ten Lakes Park, 207
Tepee Mountain, 196
Terra Tomah Mountain, 168
Thatchtop, 87
Thunder Lake Trail, 133
Thunder Mountain, 193
Thunder Pass, 191
Tileston, Mount, 56
Timber Lake, 171
Timber lake Trail, 170–71
Timberline Falls, 81
Timberline Pass, 150
Toll, Mount, 234
Tombstone Ridge, 150
Tonahutu Creek Trail, 96, 202–3
Tourmaline Gorge, 101

Tourmaline Lake, 101
Trail Ridge Road, 145–81
Triangle Lake, 265
Trio Falls, 135
Trough, The, 106
Twin Owls, 32
Twin Sisters Peaks, 113–17
Tyndall Glacier, 95

U

Upper Coney Lake, 238
Upper Lake, 255

V

Verna, Lake, 206

W

War Dance Falls, 202
Watanga Lake, 254
West Creek Falls, 44, 58
Wheeler Basin, 266
Wild Basin, 125–44
Wind River, 75
Windy Gulch, 150
Windy Gulch Cascades, 148
Woodland Lake, 252
Wuh, Mount, 74

Y

Ypsilon Lake, 53
Ypsilon Mountain, 59

Suggested Readings

Arps, Louisa Ward, High E. Kingery, and Elinor Eppich Kingery. *High Country Names.* Estes Park, Colo.: Rocky Mountain Nature Association, 1994.

Dannen, Kent and Donna. *Best Easy Day Hikes Rocky Mountain National Park.* Guilford, Conn.: Globe Pequot Press, 2002.

———. *Rocky Mountain Wildflowers.* Allenspark: Tundra Publications, 1981.

———. *Short Hikes in Rocky Mountain National Park.* Allenspark: Tundra Publications, 1986.

Leopold, Aldo. *A Sand County Almanac.* New York: Ballantine Books, 1991.

Logue, Frank, and Victoria Steele Logue. *Cooking for Campers & Backpackers.* Birmingham, Ala.: Menasha Ridge Press, 1995.

Roberts, Harry, and Adrienne Hall. *Basic Essentials Backpacking.* Guilford, Conn.: Globe Pequot Press, 1999.

Sax, Joseph L. *Mountains Without Handrails.* Ann Arbor: University of Michigan Press, 1980.

Schneider, Bill. *Backpacking Tips.* Guilford, Conn.: Globe Pequot Press, 1998.

Tilton, Buck, and Frank Hubbell. *Medicine for the Backcountry.* 3rd ed. Guilford, Conn.: Globe Pequot Press, 1999.

Field Guide to Wildlife Viewing in Rocky Mountain National Park. Estes Park, Colo.: Rocky Mountain Nature Association, 2002.

About the Authors

Kent and Donna Dannen have guided hikers over the trails of Rocky Mountain National Park and Indian Peaks for a combined total of fifty years. Both began their professional guiding activities as hike masters and naturalists for the YMCA of the Rockies and have led hundreds of hikes covering thousands of miles. Kent, a former contributing editor of *Backpacker Magazine*, freelances as a writer-photographer. He also is a recipient of the U.S. Department of Agriculture Certificate of Appreciation for his outstanding volunteer services in developing educational materials that help manage and protect the Indian Peaks Wilderness. Donna has worked as a ranger-naturalist with the National Park Service and taught photography for Eastman Kodak in Rocky Mountain National Park.

The Dannens have written three other guide books, *Short Hikes in Rocky Mountain National Park*, *Best Easy Day Hikes in Rocky Mountain National Park*, and *Rocky Mountain Wildflowers*. They live in Allenspark, Colorado, with their son Pat and Samoyed sled dog team.